FALLEN WALLS

With a foreword by
Václav Havel

FALLEN WALLS

Prisoners of Conscience in
South Africa and Czechoslovakia

Jan K. Coetzee
Lynda Gilfillan
Otakar Hulec

LONDON AND NEW YORK

Originally published in 2002 by Lidové Noviny Publishing House and the Robben Island Museum.

First published 2004 by Transaction Publishers

2 Park Square, Milton Park, Abingdon, Oxfordshire OX14 4RN
711 Third Avenue, New York, NY 10017

Routledge is an imprint of the Taylor & Francis Group, an informa business

First issued in paperback 2017

Library of Congress Catalog Number: 2004046036

Library of Congress Cataloging-in-Publication Data

Fallen walls : prisoners of conscience in South Africa and Czechoslovakia /
[compiled by] Jan K. Coetzee, Lynda Gilfillan, and Otakar Hulec ; with a
foreword by Václav Havel.
    p. cm.
    Orginally published: [Czechoslovakia]: Nakladatelství Lidové
Noviny ; [Cape Town, South Africa] : Robben Island Museum, 2002, in
series: Robben Island memory series.
    Includes bibliogaphical references and index.
    ISBN 0-7658-0229-5 (alk. paper)
    1. Political prisoners—South Africa—Robben Island. 2. Political
prisoners—Czechoslovakia. 3. Prisoners' writings, South African
(English) 4. Prisoners' writings, Czech. I. Coetzee, Jan Karel. II.
Gilfillan, Lynda, 1948- III. Hulec, Otakar.
HV9850.5.Z8R635 2004
365'.45'0922437—dc22   2004046036

ISBN 13: 978-0-7658-0229-3 (hbk)
ISBN 13: 978-1-138-51001-2 (pbk)

Contents

Foreword

It is a universal quest to seek lessons from history. Unfortunately, however, the details of the past all too frequently remain unknown. Indeed, the voices of certain heroes of our recent history who fought against oppression are slowly fading, as the details of their lives slip from human memory.

This book contains six such life histories, those of three South African and three Czech prisoners of conscience. The stories of these six patriots who fought for democratic principles help to prevent the erosion of memory. By juxtaposing these seemingly separate yet shared destinies, the authors remind us anew of the price that is so often paid for freedom and democracy.

Václav Havel,
Former President of the Czech Republic

Prelude

Introducing the Stories

War, conflict and oppression have always bedevilled human relations, and revenge and persecution form part of a continuous cycle of destruction. All too often, the coming together of people to form nations or ethnic or ideological groups is followed by fragmentation, as one group ranges itself against another for some or other reason. The very process of self-definition sets up the "other" against which the self, the nation, or the group is defined. And so the elements of conflict are set in place.

The pages of history are frequently bloody records of cruel campaigns, unjust systems, and attempts at the systematic elimination of those identified as the enemy, the "other." We are masters of the art of designing brutal systems that we unleash on those we fear or despise. And the debris of wasted, twisted human lives surrounds us, whether we find ourselves in the gleaming affluence of the first world, or in the grim wastelands of disease-ridden developing nations. There was a time when the injustices inflicted upon one's adversaries could be kept out of the public eye, when many human rights violations remained obscure. But today the evidence and the anger are inescapable, whether in the shacklands of Sudan or South Africa or in the street battles that are fought over globalization at meetings of this century's superpowers. The global village has never been as small, nor have the satellite images of CNN and Sky Television been as pervasive or persistent. But notwithstanding the media exposure of those proclaiming an alternative, individual voices are seldom heard in the fleeting media image and shallow sound bite. In a book such as this, however, the words that express the feelings, thoughts and daily experiences of victims of oppression give substance and resonance to the human suffering that continues to plague our times.

History is written by the victorious, and all too often the actual experiences of those nameless, faceless masses who are its subjects and its shapers, are silent, unsung. These pages open to public scrutiny the experience of those who have suffered one of the most extreme forms of human rights abuse: long-term political imprisonment. Each page speaks of the toll and trials—but also the personal triumphs—of incarceration. Resonating in each voice is the trauma of deprivation, the absence of all that invests human life with meaning and

1

value: family, work, the comfort of the cherished and familiar. Life behind bars is not merely a form of cruel punishment, it also embodies an excruciating form of human degradation.

Long-term imprisonment is always the first resort of the totalitarian state when confronted with the dissident. As with the banishment and ostracism of other eras, the individual is cast into a state of inner desolation. Here, life is one of discontinuity, and a primary human need—a sense of belonging—is trampled on. The life-histories that unfold in these pages describe what it feels like to be taken from the familiar, daily rituals we develop to structure our lives, from networks of support, and from the comforting sense that one can move around freely, associate with whomever one chooses, and explore the larger world of images and ideas.

Long-term imprisonment inevitably leads to trauma—both in the lived reality of the individual, as well as the state of mind that results from disruption, and deprivation. Trauma can arise not only from a particular event, but also from a persistent social condition:

> Something alien breaks in on you, smashing through whatever barriers your mind has set up as a line of defence. It invades you, possesses you, takes you over, becomes a dominating feature of your interior landscape, and in the process threatens to drain you and leave you empty. (Erikson in Rogers et al., 1999: 2)[1]

The voices that are heard in the pages that follow give form and substance to this notion of trauma as it relates to the experiences of long-term political prisoners.

Whose Stories?

These stories focus on the individual experiences of a few of those who were at the receiving end of severe forms of political violence. At one end of a global, racial and ideological divide are three South Africans—black men from the southeastern part of a country whose white minority had in 1948 voted into power the Nationalist Party. Its legacy was that of apartheid. Joseph Mati, Johnson Mgabela and Monde Mkunqwana were among those who defied the system, and consequently spent the best years of their adult lives on Robben Island—home of one of the world's most notorious penal institutions. Unlike their famous leader, Nelson Mandela, these men were among the masses imprisoned in the anonymous general cells of the island prison. The Nationalist Party was not only racist, it was also deeply sexist. The patriarchal mind-set could not conceive of women political prisoners—instead, troublesome women were subjected to relentless harassment or, like Winnie Mandela, banished to alien, desolate rural areas.

---

[1]Rogers, K. L.; Leydesdorff, S. and Dawson, G. (eds) *Trauma and life stories.* (Routledge: London and New York).

General cells of the Robben Island prison.

In the same year, 1948, at the other end of the world in Central Europe, the people of Czechoslovakia were also poised to experience the repercussions of massive political change. This was the year that marked the communist government take-over that soon led to the destruction of democracy. Jiří Stránský, Aloisie Škodová and Jiří Mesicki are representative of those who refused to accept the threat to their personal freedom and the breakdown of social justice. Their tales are—like those of the three South Africans—the plain, unembellished tales of an ordinary woman and two men who were condemned to communal cells and labor camps in some of the harshest institutions in their country, prisons that also accommodated the respected Czech leader, Václav Havel.

These six stories cry out to be heard, for they tell not only of the terrors of prison-life, but also of the networks of human support that developed. The ordeal of incarceration had, as a by-product, a system of solidarity, particularly on Robben Island. Here, prisoners soon realized that the most powerful means of mutual survival was to be found in a sense of belonging—and that the responsibility rested with none other than themselves to create this. And so a shared set of ideals ensured that each prisoner was buoyed by a powerful camaraderie—even in the bleakest months and years on that windswept island.

A remarkable feature of the Robben Island tales is the absence of bitterness and thoughts of revenge. The prison culture that developed is reflected most powerfully perhaps in the man who would, some twenty-seven years after being locked up on the island, win the Nobel Peace Prize and become a universal icon of reconciliation: Nelson Mandela. What emerges from these tales is a peculiarly African sense that human survival depends on mutual compassion and collective unity, on hope and patience, rather than the cycle of discipline and punishment that characterizes the legalistic Western view.

By contrast, the tales from the Czechoslovakian prisons and labor camps are characterized by a sense of bleak isolation and lingering bitterness. They are

To remember the victims of political oppression. Maquette in the Museum of the Third Revolt, Příbram.

largely void of camaraderie and a sharing of common ideals. It was left to the individual to delve into his or her own inner resources for the strength to survive. These stories resonate with the agony of lives that experienced the relentless assault of an inhumane system that made no distinction between the political dissident and the common criminal. For the Czechoslovakian prisoners, the key to survival lay not in collective hope, but rather in developing the sense that nothing or nobody but the individual self could provide rescue from the barbed wire, the gun turrets and the cells.

The situation on Robben Island was strikingly different. The confinement of people with exceptional leadership qualities to communal cells enabled them to strengthen their shared political beliefs, thus contributing to the establishment of a close-knit community. And so, ironically, prison provided fertile ground for the growth of a sense of meaningful existence. The prisoners benefited, moreover, from a combination of other positive factors such as political and moral support both from within and outside the country, the constant affirmation of their ideological beliefs, and a system of discipline that they themselves created and maintained. All this sustained the Robben Island prisoners throughout their long years of imprisonment.

The stories contained in this book are those of ordinary people, the details of whose lives have, for the most part, been submerged by the tide of history. This book gives the reader the opportunity to hear them out, to listen to tales that speak of determination, a firm adherence to principle, and an unflinching sense

Today the "Welcome" is for the thousands of tourists visiting one of the world's most notorious penal institutions. Previously it was addressed to prisoners who knew that they were in for hard times.

of personal truth. Among the six, some may be regarded as relatively well known within certain circles. Jiří Stránský is an established writer, scion of a family whose struggle for political—and therefore personal—freedom goes back to the early part of the last century. He represents those men and women who were singled out for prosecution as a result of a class struggle, aimed at destroying the bourgeoisie. Johnson Malcomess Mgabela was a military commander involved in the South African struggle for liberation, and a respected figure within traditional circles who performed the traditional rite of circumcision among his people, the Xhosa. Joseph Faniso Mati was well known as an organizer and educator.

"Ordinary people" usually denotes those people whose actions have had little impact on the course of history. The vast majority of us fall into this category. For many historians, the details of such lives are not worth relating, and could simply be cut from the larger history of the world. They might argue that leaving ordinary people out of the script makes little difference to the overall significance of the bigger story. It is our intention to show, however, that the constituent parts, the lives of ordinary people, are indispensable to an understanding of the whole, of the macro-narrative.

This book traces the trajectories of the lives of people that were irrevocably altered by the events that surrounded them. The ordinariness of their lives was transformed by qualities of character, by actions, that mark each person as truly extraordinary. None has been a major actor on the stage of history, yet each demonstrates the inspirational force of individual will, thus contributing to humanity's ongoing struggle to achieve social and political change. The "ordinary" voices that speak in this book are, as the reader soon realizes, far from being those of people who have lived safe, little lives.

The narratives demonstrate that ordinary people indeed exercise a unique influence on the broader story of our times. While listening to the unfolding of each narrative, we have privileged access to the traumas, the sacrifices, the hardships and disruptions that people endured in times of political upheaval under rigidly deterministic systems. The stories tell us how men and women, whether in the streets of Prague or in the townships of South Africa, reacted to the ideologies, pronouncements and rigid policies produced within two diverse, yet related, totalitarian systems of government in the period after 1948 at opposite ends of the world. We hear, and seem almost to see, how individuals in situations of extreme duress developed coping strategies, how their personal convictions and determination rescued them from spiritual annihilation.

The voices recorded here are the product of a collaborative effort between the authors and the former political prisoners. In the interests of authenticity, we have attempted to remain faithful to the original words of the narrators. Our role has been to mediate the memories of a group of people—to assist them in the task of "re-membering"—of putting together fragments of lives that may otherwise have been lost and forgotten. We hope to have recorded the cadences of the various voices, so that the reader might experience authentic voices from central Europe and from southern Africa. We have neither embellished nor sensationalized the events, nor, indeed, polished or sanitized the voices for public consumption. Our role as authors has, we hope, been a subtle, respectful and enabling one. Through our intervention, we hope to have provided the opportunity for you, the reader, to hear and understand these stories that might otherwise have remained behind prison doors, and in so doing, to have added finer details to the broad brushstrokes of contemporary history.

Society and the Individual

Ideally, society should provide opportunities for the full realization of each individual personality, as well as access to resources for a decent life. The individual should be able to enter into relationships with others, express aspirations, and participate in collective efforts for social improvement. Society should promote the well-being of all its citizens. For this well-being to exist and to grow, there needs to be an active striving for social justice, democracy, and freedom of expression. Collectively, these form the basis of an ideal society. By focusing on the life-histories of individuals, we hope to emphasize the finer workings that comprise social reality and underlie broader social movements.

When society fails to provide the possibility of living a meaningful existence, it becomes a threat to individual freedom and equality. This book presents the accounts of six individuals who experienced their society as threatening and oppressive, without respect for human life. Each of the stories describes a life that has been frustrated by an overwhelmingly deterministic ideology.

This brings us back to one of the concerns of this book: the way in which individuals experience social reality. It attempts to understand such things as the human experience of oppressive state control, and of alien physical surroundings—but it also examines the relationships, those that develop in inhospitable conditions with people who share one's daily existence, as well as the relationship with one's most intimate self. Any understanding of a broader social reality depends on an understanding of these aspects of reality. And the closest we can come to an experience of other people's reality is to allow the subjects to speak for themselves.

Each of the six life-histories represents a composite series of micro-experiences, each of which must be seen within the parameters of its particular time and place. While each life-history consists of a totality of experiences, the individual stories also exist as components of an all-embracing reality: the experience of long-term incarceration. Collectively, the stories comprise a drama of personal interaction, bargaining and resistance.

In reading the personal accounts, the reader will encounter certain unique as well as common features in communist Czechoslovakia and apartheid South Africa. The coupling of events—no matter how minor—forms links in a chain that binds the disparate yet overlapping worlds in which the narrators lived. Each of the six stories reflects the individual's particular manner of coping with a horrible reality, and therefore each should be heard against the background of an inescapable reality—the state. Its machinery enforced social control and demanded unconditional obedience. And yet, without exception, the six narrators express the desire for a more meaningful, and therefore a more human, existence.

Weaving the Strands Together

In the chapters that follow, you will listen to individual stories, each with its own experience of reality, that present a unique profile of everyday life. At the same time, however, each narrator shares the common experience of long-term incarceration. Each was exposed to, and carried the scars of, powerful historical forces, and embedded in each story is the experience of the ideological webs and political edifices that trapped the individual.

Each life-history comprises separate strands that convey a variety of experiences, while each is also a separate strand in the broad tapestry of its times. In this collection, individual stories are woven together and again unravelled as we offer a variety of perspectives on two political eras that produced icons of our age: Nelson Mandela and Václav Havel. Each story is, of course, a reconstruction, in itself incomplete; it has gaps and silences, as all our life-stories inevitably have. Yet each offers an individual view of history—a fresh angle.

Any understanding of the past is shaped by present realities and current conceptions that distort the "truth" of events. Any account of the past is inevitably the product of a process of selection, of emphasis, and synthesis: the rendering of a complete and accurate view of what actually happened at any moment eludes our capabilities. And while it may be true that the six stories here are no more than mere constructs, the imperfect products of memory— simply "stories"—they are also far more than this. For behind each is an individual whose voice speaks of a personal quest for freedom, and whose life bears the scars of struggle and sacrifice in the pursuit of whatever truth it was that compelled certain forms of dissident behaviour.

The six stories should be read together, for, while the nuances of individual experience are separately mapped, each narrative is simultaneously redefined by the experience of others who found themselves in similar circumstances. By synthesizing people's experiences into a totality, we see them as relative to one another. At the same time, a larger picture emerges, which breathes the spirit not only of the eras that shaped the two countries concerned, but also that of the international community. The past may best be reconstructed by re-collecting its fragments.

We have spoken of weavings and unravellings, of re-membering and also of re-collecting fragments. Inevitably, the final picture will be incomplete, jagged, a juxtaposition of accounts which may at times confuse rather than clarify. Yet there is no other way of struggling against the "forgetting" that Milan Kundera (in *The Book of Laughter and Forgetting*) warned against, or of ensuring that memory is indeed a weapon against oppression.

The Truth Within

In this book, six people expose their thoughts and feelings to an anonymous public. The sacrifices they made emerge as expressions of what were essentially personal experiences of truth and falsehood. Taking a stand against oppression was an authentic act of revolt against the abuse of power, the official lie—and even more than courage, it demanded firm conviction.

Defiance invited confrontation with the full force of state power. Realizing the futility of decrees and legislation, the state resorted to brute force to guarantee compliance and subordination. The rejection of state violence exposed the individual to its full machinery, however. The resultant punishment of long-term imprisonment had as its goal "rehabilitation" in Czechoslovakia and, in South Africa, the subjection of the transgressor to state authority.

The six stories trace the effects of the restrictions imposed by state power on the life of the individual. They expose the workings of state violence in the face of dissidence and defiance. Each of the narrators endured cruel coercion at the hands of state instruments whose task it was to enforce an official version of the truth. The tales reveal, each in its own way, that truth resides neither in the state, nor in any system. Instead, truth emerges from within the individual, as a profound sense of the rightness or the wrongness of things, with personal liberty its enduring touchstone. As such, truth is inseparable from personal conviction, and inextricably linked to the free exchange of ideas.

1

Setting the Stage: The Cold War

The life histories recorded in this book take place against the broad background of the Cold War. Each story recorded here is linked in some way to this larger global period, despite the individual events of each having occurred in two very different geographical locations of the world: central Europe and southern Africa. The Second World War had just ended in 1945, when a new struggle began on the world stage. In the ensuing decades, generations in different parts of the world would grow up under the threatening skies of possible global war. The era of the Cold War was characterized by the ongoing opposition of the two superpowers—the United States of America and the Union of Soviet Socialist Republics (USSR).

The influence of the USSR stretched over those parts of the world that were under the control of the Red Army (an influence that frequently relied on the help of other communist forces.) With the 1948 coup d'état in Czechoslovakia, the communist bloc included all the governments of Eastern Europe, the "iron curtain" countries, thus deepening the East/West divide of world politics. The Warsaw Pact included the USSR, Poland, East Germany, Bulgaria, Romania, Hungary and Czechoslovakia—the East bloc—while the United States of America was the unifying force which bound the North Atlantic Treaty Organization (NATO) and the western hemisphere into an opposing power bloc.

Despite the fact that this division somewhat crudely severed parts of the globe that had for geographical, cultural and historical reasons formerly been associated with the West, and included them in the Euro-Asian power bloc, the possibility of achieving world peace took precedence over the ongoing squabbles about the precise lines of the division into East and West. The two superpowers thus quickly overcame the obstacles that stood in the way of the power-sharing plan; the division of Germany, for example, was based on the post-war occupation by Eastern and Western powers, while Austria—in line with the Swiss model—was accorded neutral status.

The rest of the world—chiefly the Asian sub-continent and those parts that would soon be known as the Third World—were left little choice and therefore tolerated the power-sharing plan of the Cold War. Most of the post-colonial countries in Africa, for instance, remained coolly aloof from the broad power bloc dominated by the USA, but at the same time remained non-communist and unaligned in the arena of international affairs.

It appeared that all the parties concerned accepted the unequal division of the world as a matter of convenience. The two superpowers largely succeeded in staying out of each other's way, and in this manner extreme and provocative forms of confrontation were avoided—or at least kept to a minimum. Each allowed the other free rein within its sphere of influence. Despite this, however, frequent declarations were made, accusations levered, and symbolic gestures entered into whose aim was to remind the opposing bloc of the existence of the balance of power. And because military confrontation would inevitably have resulted in the use of nuclear weapons, it was fortunate that the USA and the USSR always reached compromise before war was entered into.

One event that severely tested the balance of power was the Cuban missile crisis of 1962. When Fidel Castro approached the USSR for assistance in attempting to achieve "a better life for Cubans," this was immediately interpreted as an act that had the potential to disturb the balance of power—a situation that was exacerbated when the Soviet government decided to install nuclear missiles on Cuban soil. Threat upon threat ensued, and eventually Nikita Khrushchev seized the opportunity offered by John F Kennedy: he would remove the missiles if America agreed not to attack Cuba. It is today clear what this episode demonstrated. The Soviet Union weighed up the effects of a change in the balance of power, and decided that the price was too high to pay. A similar dilemma had earlier faced the USA in 1953, when it was decided rather to accept the reinstatement of communist power in the workers' uprising in East Germany than to intervene. The USA adopted the same strategy in 1956 when the Soviets invaded Hungary to quell the revolution. The policy of the West was one of non-interference in the Soviet domain.

Throughout this period, the Cold War was based on the principle that the destructive potential of a catastrophic war between East and West had not been eliminated by the outcome of the Second World War. The West regarded the communist system as having an insatiable will to power, with only one objective: total world domination. The struggle was, therefore, viewed not only in military terms, but also had an ideological dimension. The West, for example, saw communism as a system that threatened to replace western religion and democratic values with a merciless, godless tyranny. Freedom in its most fundamental form was regarded as being under threat. The only acceptable strategy for Moscow was one of "no compromise." Just as the USA feared Soviet world domination, so Moscow was concerned about the USA's influence in those parts of the world not under the occupation of the Red Army.

Neither the West nor the communist bloc admitted to having flexible strategies. On both sides of the divide there was one ever-present obsession: to remain at the forefront of the arms race. So intense was this obsession that a deaf ear was turned whenever anyone dared suggest what madness it was to militarize the world. For never before had a military-industrial complex of such magnitude been established during peacetime—and for no other reason, as history would show, but to act as a deterrent to the opposing side.

Although the arms race gave the Cold War the appearance of military confrontation, it was the political results of the Cold War that were most telling. With the world divided into two camps, the communists had disappeared from most Western governments, reduced to the status of political outsiders. In the USSR, on the other hand, non-communists had been eliminated from the "multiparty people's democracies," and Soviet control was strictly exercised in all Eastern European states. As a result, politics in the communist bloc had become increasingly monolithic.

By the early 1960s the Cold War was characterized by negotiated settlement. Western Europe experienced general prosperity, and the USSR economy was also on a sound footing. In fact, the communist economies revealed even faster growth rates than those in the capitalist West, and in the field of technology the development of Soviet satellites and spacecraft outstripped Western efforts. During this period the two superpowers agreed to remain in direct contact, and a telephone "hot-line" was installed between the White House and the Kremlin in 1963. Also, various agreements, such as the Strategic Arms Limitation Treaty (SALT) and limitations on Anti-Ballistic Missiles (ABMs) were concluded.

But the thaw between East and West proved to be of short duration, and by the middle of the 1970s a second phase of the Cold War was entered into. One of the main factors was the sharp increase in the price of oil after the formation of the Oil-Producing and Exporting Countries cartel (OPEC), which now controlled the much-needed commodity. Leonid Brezhnev, Khrushchev's successor, immediately found himself in a favorable position. The USSR escaped the oil crisis because large quantities of oil and natural gas had just been discovered on its territory, while in the USA, the effects of the energy crisis were exacerbated by ten debilitating years of war in Vietnam (1965-1974).

New conflicts and revolutions soon arose that caused new upsets in world politics. For instance, the 1974 revolution in Portugal did more than simply establish a new government in this small European country. The communist governments and revolutions in its former colonies—Angola, Mozambique, and even tiny Guinea-Cape Verde—opened the way for the rapidly expanding Soviet fleet to establish new bases on both sides of the Indian Ocean. The Shah of Iran was also toppled during this period, opening the way to a new conflict between the Muslim/Arab world and the west, and threatening oil supplies. The Brezhnev-led regime in the Soviet Union seemed to be overcome with self-satisfaction and bravado. From its overweening self-confidence in the handling of international affairs, to increased defence spending and excessive investment in heavy industry, the Soviet Union seemed determined to entrench its role as a global superpower.

Inevitably, concerns were raised in the USA. The path of collision embarked on by Ronald Reagan's new administration went hand-in-hand with a fanatical fear of the Soviet military threat and a belief in the inevitability of an apocalypse. Americans citizens were urged to abandon the chaos of the Richard Nixon-era that had erupted in the shadow of the Watergate scandal. Gradually, the U.S. economy began to dominate the world and an ever-strengthening dollar soon overshadowed the massive and once-powerful economic system of the USSR that was largely dependent on heavy industry. Where exactly the turning point in the balance of power occurred will doubtless become clearer as history unfolds and a clearer perspective on the past emerges. The fact remains, however, that the crude and inflexible economy of the USSR, which up to the mid-80s had led in the production of various commodities, began to collapse in a dramatic manner. In the USA, however, the economic explosion in Silicon Valley, spread by the cyber network and producing software that provided for a large variety of modern needs, launched the economy into an era of unprecedented prosperity.

Both parties in the Cold War eventually came to the realization that the nuclear arms race and the arms build-up would lead to nothing other than a catastrophic outcome for the whole of humanity. Mikhail Gorbachev made a significant individual contribution to the defusion and conclusion of the Cold War—processes that received added momentum after the summits of Reykjavik (1986) and Washington (1987). Nevertheless, forty years of suspicion, lack of understanding and enmity could not simply be removed. Neither, for that matter, could Soviet industries that had been designed exclusively for weapons-production and the servicing of military systems be transformed overnight to fit the needs of a rapidly changing society.

But the legacy of the Cold War that is likely to linger the longest in the contemporary world is its human consequences, the individual traumas suffered by so many ordinary people. Hundreds of thousands of people's lives were changed forever by the ripple effects of the Cold War and international conflict, and thousands more were directly at the receiving end of brutal and dehumanizing acts. There are many stories that need to be told, and much that needs to be written about the personal suffering of ordinary individuals whose daily lives were casualties of global power-struggles and political conflict during the decades following World War II.

This book offers an opportunity for a small, disparate group of people who lived during these tumultuous times to tell their stories. The personal trajectory of each person's life is linked in an integral way to the contemporary history of the Cold War era. In one hemisphere of the globe, three members of the Slav nation that is today known as the Czech Republic tell their stories—elements in a larger narrative of a nation that found itself on the fault line of East and West. For no other reason than geographical location, ordinary men and women such as those whose life histories are recorded here, were innocently and without engaging actively in war and destruction, drawn into the political turmoil of the Cold War. It is people such as these that may be said to be among the bravest of the victims left behind on the battlefield of history.

And on the other side of the world, at the southern tip of Africa, three Africans recall how their lives were irrevocably changed during this same period. A small parliamentary majority brought the Nationalist Party to power in South Africa in 1948—a minority government that lost no time in aligning itself with the outspoken anti-communist leadership of the USA. These same white Afrikaner Nationalists who had, a few years previously, refused to fight "England's war against the Nazis," now offered few objections to sending troops to fight alongside the Americans and their allies in the Korean War in 1950. From then on, throughout the Cold War, Afrikaner Nationalists accepted U.S. hegemony and claimed U.S. support.

In order to bring the six stories in this book into sharper focus, it will be necessary to examine the particular histories of South Africa and Czechoslovakia more closely. It is, of course, not possible to render the full complexity of the historical period by focussing exclusively on only a few particular beacons. But it needs to be emphasized that completeness is not what is aimed at here. With a few broad brushstrokes, we hope to sketch the period that followed in the wake of World War II, and, by adding a couple of finer lines, to trace its repercussions by examining certain milestones in the respective histories of two countries at opposite ends of the globe.

The histories of Czechoslovakia and South Africa during the decades of the Cold War differed in significant ways. So, too, the military and economic rivalry of influence of the Soviet Union and the USA affected the people of these two countries very differently. Yet, even so, there were several points of contact in the experiences of those who suffered oppression. In both countries, the majority of people were affected by an official, doctrinaire rigidity, and endured the effects of the Cold War—official corruption, crimes against humanity, and state oppression.

The effects of the Cold War intensified suffering both in Czechoslovakia and in South Africa, and this compelled many individuals and small groups to take a stand. Political and economic oppression generally result in resistance and revolt, and when individuals—encouraged by the support of others—pit themselves against structural violence, a set of commonly held political and ideological beliefs frequently comes into being. This book focuses on particular individuals who went against the tide and fought for democracy and freedom for their two countries. And while the manner in which they went about this might differ, what is strikingly similar is the passion and conviction with which they acted to defend their particular truths.

2

The Context of the South African Narratives

What is it that makes ordinary people commit acts that jeopardize their personal freedom and happiness? What inner compulsion makes them risk imprisonment and even death? The question is as old as Socrates and Spartacus. In the case of the six narrators of this book, it was the threat to their personal freedom and the obstacles put in the way of the achievement of personal happiness and fulfilment that caused them to take the risks they did. Resistance is the fruit of awareness and a profound sense of personal and social injustice. It results from the perception of threat, a sense of frustration, as well as anger and outrage. More than anything, perhaps, it was the will to live, the refusal to capitulate, the assertion of the self, that caused these people—and millions like them throughout human history—to tackle, in their small ways, political and social systems that were at once foreign and frightening.

The Nationalist Party and Its Leaders: 1948-1978

After 300 years of colonial rule and three decades of Commonwealth membership, a small parliamentary majority brought a minority of whites to power in 1948. Since the main aim of the Nationalist Party of D. F. Malan was to remain in power in order to advance the interests of whites—in particular those of Afrikaners—its intention of changing the structure of South African society soon became evident. Nearly half a century of concessions and government by military strategists (such as General J. C. Smuts), and pragmatists gave way to the rule of ideologues and technocrats. Within a year, whites in South West Africa (now Namibia) were granted the right to choose six members to represent them in the South African parliament. At the same time, the right of Indians to elect parliamentary representatives was revoked, and shortly afterwards, in 1951, a set of processes was put in place to remove coloreds (people of mixed race) from the voting roll. Just before the 1953 general election, the Nationalist Party changed the borders of constituencies to their advantage.

More than any of its predecessors, this government was determined to remain in power, using whatever mechanisms were necessary and exploiting the power of the state to the advantage of the Party. For example, senior officers in the defence force were replaced by Nationalist Party and *Broederbond* supporters—the latter would, indeed, for decades to come, exercise control over all facets of Afrikaner politics and society. Top positions in the judiciary, the civil service, the South African Broadcasting Corporation (SABC) and the South African Police were given to members of the government's inner circle. The *Broederbond* and the Nationalist Party began to exercise control over every aspect of the social structure that fell under the jurisdiction of the state, including the South African Railways, the Electricity Supply Commission, the Iron and Steel Corporation and the Prisons Department.

The 1953 election resulted in the Party achieving an enlarged parliamentary majority and a further strengthening of its hold on the state machinery. With the retirement of D. F. Malan in 1954, yet another step was taken in the direction of consolidating Afrikaner state control. Malan's successor, J. G. Strijdom brought to the fore a new dimension of power. Representing powerful groupings of white workers and farmers, he was far less circumspect than his predecessor in marshalling Afrikaner nationalist ideology in the sphere of race relations. Malan's roots had been in the more liberal-minded Cape Province, but with Strijdom in power, the political scene was soon under the control of groups with far more extreme ideas and interests. Afrikaner *baasskap* was declared, defined and implemented, and apartheid became the overriding policy.

After ten years of Nationalist Party rule, in 1958, Strijdom's death brought to power a man with whom apartheid would become synonymous: H. F. Verwoerd. From 1950 as Minister of Native Affairs, and again from 1958 to 1966 as Prime Minister, Verwoerd dominated the racial policies of the Nationalist Party. His pre-war German education, his ambitious zeal and his peculiar race-based logic ensured him a large following. According to Verwoerd, there was only one "constructive plan" that could work in the South African context. This grand plan had as its goal the advancement and protection of Afrikanerdom, and therefore of the white race. Nationalist policy exploited to the full the Afrikaner's fears of racial mixing and racial degeneration. The prevailing climate was one where the question most frequently asked at the conclusion of a debate about race was: Would you permit your daughter to marry a black man?

At the same time, however, Verwoerd fundamentally altered the terminology of apartheid, promoting euphemisms such as "separate but equal" cultures, nations and homelands. The term apartheid was itself replaced with "separate development," and references to "Natives" gave way to the term "Bantu" (a Xhosa/ Zulu word meaning "people"). These changes represented an important pillar of Verwoerd's policy: quasi-independence for areas designated "homelands" for various black groups. Accordingly, 8 percent of the population was to be squeezed into 13 percent of the land—and often the least hospitable parts, at that.

The other pillar was to declare South Africa a republic, and to resign from the Commonwealth. Both these aspects of Nationalist Party policy came into being in the context of a far larger process, namely, the decolonization of Africa. Shortly after Verwoerd announced a referendum to gain the support of the white electorate for a republic, the British Prime Minister, Harold Macmillan, delivered his famous "winds of change" speech in the South African parliament. In it, he described the irresistible tide of African nationalism that he had encountered on his tour of various parts of the African continent. He made it clear that Britain would not support the apartheid policies of the South African government, arguing that legitimate political power could only be gained on the basis of the principle of individual merit. Verwoerd's impromptu response was a reiteration of his government's position: the defence of the rights of the white man—a "European minority"—on a black continent.

After the general election of 1966 the Nationalist Party again increased its majority. Shortly afterwards, the fifth anniversary of the Republic was celebrated and the country experienced unprecedented economic prosperity. But on 6 September, as he was about to address parliament on an important matter of policy, Verwoerd was fatally stabbed. A large section of the white population felt abandoned and afraid, for the architect of a policy that protected and promoted their interests had summarily been removed. In reality, however, no political vacuum was left in the wake of this event. Verwoerd's successor was the Minister of Justice, B. J. Vorster, and it soon became evident that the policy of apartheid would continue to be carried out by the collective will of the Nationalist Party leadership and top civil servants whose positions were the result of careful political screening.

Under the leadership of Vorster, the policy of apartheid was elaborated. What structures could be set in place to govern the urban blacks? Would it be possible to incorporate urban blacks into local government by means of Community Councils—particularly after the schools uprising in Soweto in 1976? Should black control be extended in homeland governments? In addition to addressing these issues, Vorster also tried to include coloreds and Indians in a revised constitutional system. As part of this plan, the Colored Representative Council, the South African Indian Council and the white parliament would refer legislation that was of general community interest to a Council of Cabinets, presided over by the State President. Some white South Africans saw these adjustments as the beginning of a series of concessions that would eventually bury apartheid. But for most blacks, coloreds and Indians, apartheid remained a formal structure that fundamentally violated their human and citizenship rights.

During Vorster's administration, resistance against apartheid gathered momentum. The Black Consciousness Movement (driven by Steve Biko), the Black People's Convention, the South African Students Organization as well as several other organizations mobilized public opinion. Increasingly, terrorist attacks were launched, not only from neighbouring territories, but from within the country as well, as acts of resistance increased. Two months after Steve Biko's brutal death in detention, and a month after the clampdown on Black Consciousness organizations by Minister of Justice Jimmy Kruger, South African whites again went to the polls in the 1977 general election. This time, the Nationalist Party won a record number of 134 seats in parliament.

In September 1978 Vorster resigned as Prime Minister and was made State President (in place of Nico Diederichs who had died in office). Barely eight months later, the government "Information Scandal" resulted in Vorster's political career ending in disgrace. He was succeeded as Prime Minister by P. W. Botha, ex-Minister of Defence, whose administration was characterized by an oppressive state of siege involving draconian legislation, a succession of states of emergency, and huge increases in military spending. Botha controlled his cabinet, parliament, and extra-parliamentary opposition with brute force. But it became increasingly evident that the tide of resistance could not be held in check indefinitely.

Living under Apartheid

There are various definitions of the policy of apartheid in post-war South Africa, and a glance at history reveals that each apartheid leader gave a particular slant to its interpretation. But however apartheid was interpreted, certain characteristics are central to the notion. Throughout its years in office, the Nationalist Party had but one ultimate goal for apartheid: the preservation and protection of *Afrikanerdom*. In effect, this meant the protection of white power and the advancement of the white racial group. While biologically based racism was not an essential aspect of Nationalist rhetoric, its everyday discourse was, however, peppered with crude racist statements. In addition, every aspect of an individual's life was to be determined by his or her racial origin. Race determined what sort of medical care you received, what your educational opportunities would be, where you could live, whom you could marry, what public amenities you could use, and whether you could own fixed property in certain areas. Your race determined your life expectancy, how far you lived from your place of work, and even access to alcohol. Everything was linked to race.

South Africa was not the only authoritarian regime in the world. It was also not the only country where segregationist attitudes were to be found. The latter were prevalent even in the USA, the world's leading democracy. But apartheid in South Africa was a far more pervasive—because legislated—system, and it increasingly went against the tide in an era of decolonization and majority rule. The core of apartheid's legislative programme and the political projects associated with it clashed sharply with post-war sentiments. Nevertheless, an exclusive nationalism, combined with a social system entrenched by a plethora of apartheid laws, resulted in a unique political system that increasingly drew the majority of the population into its vast network.

A central aspect of apartheid policy was the system of race classification (Population Registration Act of 1950). With this as its point of departure, the comprehensive system of apartheid pursued its ideal: maximum separation of the races in all spheres of life. The Mixed Marriages Act (1949) and the Immorality Act (1950) prohibited marriage and sexual relations across racial boundaries; the Group Areas Act (1950) and the Prevention of Illegal Squatting Act (1951) allowed geographical zones to be defined according to race, and for people to be confined to these zones; the Reservation of Separate Amenities Act (1953) led to separate and unequal public amenities—resulting in "petty apartheid" such as the reservation for whites only of public swimming pools, buses, parks, benches, post office counters and liquor outlets; the Bantu Education Act (1953) provided for a separate and highly unequal education system for blacks.

With the establishment of the Group Areas Board, large-scale dispossession and forced removals took place. The colored and Indian population groups in Cape Town and Durban were especially affected by this legislation. It is estimated that 600,000 people in these two cities alone were removed from their houses and businesses. In the wake of this, it frequently happened that building companies and property developers bought houses at bargain prices, effected improvements, and sold them as "whitewashed cottages" to whites. District Six in Cape Town lost its 60,000 inhabitants and the city's architectural heritage suffered as historic Victorian houses were razed. An inner-city wasteland with a few scattered churches and mosques are all that remain today as testimony to the government policy of the time. In other cities and towns, similar forced removals took place, and among these were Sophiatown in Johannesburg and Marabastad in Pretoria.

Apartheid also played a role on the labor front. Legislation in the 1950s resulted in the reservation of an increasing number of job categories for whites. Blacks were not allowed to hold positions of authority over whites, and unions with black and colored membership were forced to establish separate branches and to appoint white executive managements. The policy of job reservation and the ready availability of work in a growing civil service reduced white unemployment, thus significantly reducing the number of poor whites.

One of the central pillars of apartheid was the migrant labor system, which provided cheap labor for the mining industry. Strong influx control measures were implemented to deal with the problem of increased urban growth, thereby limiting the development of a black urban working class. In addition, with the large numbers of workers who were forced to remain in rural areas, white commercial farmers were freely able to exploit farm workers. A further way of maintaining the low cost of labor was to import migrant workers from Zambia, Malawi, Angola, Tanzania, Zimbabwe, Botswana, Lesotho, Swaziland and Mozambique. The importation of cheap labor helped, furthermore, to maintain the traditional role assigned to the South African Bantu Reserves, namely to ensure that black South Africans had a fixed place to live. Section 10 of the 1952 Urban Areas Act, which regulated both the movements and the rights of blacks, became a useful instrument in stemming the tide to the cities. Only those blacks who could prove that they had been born in a city, or had worked for one employer for an uninterrupted period of ten years, or who had been living in a city for fifteen years, were permitted to live with their wives and unmarried children under the age of eighteen. Everyone else had to register as a work seeker within seventy-two hours of arrival in an urban area. If they did not succeed in finding work, they were simply sent back to where they came from. A whole web of laws thus regulated the movements of black people.

A further aspect of this complex mechanism of social engineering was the Bantu Education Act of 1953. Its funding and administration were relocated from missionary societies and provincial departments to a single centralized control point: the Department of Bantu Administration. The government blatantly claimed that the majority of mission schools placed too great an emphasis on academic education, that English as medium of instruction alienated blacks from their language and culture, and that the liberal ideas these schools transmitted posed a danger to the state. Henceforth education would take place in the mother tongue—at least until the eighth year of education. After this, Afrikaans and English would be used, with a strong emphasis on technical education. Strong criticism was levelled against this "education for barbarism" which was rejected as a system of "education as retribalization to produce a cheap but not entirely illiterate labor force." The huge discrepancy in education spending between white and black children further emphasized the nature and purpose of apartheid education: the training of the masses to fulfil their pre-ordained subservient role in the social structure.

The apartheid system was also aimed at establishing local and regional governments in the reserves. Huge numbers of black farmers were removed from agricultural land and relocated to urban zones inside designated homelands—fragmented territories which would gradually be consolidated. The establishment of decentralized industries on homeland borders was encouraged by means of tax incentives. But not all these proposals were implemented. For example, Verwoerd rejected the idea of the consolidation of land because this would undermine the role of tribal headmen and local chiefs whose support was crucial to the success of the Bantustan policy. Because he recognized the power and potential of African nationalism on the continent, Verwoerd saw the homeland policy as a means of effecting a type of "internal decolonization." But there were many anomalies in his theory. The most glaring, perhaps, was that the white population, with its diverse national origins, was seen as one group, while black groups with divergent cultures, languages and history were separated into rather arbitrarily defined ethnic groups or minority nations in a policy that served the regime's divide-and-rule policy and its ultimate goal of racial domination.

Resistance: 1949-1964

South Africa has always been a country of conflict. One of the greatest sources of conflict may be traced to the dedicated enthusiasm with which a section of the population (white, and overwhelmingly Afrikaans-speaking) identified themselves with the utopian visions of leaders such as Malan, Strijdom, Verwoerd, and Vorster, and ignored the aspirations of the disenfranchized majority which rejected the racist foundations of Nationalist Party policy. Shortly after the assumption of leadership by the Nationalist Party in 1948, voices could be heard among its following favoring the right to self-determination of black people. But the black majority had plans of its own. At the 1949 conference of the African National Congress (ANC) it was formally accepted that more militant methods of resistance were needed. All forms of white domination were rejected, and voices rose in support of mass struggles by means of boycotts, strikes and civil disobedience.

Throughout the 1950s the resistance of the ANC coincided with the anti-colonial movement in the rest of Africa. Colonel Nasser's anti-imperialist revolution in Egypt in 1952, the independence of Libya the same year, and that of Sudan, Morocco and Tunisia in 1956, Guinea in 1958 and a host of other African nations during the 1960s, all served to keep alive the hope of liberation in South Africa. But the Nationalist Party had already made it clear in 1950 that it would not tolerate resistance, and the Unlawful Organizations Bill (later re-christened the Suppression of Communism Act) drove a significant section of political discourse underground.

By 1951 the strategy of mass resistance had gained wide acceptance. It was directed at the pass laws (each black person who lived and worked in "white" South Africa had to carry a pass), the Bantu Authorities Act, the Group Areas Act, the Separate Representation of Voters Act and the Suppression of Communism Act. Government was warned that if these laws were not repealed, a Campaign for the Defiance of Unjust Laws would be called. The goal was to involve large numbers of ordinary people in street protest action against laws relating to separate amenities as well as those enforcing racial segregation. Groups of black people defied "Europeans Only" signs at railway stations and other public places, queued at Post Office counters reserved for the exclusive use of white people, and appeared on the streets without their passes. More than 8 000 people were arrested within a short period (approximately 6 000 of these were in the Eastern Cape), and all of them refused to pay fines. Jails were soon full to overflowing. Besides imprisonment, bannings took place, and the government used the Public Safety Act and the Criminal Laws Amendment Act against those who defied the law. While the Defiance Campaign was subsequently called off, the M-Plan (Mandela Plan) was soon put into place: ANC supporters were organized into small cells at grassroots level which were linked to the district and regional leadership of the ANC through a network of structures.

Resistance was taken to another level at the Congress of the People held on 26 June 1955 in Kliptown, near Johannesburg. Some 3 000 people participated, and, encircled by armed police, the meeting discussed and adopted clause after clause of the Freedom Charter. The latter codified the demands of the masses for a non-racial South Africa with political rights for all. It also gave expression to a desire that all national groups be treated equally, that everyone had a right to social security and a good education, and that the country should live in peace with other countries.

Throughout the 1950s, various black communities expressed their opposition to government policy, and the ANC Women's League frequently formed the vanguard. The climax of the anti-pass campaign was, indeed, the march of 20,000 women to the Union Buildings in Pretoria on 9 August 1956. Notwithstanding Prime Minister J. G. Strijdom's refusal to grant them an audience, the women's voice was heard nationally, and they left thousands of petitions at his door.

An increasing tide of resistance resulted in the government taking drastic action, and in December 1956, 156 people—including leaders of the Congress movement—were arrested on charges of high treason. They were accused of orchestrating a countrywide movement to overthrow the government—a movement that was, according to the charges, inspired by international communism. The Freedom Charter was viewed as a communist document, and the ANC and its allies were accused of having a policy that promoted violence. A formidable legal defence team (which included Nelson Mandela, Oliver Tambo and Joe Slovo) succeeded in having the charges against all the accused dropped, and the state's attempt at intimidating the liberation movement and labelling its leaders communists, failed.

Resistance to the government's oppressive and degrading legislation increased, and on 21 March 1960 the police shot into a crowd of unarmed anti-pass protesters at Sharpeville, where sixty-nine were killed and 180 wounded. That same night, the people attacked police in Langa in the Western Cape, burned municipal offices, cut telephone lines, and blockaded roads, and on 30 March Pan Africanist leader Philip Kgosana led a march of 30,000 in Cape Town in protest against police brutality. The ANC and the PAC were banned on 8 April 1960, a State of Emergency was declared, and more than 2 000 activists arrested. This marked a significant moment: denied the right to operate legally, the liberation movement was outlawed.

With so many leaders in detention, the burden of continuing the freedom struggle lay heavily on the shoulders of those leaders who were forced into hiding. Underground structures were set up, and, through a system of small cells, information was passed on and strategies secretly devised. After the lifting of the State of Emergency a group of ANC leaders called a consultative conference in Johannesburg where the demand was made that a National Convention be called before 31 May 1961 (the day set aside for the founding of the Republic). The Convention had to consist of the elected representatives of all South Africans, irrespective of race, color, or creed—a demand rejected outright by Verwoerd.

Meanwhile, a police search continued for Nelson Mandela. In June 1961 discussions were held concerning the future direction of the liberation struggle, and it was concluded that the use of violence was unavoidable—but also that all acts of violence would be under the strict control of the political leadership. A military wing was, accordingly, established, a sabotage campaign embarked on, and plans made to launch a guerrilla war against the regime. And so, in November 1961 *Umkhonto weSizwe* (The Spear of the Nation) was founded, and on 16 December 1961 the first explosions took place at government buildings and electrical power installations.

Despite increasing international pressure on the South African regime, the stifling of political opposition continued. In November 1962 the United Nations General Assembly recommended that economic and diplomatic sanctions be instituted against South Africa. However, because South Africa was included in the Western bloc during this period of the Cold War, it was not severely affected by this decision. Sanctions were not mandatory, and were ignored by most of South Africa's trading partners, though the UN resolutions did result in newly independent countries choosing not to establish diplomatic relations with South Africa. Thus began the gradual isolation of South Africa within the Western power bloc.

A cycle of violence ensued as an increase in underground activities against the state resulted in renewed acts of retaliation and oppression. On 1 May 1963 the government enacted the General Laws Amendment Act (widely known as the "90-day Act") which allowed the police to detain suspects for ninety days without charging them in a court of law. Detention orders could be renewed after ninety days, which effectively meant that a person could be detained for an unlimited period. With hundreds of its leaders in detention, the liberation movement struggled to keep the flame of freedom alive.

The movement experienced a particularly severe setback when, on 11 July 1963, police raided *Umkhonto weSizwe* headquarters in Rivonia, Johannesburg, arresting the entire leadership of the High Command. This led to the infamous Rivonia Treason Trial, and a year later, on 11 June 1964, the leaders of the ANC and *Umkhonto weSizwe* were found guilty. Mandela was given a death sentence, which was later commuted to life imprisonment. Nelson Mandela, Walter Sisulu, Govan Mbeki and many others were immediately taken to Robben Island where they were held in single cells for nearly three decades. This was the same year that the three former Robben Islanders who tell their prison tales in this volume, were sentenced and brought to the prison that would become a symbol of the heroic defence of truth and justice.

The Robben Island Tales

The accounts of three former Robben Island prisoners in the chapters that follow should not be seen as a comprehensive and representative picture of life on the Island. These three were all from the Border region (mainly East London, Mdantsane, and Grahamstown) in the Eastern Cape. Here, resistance against apartheid was part of everyday life in the 1950s and 1960s. Each of those who tell their stories experienced the daily reality of apartheid: the carrying of a

The prison on Robben Island: condemnation, punishment, captivity and isolation.

reference book (*dompas*); regular humiliation as a result of being considered a second-class citizen; inferior education, housing and health-care. Each prisoner participated in acts of resistance from an early age: organizing for the ANC and its youth league; attending meetings where national leaders (such as Professor Z. K. Matthews, Chief Albert Luthuli and Nelson Mandela) spoke out against apartheid; participating in acts of civil resistance such as defiance campaigns and strikes. Eventually, each considered the option of an armed struggle. Perhaps the legacy of prolonged racial conflict, stemming from the nineteenth-century frontier wars between Xhosa and white settlers (who were supported by the colonial government in Cape Town), provided the impetus for continued struggles in the troubled Border area. Indeed, the symbolism of this popular name for the region should not go unnoticed. The broad band of territory between the Great Fish and Kei rivers was meant to act as a border or a buffer zone. This troubled stretch of land was the birthplace of many political leaders in contemporary South Africa. It also provided fertile ground for active resistance against oppression and a training area for active involvement in the national liberation process.

The stories told in the following three chapters provide a door to understanding the grassroots experiences of the large number of "ordinary" Robben Island political prisoners—those who spent many years with their comrades in common cells. These stories will not give us a full understanding of the total picture of life on the Island. Nobody is able to reconstruct the full impact of the entire experience of any one political prisoner, for aspects of one's personal experience are always elusive. Life experiences are like books on a library shelf—one can constantly reshuffle and rearrange them, or unpack new titles. Clearly, life histories can also be evasive. They are made up of fragments of information, and, depending on what we wish to uncover, and how we order these fragments, different perspectives emerge. The process of reconstructing life histories is thus necessarily selective.

The three life stories here draw our attention to the trauma of long-term imprisonment. The fragments are necessarily incomplete, though the chapters do try to convey some conception of the whole. This collection of stories reveals aspects of a specific era. It tells us about broader social and political issues, about the role of these forces on the Island, and also about the interplay between social processes and the different individuals who tell their stories.

As we have seen, the years of authoritarian rule in South Africa were marked by a range of human rights abuses. It is not the intention of this book, however, to analyse these abuses. Nevertheless, as part of the context, aspects of legislation, economic and social structuring, as well as repressive machineries introduced to maintain power and control have been briefly examined.

Not a single aspect of the lives of South Africans—black, as well as white—was left untouched by apartheid. The white minority experienced a privileged position while those classified "non-white" were caught up in a web of oppressive laws that influenced their everyday lives. Those who lived under oppression had little option but to accept their predicament, as the yoke of oppression became an inescapable part of existence. But the lives of those who tell their stories in the following three chapters are exceptional. Their resistance put them at great personal risk, and each of them eventually stood trial and was sentenced to long-term imprisonment on Robben Island.

The upsurge of resistance against the establishment of the apartheid system could not have gained ground without the support of the masses of oppressed people, even though this support was not always overt. Oppression was directly linked to race, and the keystone of the system was enforced separation on the basis of race. Those at the receiving end of injustice found themselves grouped together, and, because of the clear racial divide, it was possible for them to engage in organized opposition. Living together in oppressed communities contributed directly to the development of a strong awareness of belonging to the same group—of being in the same boat. Increasingly, the everyday situation of "non-white" South Africans called for the use of mass resistance through boycotts, strikes and other forms of civil disobedience. The fact that the regime managed to maintain control over every sphere of existence can largely be attributed to its massive military power and its growing control of financial and mineral resources. Moreover, it received continued support from many of its Western allies and callously used law as an instrument of total oppression. Indeed, the law determined all aspects of people's everyday lives in South Africa.

Apart from determining all aspects of the social structure, the law also prescribed how and what people should think and what they were allowed to do—the Unlawful Organisations Bill of 1950 (later promulgated as the Suppression of Communism Act) forced the Communist Party of South Africa to go underground; the Public Safety Act and the Criminal Laws Amendment Act threatened extremely harsh action against people who defied the law. While the Defiance Campaign (resistance to the pass laws in particular) was eventually called off, other forms of struggle emerged, including the beginnings of opposition to Bantu Education, the formation of trade unions, and the women's movement.

All three of the former Robben Island prisoners refer to aspects of the social functioning of the law in their narratives, thus indicating their experience of the law as a powerful instrument of social engineering. By means of various administrative measures, apartheid laws collectively determined what was "good" and what was "bad" in all areas of social life. The legal system became a mechanism to maintain a segregated society and to mete out punishment to those who resisted. Inevitably, resistance brought the three into conflict with the regime and they were subsequently arrested and charged. The sentences they received at their trials were harsh, condemning them to many years of imprisonment.

When they arrived on the Island it was made clear to them that they were in for a hard time. They were at the mercy of their warders, and in many ways these agents of the state attempted to violate their private worlds. By compelling prisoners to behave in certain ways and exposing them to degrading practices (such as forcing them to wear inferior prison clothing, using derogatory forms of address, setting common-law prisoners against them), an attempt was made to dehumanize them. The state and its agents were aware that once a person loses his sense of self-worth, the destruction of his personality will follow.

In the following chapters, three former Robben Island reflect on their lives and their time on the Island: they talk about themselves and how it came about that they ended up in court having to face political charges. All three arrived on the Island in the same year—1964. All three travelled the same route (though not together), transported by truck from East London and Port Elizabeth via George, where they slept over in police cells, before being bundled off to the Island by boat. In each case, it was their first trip out to sea.

They tell about their arrival on the Island and the reception they got. They go on to describe their daily routine and prison work, reflecting also on their relations with prison warders and the different forms of brutality imposed by the latter.

The stories reveal much about the prisoners' concern for their fellow inmates. Not only did they strengthen one another with support and encouragement, but they also prepared themselves for potential problems with their families and loved ones. A great deal of energy went into political discussions, studies and reflections on the struggle. The stories lift the veil on the activities and concerns of ANC and PAC structures on the Island and the maintenance of discipline within these structures. After several hunger strikes, conditions slowly improved as a result of political prisoners taking a stand against the harsh treatment they received.

The three tales contain dramatic evidence of strong-minded people who were determined not only to liberate their people, but also to maintain important aspects of their own identities and culture—including, in Johnson Mgabela's tale, the traditional circumcision rite performed on 361 young Xhosa political prisoners on the Island. Like the other stories, this story dramatically reflects the emotional sacrifices endured by human beings separated from their culture and their loved ones.

3

Joseph Faniso Mati: The Organizer

Heading for Trouble

You ask me where did it all start? I don't know. It might even go back to my birth. I was born on a farm near Adelaide where politics seemed to enter your system with your food and with all the other things about being a child. That was the farm of Errol Moorcroft's parents. He later became a member of the opposition in the white parliament. On that same farm was born Makhenkesi Stofile, who became the premier of the Eastern Cape. I was young when we left the farm but I can still recall that life was not very difficult. There was no shortage of food. We ate green things and fruit from the fields and there were quite a lot of rabbits and other animals for meat. Sometimes we even got some mealies harvested on the farms. When it came to health we had very few problems.

I can't remember exactly why, but later my father moved to Adelaide to work on the railways. I suppose it became difficult on the farm and there was no money. We were seven children and I am the eldest. My brother who was just younger than I died in Adelaide and one of my three sisters also passed away. Things started to change for us there and life became very difficult. In addition to his work on the railways my father would sometimes go and work on farms and shear sheep. But there was very little money. Even our health started to suffer. On the farm my grandmother would give us medicine when we got the 'flu or when it was a stomach-ache she would mix herbs with milk. We would drink it to clean our stomachs. In the town we no longer had that. From Adelaide we moved to Port Elizabeth where my father worked for the railways in the harbor.

When I was at high school our teachers encouraged us to go and listen to our leaders: Professor Z. K. Matthews, Chief Albert Luthuli, Nelson Mandela. In the township where I stayed in Port Elizabeth, I attended meetings—open-air meetings. Listening to these speakers always brought the same questions to my mind: Why is the situation in our country like this? Why are we treated differently? Why did that man at the hotel in Adelaide, who asked me to clean his car, beat me up and wet me with the hose-pipe when a little bit of water got inside the car?

Joseph Faniso Mati in 1991

From an early age I became involved as an organizer for the ANC Youth League and as a street steward, somebody who was involved in the executive of the ANC branch. Not only was I involved in organizing but I also assisted the people. Most of them were uneducated and when there was a problem at home they would call me to write letters and to give advice. They gained confidence in me and it was easy for me to organize them. I was always with them. Most of our people supported our views. When I asked a person to join the organization—even if the person had no money for a membership card of the ANC—that one would say: "Oh, my child, who is not a member of the ANC? We are all members of the ANC!"

At first we focused our efforts on organizing the people. When a newspaper reporter—I think his name was Gideon Khumalo—splashed the scandal of people having to work like slaves in potato fields at Bethal, the Congress Alliance stepped in. Khumalo revealed that several who didn't have a reference book had to go and work in potato fields. Some of them even died and were buried there. Hearing this, we decided that potatoes must be boycotted. We used young girls to help us. Young girls are very good at smelling out potatoes and they would go out into the streets. When detecting the smell of boiling potatoes they would go inside that house and tell the people not to use potatoes.

This boycott was directly linked to our campaigns against reference books. The government started the pass system among men and later decided to extend it even to women. This became a very serious matter because it was against our tradition. A woman was required to take off her *doek* (head-dress of scarf wound round head) when being photographed for the pass book. And she was called by the surname of her husband—something which was not done, especially in the rural areas. It was our custom that a woman keeps her father's clan name even after marriage. So there was a big resistance. I remember the reaction of the people when a fellow from parliament addressed a meeting in Port Elizabeth to explain the reference book system: "No, this is nonsense! You can't come and tell us this. You are from that mental asylum called parliament and you come and talk about this! Go to the police station and find out from the police what is happening. Let the police show you the injuries of those who were arrested; let them show you the pregnant women who were caught without a pass."

There were other campaigns as well, like the bus boycott of the early sixties. When the bus fare was increased by one penny, the people decided to boycott the buses. A penny at that time was a big thing. Our activities intensified but our main focus remained the pass issue. The police shot many people at Sharpeville and Langa precisely because they were fighting against the passes. We burnt these reference books. At that stage the government decided to ban the ANC.

Later, there was talk of embarking on an armed struggle, guns would be used and some petrol bombs. It was clear that we were heading for trouble. The mood of the youth was that we should fight. In 1959 I was elected a member of the National Executive of the ANC Youth League at the conference in Durban and my involvement increased. When the ANC was banned, we went underground. I was recruited to be a member of *Umkhonto weSizwe* and had to go to Johannesburg for training. It wasn't like later on when people went across the borders; we were trained inside the country. They taught us how to dismantle guns and how to shoot. We also received training to make bombs, Molotov cocktails, napalm bombs—and to sabotage motor cars. Things turned ugly, and for a few of us the war had started.

Although we knew that the war had begun, our targets were not supposed to include people. We were trained for using dynamite and gelignite to blow down pylons. Another target was to blow up goods trains, especially those carrying petrol in large tanks. We were also using plastic bombs to destroy and disrupt power stations. There were many targets such as these and we would have discussions to decide which targets to go for. We used all our contacts and every bit of information to get hold of the things we needed. In Adelaide a regular goods train coming from Fort Beaufort would carry a red flag, indicating that it had some explosives on board. They stored the dynamite outside the town and one of my duties was to break into the storage place and to steal the dynamite. Around that time I was working in the municipal laboratories in Port Elizabeth and we got some chemicals from there. Sometimes our friends who worked at other factories or druggists got us the things we needed.

When joining *Umkhonto weSizwe* we had taken an oath that we would fight for the ideals of liberation—even by having to die. All along we knew it was work with risks. Personally I knew that one day I would be arrested but I felt that it was my duty to perform these tasks. Although I sometimes thought about the dangers, we never discussed this in the group I was working with. We realized that some of us might become *iimpimpi* but it did not change our commitment.

Things started to heat up. During the State of Emergency in 1960 I went into hiding. My job was to look after the families of those who were detained. Very little normality remained—always on the run, always dodging the police, always looking over my shoulder. So when they got us it was not a great surprise. I suppose we realized it couldn't continue. You see, there is a friend of mine, he is a Member of Parliament now. We were arrested together at my place. Now, the day we got arrested, I said: "Hey Ben, we are going to go for a high jump, my friend. We must be prepared now; we are going to go for a high jump."

So we told ourselves that we were going for a long period to prison. I am not saying that we simply accepted the fact and that there was no feeling—suddenly we were cut off from our families. It was very painful. But, because of our political involvement, we had known that we could get arrested. Even worse, we had known that our involvement could lead to our death.

It all happened very rapidly. I was arrested in 1963. It was the end of the month—exactly the end of July. They came rushing to my home at seven in the evening. They got information from one who had been arrested in Humansdorp. So he spilled the beans and he told them. Then they started picking us up—all of us. The twenty-nine of us arrested that day were all *Umkhonto weSizwe* people.

Because they had arrested us under the new Sabotage Act, life was very difficult. The Sabotage Act was harsh and we would get no visitors and no lawyers. We were not prepared that there would come a stage when we would be arrested and be alone in a cell where we would be tortured. During this time it was common that the police would try to trick some of the fellows. Referring to a leader, the police would tell the others: "No, Joe has told us everything. You can just as well speak. Joe has said it all." Some thought that if Joe had said everything, then there was no point in them keeping quiet. This is how they fooled us and why many more were arrested.

They kept us in solitary confinement for about two weeks. We didn't know where we were. Nobody would tell us. One chap saw on a windmill the place name Thornhill and we assumed that we were in Thornhill. In the cell was no light, no blankets—only a sisal mat. They gave us old porridge full of ants and for the whole two weeks we had no opportunity to wash. From there they took us to Walmer police station where we could at least clean ourselves. They also gave us blankets but the blankets were full of lice. One fellow amused himself by looking for the lice and killing them. When we complained, they sprinkled DDT on the blankets and in the cell. Only much later did we learn about the danger of DDT.

I did not suffer physical torture, but several of my comrades did. They were handcuffed and had to stand the whole night. I remember someone complaining: "Hey, my head seems as if it is full of water." When I asked what happened, he said: "The police kept hitting my head against the wall." Fortunately I escaped this kind of treatment. They used other methods on me. Sometimes I would wake up at night hearing somebody calling my name. Only that—just my name. Sometimes the voice would add: "Speak the truth. Just tell them everything." When waking up, still exhausted by hours of interrogation you wondered whether the voices were real. I sometimes wonder even today.

Although we were arrested on the same day for more or less the same acts, we were not tried together. Different trials took place in different courts—probably to defuse any possible protest by the people. My case took place in Port Alfred. The main charge was sabotage. All of us belonging to *Umkhonto* were charged with sabotage. Six of the twenty-nine of us arrested that same day in July of 1963 were sentenced to death and I received ten years. Shortly after the trial a few of us who got long sentences were taken from Port Elizabeth to Robben Island.

The journey was by truck. We were in the back of this truck. Two-two we were manacled and shackled together—arms as well as legs. We stopped over in George and slept there in police cells, still chained. Then on to Cape Town to the harbor and onto the boat to the Island. My first journey on sea: I had never been on a boat before. There I was, sitting in the belly of this boat, next to my comrades—some of them got quite seasick. All the time we were handcuffed and chained together.

Arrival

And what a reception on Robben Island! The warders shouting instructions for us to get onto the truck for the short journey to the prison cells. Even taking us down from the truck, they didn't care. Some were beaten, some would fall down, because each one of us was still chained to a comrade. The warders were ruthless. They treated us more ruthlessly than they treated the criminals. I suppose the intention was for us to die on Robben Island—if not our bodies then at least our spirits.

And what a reception on Robben Island!

We later heard that even the Justice Minister, B. J. Vorster, visited Robben Island after our arrival, to celebrate. The Security Branch in Port Elizabeth also had a big party. They were convinced that they had broken the backbone of *Umkhonto weSizwe*. This rubbed off on the warders and I remember one saying: "You dogs, do you think you can rule South Africa? You want to become the cabinet! You want to take over! But who are you? You want to mess up this country like other states in Africa! This you will never achieve!"

It was April '64 when we arrived on the Island. There was no proper clothing. You can imagine, people who were used to wearing shoes and when they got there there were no shoes. We were going to the quarry barefoot and the warders would enjoy themselves and even call their children and say: "*Kyk hoe loop hulle!*" Because it was difficult to walk. We were not used to that. It was difficult to get shirts, or trousers, or anything, even a mere khaki handkerchief. Common-law criminals were being put in charge in the stores and the kitchen and corruption was rife.

For us it was the first time to experience the scheming and the plotting of the prison underworld. Most of us had been arrested and detained previously but we had no experience of these kinds of prison conditions. So when we arrived there, we got a very, very bad reception. In addition to the bad food and the inadequate clothing, we initially had to stay in the *sinktronk*. These cells were very cold, especially during that first wet Cape winter. Everything was bad. Even the blankets were full of lice. And when we got ill we were afraid to go to the prison hospital. Most of us were convinced that the warders hated us and that we would die in hospital.

On with the Struggle!

Fortunately, when we got to Robben Island we found that the ANC was already organized. There were group leaders and a structure. So when we got there we were called by these people who were in charge. Then they would brief us and tell us that things were tough: "This is what you must do and this is what you must not do." They would tell us: "Comrades, you must know that we are arrested here—we are in prison and the conditions are bad. So you must understand that the struggle continues. We have got to make the conditions better in prison. We are going to fight for many things. And fighting for these things will entail suffering."

But our joint struggles also provided ways in which we could grow together. Each time, we would discuss our complaints—in all the cells. We would decide on a delegation to go to the authorities and put forward these complaints. Initially, we were always getting negative responses, but we continued discussing: What must we do now? If we had decided to embark on a hunger strike, then we would discuss how to prepare for that hunger strike. A hunger strike is a painful thing because it is a sword with a two-edged effect. It affected us because after a hunger strike of five to six days it would take a time to recover.

Although we suffered as a result, we realized that this was one of the few ways to register the points that we wanted to make to the authorities. Each time, we tried to get the message of a pending hunger strike to the people outside. They had to know that we were resisting oppression—even inside.

I don't know how many hunger strikes we embarked on to try and fight all the conditions. We made representations to the officials but they would do nothing. Until a breakthrough came. The International Committee of the Red Cross was allowed to visit us. So what happened? People from Pretoria came before the International Red Cross arrived. We put all our complaints to this group from Pretoria, but, as we put our complaints, these fellows became very hostile. I remember one incident. I was on the committee that was putting complaints through to the authorities on behalf of the rest of the prisoners. One of the group from Pretoria—I think he was a general in the Prison Services—started talking about other states in Africa, about military coups, and about us thinking that we can rule the country. Then Harry Gwala from Natal said: "*Ja,* it is true. Many bad things have happened in Africa. But nowhere in the world was a Prime Minister stabbed during daylight right inside Parliament!" He was of course referring to Dr. Hendrik Verwoerd. When Gwala said this, the officials got really mad. They immediately demanded our tickets which contained our prison numbers and wanted us to be punished for all that we were presenting to them. After these fellows had gone, we presented our complaints to the International Committee of the Red Cross—all the things we had said to the government officials as well. We were hoping that they would take our complaints to Jimmy Kruger and to the other ministers at that time.

I remember one member of the Red Cross saying in the presence of Robben Island prison officials, as we were putting our complaints: "I was in Uganda during the time of Milton Obote and the Minister who was responsible for prison services was himself being put in prison at that time. Now this fellow was complaining to us, the International Red Cross, about the food in the prison where he was kept—food that was provided and prepared in terms of the guidelines which he himself drew up." What this guy was saying, was that Kruger and the others must be careful. Some day in future the shoe might fit on the other foot.

Many complaints were put to the authorities—about food and clothing and facilities and working conditions and health services and general treatment of prisoners. One of our main arguments was that we should not be regarded as common-law prisoners. Our status must be prisoners of war. Our insistence on being prisoners of war made them very angry and hostile. But slowly things became better as time went on—because of our struggles.

Our Warders

The attitude of some of the warders also changed as our situation changed. When we arrived there, they were told by their superiors: "These people are very dangerous. You must not befriend them." Soon they realized that we were normal human beings and that we were not criminals. And that left a question mark on the minds of the ordinary warders. Why must we not speak to these people? If a warder loses his watch, we would pick it up and give it to him. And we were not engaged in many of the other things that criminals do in prison. Gradually we started to talk to the warders, and they with us. Once in a while a warder would agree to take a letter with him to Cape Town and mail it without informing the prison censor. Although they were not aware of it, they helped us in telling the outside world a little about life on the Island. Some of us who served shorter sentences later left Robben Island and a small number of these guys even went abroad to campaign in Britain or in America or at the United Nations. In this way we reminded the world of our existence.

We even encouraged some of them to study: "Look, man, you will never get promotion. You must do something; you must study. Sacrifice some of your time and money and pass JC (Junior Certificate), pass matric. You cannot become a lieutenant if you don't have matric—so you must study." During the course of time we started studying together with them; in fact, teaching some of them. The fellow who was in charge of us at the quarry was a ruthless person. But after some time some of us managed to help him with his studies, and he passed. He was later promoted. Some warders were even taught by Mandela and others in the single cells. When they were on duty for night shift they would take their books to be corrected by the Masondos, the Mandelas and other people there. So in that way we made quite a number of friends.

But these friendships remained friendships of a particular kind. We were still prisoners and they were the warders. Remember, the type of warder that we got on Robben Island when we arrived there was the old type. Some of them were in their forties up to their fifties, and so on; a very hostile, uneducated lot of people. All they knew was that a kaffir was a kaffir—you have got to mistreat him. They never made any effort to try and change us. All that they knew was that a disobedient prisoner had to be beaten and made to go hungry. What happened was that we were the people that wanted to change the warders. We told them point blank that a prison sentence cannot rehabilitate us. We will remain committed to the struggle. We even discussed among ourselves what we were going to do to reform the prisons when we went free. These people had messed up the prisons. Many of the senior warders got promoted to their senior ranks by virtue of the fact that they had been working in prison services for a long time. They were completely set in their ways.

Maybe one should try and understand the dilemma of the senior warder. On the one hand, there was the group of common-law prisoners who were overly subservient. In any one sentence that a criminal would utter to a warder he would use the term *Baas* several times: *"Baas, 'seblief Baas, kan ek 'seblief in die kombuis werk, Baas?"* All the criminals would do that in order to get the smallest of favors. And then there were us. We spoke English to them and when addressing them we used their ranks. If he was a captain we would say Captain So and So; if he was a lieutenant, Lieutenant So and So.

All the warders were Afrikaans-speaking and all of them were white. In many ways they represented the government of the day, the Nationalist Party. But even on the Island we noticed elements of the political and cultural differences which crept into Afrikaner unity by the end of the 1960s. Among themselves the warders often labelled one another as *"Verkramp"* or *"Verlig"*—labels from which we could gather that there were cracks appearing in the facade of Afrikanerdom. At least there were some changes on the mainland—a mainland that most of the time seemed to be as immovable and rock-like as Table Mountain on a clear day. The warders were products of that specific period in our history. They reflected some of the changes which were taking place in society. Some of them became very angry about what was happening outside. They were very much against any form of international pressure which could lead to changes on the Island as well as on the mainland.

From the moment we set foot on the Island, we realized that the warders were not there to look after our interests. Their attitude and the way in which they treated us made us afraid even to go to hospital when we were ill. We thought: They hate us so much that we should not take medicine from them. They hated those of us with higher qualifications even more. Andrew Masondo, who was a lecturer at Fort Hare before he came to the Island, was one of those who suffered most. I knew Masondo from outside—we worked together. But when I found him on the Island I thought: Hey, this man is finished! He was very thin and when he scratched himself the blood that came out was almost black. He had attracted most of their anger and beatings for the mere fact that he was educated. Warders would say: "All teachers must come this side." Then they would ask: "Have you got a driver's licence?" Those who said yes, they used to be put outside, they would be made to push wheelbarrows. Those were the ones that they hated most. They had to push those wheelbarrows with the narrow iron wheels through the soft sand of the Island.

Most of the forced labor that we were required to do on the Island was meant to humiliate us and to break our spirits. At first we had to do piece work. They gave us each a heap of stones and we were to crush them. It was hard labor and some of us could not manage the quota. If a person was unable to crush the amount of stone, his ticket was taken and he was given a spare diet. He would not get food for three meals or he would be sent for isolation to the single cells as punishment. Later on, we fought the question of piecework. With the assistance of a firm of lawyers in Cape Town, we challenged the right of the warders to force us to do a required amount of work.

Before the piecework issue was resolved the warders would be roaming around us and constantly complained about our slowness. And the way in which they expressed their dissatisfaction was always meant to humiliate and to hurt. They would ask you to take a stone from this end and to put it that end.

At least there were some changes on the mainland—a mainland that most of the time seemed to be as immovable and rock-like as Table Mountain on a clear day.

Tomorrow they would demand that you bring that same stone back to its original position. Sometimes you had to take a spade and do some work in an open space. Nothing was going to be done there—and you knew it. These people were only trying to destroy your spirit.

Later on, when they had done away with piecework, we decided on our own that we need to do some work. In prison the warders can destroy a person by forcing him to do senseless work. But you can also destroy yourself by doing nothing. We realized that we needed to do something physical because there was very little opportunity to exercise. You can't just hang around day after day. So we sometimes asked the warders to give us spades to go and do something to keep ourselves busy. Some of the youngsters who came in after 1976 couldn't understand this. They refused to work and we often told them: "You can't just sleep for the whole day; you are going to die here!"

Those of us who arrived on the Island as part of the first group of political prisoners could see a change in the attitudes of the warders. Later on we realized: No, these people are different from the older generation of warders. The older generation were not promoted because of their education or because of new qualifications. No, they were senior warders merely by virtue of the fact that they had been in the prison services for a long time. And for them there was only one way to treat a prisoner: Beat him and take his meals away. But later on the Prison Department was changing and they were sending educated young prison officers. They are more like ordinary people. Sometimes we would discuss with them the changes in the country. These changes were taking place whilst we were on Robben Island. Towards the end of my stay some of the younger warders would confess: "It is very difficult for our parents to understand, but all people have to stay together in this country."

A Day in Our Lives

Ja, well, everyday life on the Island was rather boring. Early in the morning the bell would ring and everyone had to make his bed, fold his mat, go to the bathroom, wait for the warders to open. And when the cell was open, we would go to the kitchen. There was no regular inspection of the cells during the week—it was inspected only on Sundays. During the day the warders could inspect or search the cells as they pleased—we were not there. Of course, we had our own cleaners who were doing the cleaning.

When we got there in 1964, the food was very bad. That was one of our main complaints. They gave us mealies and porridge in the morning—too little porridge and without sugar. The coffee was just like water with almost no taste. The rest of the day's food was nothing better. In fact, I never thought I would finish my ten years there.

At first we would get our breakfast food from the kitchen and all of us had to sit and eat there, next to the kitchen, in an open space. We were forced to remain in rows—to squat there in the open air, looking at the back of the person in front of you. There were no tables and no chairs. To make things even worse, we were constantly bothered by the insatiable seagulls. They loved to come down and to disturb us, because they loved our food. Even on cold and rainy days we would be squatting like that—gulping our humble porridge. Later on, a hall was built next to the kitchen and we would eat in the hall; sitting on chairs. We then would even have a prayer in the morning before eating our food. Things were getting better at that time. Later on we could even take our food to the cells and eat there.

We would get our food from the kitchen and all of us had to sit and eat there, next to the kitchen, in an open space.

The food that we got on the Island—you know the semels *which was given to cows and horses on the farms? They took something like that and cook it for us.*

After breakfast we would go out with the *span* to work. Most of us worked at the stone quarry. Some were breaking the cliff at the quarry, some would pull stones, the majority would chop the stones. We had to walk to the quarry. There were many of us—hundreds of us—and we would walk in this fenced-in area, in this fenced passage. The warders were just on the outside of this passage, armed with guns and dogs. Even at the quarry, whilst we were working, the warders were there. Some were amongst us, others were standing on the outside with guns and some others were manning the guard posts.

During the day we had a lunch break—food was brought to us at the quarry. Later in the afternoon we went back to the cells and had our meals. By just after five o'clock we were locked up again in the cells. We soon realized that it was essential for us to be constructively busy during these long evenings. It was indeed a very dangerous possibility that we could become mentally deranged—living like this for ten or sixteen or twenty years, depending on the sentence. Sitting there; thinking of your family, your wife, your girlfriend; feeling sorry for yourself.

So, back in the cells by late afternoon, we would eat our food and after a while some people would wash, others would be chatting, others would rest. In order to avoid a situation of people simply hanging around, the leaders decided that we must get busy in studies and in other forms of activity. These study periods were taken seriously. We appointed study officers from among ourselves. The role of the study officer was to declare the study period and to close it afterwards. Several things took place during this period but the ANC Disciplinary Committee (DC) concentrated on encouraging and enforcing two things in particular: studies and political discussions.

Section D—the communal cells

The DC controlled life in the cells. It was there until I left Robben Island. The DC was not elected, it was appointed. We did not know who appointed the DC and we did not know who exactly were its members. But the important thing was that the people knew very well that there was a DC. Members of the DC were appointed in each section. When I became a member, somebody just told me: "You are now a DC member." Then he explained to me how to behave and what I should do as a member. The main function of the DC was to see to it that there were political discussions. In prison the food of the politician is discussion; political discussion. Nobody should be excluded and nobody should be allowed to loiter in the yard. Everybody had to go out with the *spans* to work. People should not get themselves involved in smuggling food or forming small groups. The DC was very successful in keeping us together.

"People must study," the ANC would repeatedly say. If you got a matric, you had to teach others how to read and write, had to teach those who were attempting standard six or the junior certificate. Every person on the Island knew that he had an obligation to teach others. Later on when we managed to get study rights the teaching was more formal, but initially we specifically tried to help those who couldn't read or write.

We even had societies: A Science Society and a Literature Society. People would come and ask: What is it to have 'flu? Explain this thing of 'flu. Somebody might prepare a topic from the few books which were available in the prison library and introduce a discussion. Other questions posed during these study periods were: Is there such a thing as a flying saucer? What is the biological evolution of man? How can a man be changed to become a woman? Some of us were interested in this question because sex-change operations were mentioned in newspapers. Others wanted to know: How do spaceships go up? On one occasion I was enthusiastically talking about the rotation of the earth.

More and more questions came up and I finally thought that I had explained this phenomenon in full. The next morning one of the comrades triumphantly exclaimed: "Hi, Joe, you were saying the earth is rotating, but this book of mine is still here where I put it last night!"

Rivalry

Of all these committees and societies the Political Committee was the most active. As I said, the two things that the ANC concentrated on enforcing and encouraging were studies and political discussions. The political discussions focussed at first mainly on the rivalry between ANC and PAC. When we got to the Island, the PAC were very hostile towards the ANC. They were often accusing the ANC leaders of selling themselves out to the Jews. They found it unacceptable that Ruth First and Joe Slovo could play an important role in the ANC. They believed strongly in "Africa for the Africans"—in the narrowest sense of the word. Today their interpretation is different, but at that time when they were saying "Africa for the Africans," they meant exactly that. I remember Mtupingo addressing a meeting here in my cell: "If we take over at twelve, quarter past twelve we nationalize, twenty past twelve we take all the Indians to a boat and we send them to Bombay and we chase all the whites into the sea; even the coloreds have no place with us."

There was this strong hostility, and they were constantly accusing us of being traitors and Communists. At times the lies which they spread were very scandalous. They would talk about big parties in Cape Town, attended by ANC leaders, where Jewish women would expose their thighs to these leaders and they would fall for that. We tried to discuss these lies with their leaders, but to no avail. On several occasions we challenged them to open debates about the history of South Africa. We would quote from history books and would try to show them: Look, man, history is against what you are saying. We pointed out examples where people clearly stated that black and white can live peacefully in this country—sharing everything and accepting that both groups had a claim to this land. Our position was that most white South Africans were born in South Africa and most of them speak Afrikaans—not some European language.

These wrangles with the PAC continued for quite a while. They would be attacking us almost every weekend, because over weekends we had lots of time to discuss and to talk. Later on, our leaders tried to convince us not to become involved in arguments. By then the ANC had become the majority on Robben Island and the leaders wanted to make it clear that it would serve little purpose for the ANC and PAC to continue their arguments. I remember a wise remark by one of the ANC members: "Look, man, if there is a big truck running down the street and there are a lot of young dogs barking at that truck, you will be wasting your time by chasing these dogs if your purpose is to stop the truck. We are concerned with the destruction of this minority regime in South Africa and with the destruction of Apartheid. Why worry yourselves about the PAC?"

But for most of us the ongoing broadsides of the PAC were irritating and annoying. We wanted to refute their statements and to rebut their claims. At last the leadership agreed: Okay, we only give you two weeks to try and convince them; after two weeks there should be no more arguments and debates with the PAC.

I clearly remember those times. For two weeks we went full-out and boldly tried to convince them that we were right. With the arrogance typical of hot-headed, highly politicized people, we launched our conversion campaign. In addressing a group of PAC supporters I would introduce my arguments (with applause from my comrades) by saying: "Look here, man, you know there was a Chinese philosopher who once said that if you have a garden and if you don't start plucking the weeds whilst they are very young, you must let them grow so that you pull them out with the roots. And I am going to do that to you today. I am going to pull you up with the roots because you have been telling lies here on Robben Island for a long time."

Only later in life did I come to realize that political ideas and persuasions do not change easily during heated and emotional debates. Humiliating remarks often reinforce positions. But at that stage we were satisfied that we had challenged them to a debate about South African political history and that we had refuted their claims. For everything we had an answer: You are saying we are communists. Come, let us tell you about communism. We will ask a communist from among our members to tell you about communism.

So there was that tension and conflict between us and the PAC at first. But later it died down—not simply because we were the majority, but also because we realized that our squabbles did not lead to anything constructive. Other issues came up. When the younger group came in during the seventies we were confronted with new debates: the Black Consciousness business. Initially we didn't know much about it. Some of us had had contact with members of student organizations at Fort Hare and other places, but now new political and social movements were appearing on the horizon. Terror Lekota, Popo Molefe, Eric Molobe—they brought new debates and new arguments to the Island. These young guys thought that it was going to be an easy thing to get the ANC and the PAC together to fight as one organization. Later on they gave up on this idea and joined the ANC. We never managed to unite these two forceful players on the liberation scene.

Staying Sane

As I said, if you were not constructively busy in prison, it was very dangerous, because you could become mentally deranged. You were sentenced, maybe to sixteen or twenty years, and it was no use thinking about your wife, or your girlfriend, or your children. There was nothing that you could do. So in order to stay sane and to avoid worrying about your loved ones, you had to get busy in studies, in discussions, in sport, in reading—later on even playing games like scrabble and chess. We enjoyed playing soccer and rugby. Some of us even played tennis. The ANC structures on the Island saw to it that we were busy. There was the Higher Committee—the Mandelas, the Sisulus—operating from the single cells, and there was the Disciplinary Committee on our side where the majority of the people were staying. We were very strict. People were not allowed to become engaged in corruption or any other thing. Everybody had to go out during the week with a *span* to go and work. Together with other organizations we would also have committees on sport and entertainment—in particular, plays and music.

But the one activity that dominated our stay on the Island was the political discussions. No-one who spent time on the Island can say that he hadn't been strengthened politically. It was as if we couldn't get enough. There were those who wanted to discuss politics every day. They discussed politics at lunch hour in the quarry, they discussed politics in the evening. They read a lot about politics in books and magazines. Most of the formal political discussions were organized by the ANC structures over weekends. On Saturday afternoons there were discussions in each cell. The topic would be decided on by the political committee and the cells would discuss what the political committee recommended. We often discussed the history of South Africa. It was one of the main themes with the ANC: focussing on where we came from and where we were heading. From here we would continue to discuss other countries around us— Mozambique, Lesotho, Angola; the formation of the OAU and even issues like the Middle East and the question of Ireland.

At first we were desperately trying to get hold of newspapers. We would steal them from the rubbish dump or from where a warder would put them. We would bribe the criminals, who were given more freedom of movement in that some of them worked in the village of the warders, to bring us whatever they could lay their hands on. In later years, when we had free access to newspapers, the situation was sometimes unbearable. Some of us would go to bed early so that we could read the newspaper during the night—when those who read it first were sleeping.

Having newspaper reports and cuttings available, the news analysis became more systematic. The analysis would, for example, be based on the Middle East crisis and somebody would lead the discussion. Or it would be on the IRA and the Irish problem. Or we would be discussing revolutions in other parts of Africa such as Kenya with the problems caused by the Mau-Mau. Wherever there was a crisis or a big event in the world—we would debate it. The main focus of these discussions was on South Africa and on what was happening in parliament and in the rest of the country. There we would be, sitting in the cell, arguing or listening. One person would lead the discussion, others would make contributions or ask questions, the rest would sit listening. That is how the ANC discussed politics on the Island. The other political groups did not participate in these discussions. They had their own meetings and I don't know what they

One part of the prison was divided into four cells—two on this side of the passage and two on the other side. More or less 70 people shared a cell.

discussed there. Ours were serious discussions—no applauding, no clapping of hands. It was a serious affair—organized by the political committee for when we were locked up in the cells. At first it was more difficult to arrange these discussions because we were under close scrutiny. But as time went on we could have these meetings without any fear of interference.

Although politics dominated our discussions, it was only natural that we thought about our people outside. Sometimes, you know, that thing of being a man, longing for your wife and especially because most of us were still young, we felt: Hey! I am getting old here. Certain things I cannot enjoy because of my stay in prison.

But then, through discussions with some of the others, we encouraged each other. When you fight for freedom these things have got to happen. Thinking and talking about our own feelings and experiences, and knowing that it is inevitable that things can go wrong in our families, we also discussed matters such as what might happen to people when they got out of prison. You might find that you had lost your family. Not all of us could maintain contact with our families. Some were arrested when they were still young, and when they got out of prison they found that their lives and their family were in tatters. I mean, the family were human beings too. You got married when you were still young. Could you expect your wife to wait for you for fifteen or twenty years? You started asking yourself the question: What would I do if it was my wife who was here? What would I be doing outside?

So we had these discussions on Robben Island and sometimes we were very frank. We would talk about it and say: Hey! Look here! When we go out we will find that terrible things have happened. Maybe your wife is not going to be at home. Maybe you will receive a letter whilst still on the Island, telling you that your wife is doing this and that. And what would your reaction be when you get outside? Although it wasn't easy, we realized that we had to talk about these issues. We had to prepare ourselves and teach ourselves to endure these problems. When we got out, there were many of us who did not find their wives at home. Many of the fellows were divorced—no wife at home. They were remarried. Or others got kids by some other men. And that was something the ANC were doing in prison—preparing us for this kind of thing.

Despite talking about the possibility of problems in one's marriage, and despite being prepared for it, one was still missing the wife; not being able to be with her; thinking and worrying about what was going on there. And although we were discussing other revolutions like the Chinese Revolution and what happened there, the Mau-Mau Revolution and what happened there—pointing out that people often got separated for good—it didn't take away the pain and the longing. We kept on saying to each other: Our loved ones are struggling outside as well. But we shouldn't be thinking too much about the outside. We are here in prison and we can't change it.

In other ways, we also tried to encourage each other. I remember what my fellow-prisoner, Dr. Pather, who was a medical doctor, always told me. He pointed out the advantages of being a prisoner. You are sleeping enough; you don't eat lots of junk food; there is no liquor; there are no women. Maybe you would have died at an earlier age if it wasn't for prison and for all these factors. We wanted to look at the bright side, but it wasn't easy. When you sit there with your plate and swallow the unpalatable food, the reminder that the food on the plate was recommended by dieticians did not really contribute to changing its smell and its taste.

Something else which managed to make the years more bearable was the opportunity to study. In the afternoon we would come back to the prison after having been out with the *span* to work. We would eat and be locked up by about five o'clock. A long night was lying ahead. After some chatting, washing and resting, the study officers would declare the studies. Some people would teach others, some would work on their own. Some people would go to sleep earlier—nine or ten o'clock was regarded as late. We read a lot—the *National Geographic* magazine, the *Farmer's Weekly*, other magazines and newspapers. We would never have had the chance to do this if we were not inside. Sometimes an assignment for UNISA (University of South Africa) could bring about only three or four hours of sleep for the diligent student. It didn't really matter when one was going to bed. The lights were always on. We later got used to it and it was only after my release that it occurred to me that a light was supposed to be off at night. We all slept with the light on.

The situation in the cells after lock-up time changed dramatically in later years. At first we struggled to get hold of any piece of news. We would devour one single newspaper report and often people would transcribe pieces of information so that it could be distributed to other cells. Later on we could subscribe to newspapers and apply for study rights. It then became a problem to deal with all the news and all the ideas. Around the 1976 Soweto uprising a new generation of political prisoners added to the flood of information. For some of us the days got longer and longer. It wasn't possible anymore to absorb and debate issues as they became available. In a way we missed the order and the discipline of our initial search to remain in touch with the world on the mainland.

Talking about the younger generation of prisoners who joined us towards the middle seventies reminds me of the need to introduce circumcision[2] for some of them. We realized that most of these youngsters were to stay in prison for a long time and that circumcision was necessary for them. It was all done clandestinely. We did not know when it would happen and the ANC pretended as if they did not know about it. There were no celebrations afterwards and we would only discover it that following day when we were going to play soccer and found that most of the youngsters were not there.

They had been circumcised by Mgabela—in small groups together. They would stay in the cell the following day or two—no water, their wounds being dressed by Mgabela, sometimes suffering from severe pain. All of this was done with the connivance of the person in charge of the hospital.

Just as there were no celebrations after circumcision, there were no celebrations of birthdays or of individual achievements. We did, however, celebrate annually the formation of the ANC way back in 1912. On this occasion somebody would read out a paper written by maybe Mandela, Toivo or Neville Alexander. Thereafter we would sing some of our freedom songs. Sometimes we briefly celebrated the independence of one or other African country.

Once in the Struggle, Always in the Struggle

In 1974 I left Robben Island, having served the ten years of my first sentence. Being back among the people, I looked at the conditions around me and concluded that the situation was more or less the same as before my imprisonment; there were no major changes in the country. And I wasn't the only one to think like this. A number of us felt this way: Jacob Zuma in Natal, Griffiths Mxenge in Johannesburg. Not only were there no changes in the political field, but we could also feel that there was something wrong with the ANC. It wasn't functioning as it should. We discussed it among ourselves and concluded: "No, man, there is something wrong. We know the ANC. If it is active inside the country, it cannot be difficult for us to know about these activities."

Fortunately for the ANC, a few of us were released from Robben Island at the same time—some strong fellows from Natal, the Transvaal, the Western Cape and the Eastern Cape. So we all felt the same and we tried to devise a means of

---

[2]Circumcision forms part of traditional rites among many African communities. It marks the advent of adulthood and formalises the position of men within the power structures of adult society.

contacting each other. We also thought we must make contact with the external mission of the ANC. Some of us should go out of the country to find out what was going on. In 1975 I found myself—called by the ANC—in Swaziland.

Now, I was still serving a banning order when somebody from Swaziland arrived at the place in Mdantsane where I stayed. He explained that some Robben Islanders passed through Swaziland on their way out of the country and they persuaded the organization to make efforts to contact us. We spoke about the risk and the fact that the police seemed to be more active than previously and that I was not allowed to leave the East London area. To cut a long story short: in late 1975 I arrived in Swaziland.

It was soon clear that the ANC had many problems outside. Some of the leadership, called the Group of Eight, were expelled because they were brewing up trouble. They planned on toppling Oliver Tambo and taking over. As a result they never made any effort to build the organization. That became my duty and I started by making contact with the Western Cape. It turned out to be more difficult than I initially thought: Cronin, Jenkins, and others were all arrested and new ones had to be drawn in. And there was also the problem of distance. The Western Cape, Swaziland, and Lusaka are all remote. But we had to get things going and arrange for *Umkhonto* recruits to be sent out from the Western and Eastern Cape through Queenstown up to the Transkei, Matatiele and other places, to Swaziland.

There were a few close encounters. In December 1976 they caught me on the Swaziland border. Fortunately I only had R150 in my pocket and they believed me when I pretended to be a tramp—going nowhere in particular. That day I used my experience of criminals on the Island and I flooded my sentences with *Baas*, mixing Afrikaans and English: "*My Baas, kyk hierso my Baas, ek gaan nêrens nie, my Baas. I am just travelling, my Baas!*" I escaped arrest that day and I seriously considered withdrawing from these activities. I did not want to go back to Robben Island. But I realized: I have to do it. It is a question of risk but the work should continue.

Because of my behaviour my banning order was lifted by the end of 1976. According to the Security Police I was a good person. So they didn't know about my ANC work, which became more and more intense. My activities took me to Maputo where I met with Tambo and Slovo. But sooner or later I had to run out of luck. It came in June 1977 when they picked me up at the border post, Golela, with stacks of June sixteen leaflets and some R3,000 on me.

Long periods of interrogation followed before they took me back to East London. In the end I was charged on a few counts: using my premises for ANC activities, carrying money for the organization, being a member of a banned organization, and so on. I got five years. So I went back to Robben Island where I served most of this sentence. They introduced a Release Board and I was one of the first ones, together with a few Namibians, to be released by this Board. Instead of November, I came out in July 1982.

Shortly hereafter we had the first State of Emergency and they detained me in East London for two years. It was only after we had embarked on a hunger strike in all prisons that they released some of us. I was detained for being active in the United Democratic Front (UDF), where I was the publicity secretary for the Border region. When they detained me the Security Police asked me: "Do you know why we lock you up? We know you are there for the ANC. You want to change these UDF things into ANC. That is why we detain you."

Retrospective

As one would expect, life on the Island had its own pattern. In looking back, my whole sentence seems to be just one long episode—my arrival, the years which I spent there and my departure. It was one comprehensive experience. From time to time something exceptional happened. There was the time when many of us were struck by what was called Asian 'flu. One of the brightest young men on the Island, also from Port Elizabeth, died as a result of the 'flu. Another thing was the earthquake which rocked the Island in the late sixties or early seventies. We had already been asleep when the tremblings started. The whole earth was shaking, and the cell with it. Everyone was woken and many started to scream, and even to cry. We were truly panicking. The next morning we complained to the warders for not unlocking the cells. Mandela even wrote something himself about this episode and it was sent to Pretoria, but there was never an outcome to his complaint.

Although my time on Robben Island forms part of our struggle for freedom and is therefore closely interlocked with the liberation history, it was of course also a period in my own personal life. I sacrificed with my comrades for a common cause, but I also suffered deep inside. Knowing that we had to do what we had to do established a bond and strengthened us. But at night, when the political debates and the study periods had ended, and when things started to quiet down, you couldn't help thinking about your loved ones. I didn't even know the full extent of their suffering. When I was taken away to Robben Island my wife was expecting a child. The child was born when I was in prison and the news of the birth of my son reached me soon thereafter. But what I never heard was that this baby didn't survive for long. Only after my release did I realize that the people at home withheld bad news from me because they didn't want to add to my suffering. Even my sister: I only found out when I came out that she had long passed away. All the time I thought my sister was still alive. They decided not even to tell me of my sister's death, notwithstanding the fact that in our culture it is very important for all relatives to mourn together.

When they told me about the pain and the grief of the tragedies experienced in my absence, it was as if my heart was ripped out of my body. There my wife was, telling me with tears flowing down her cheeks: "Our son died because of the difficulties I had. *Yo!* It was not even possible to get food!"

How she did it, I don't know, but she managed to bring up the other kids. Although everyone was battling to survive, her brothers and some other relatives assisted her and the children. Those were very tough times. She regularly told the kids: "Your father is on Robben Island." This idea of a father who was living far away, whom they can't see, didn't really help to keep alive the family ties. When I came out of Robben Island I was sent to Mdantsane. I was not allowed to go back to Port Elizabeth where they lived. When I did manage to pay them a short visit we could all see how confused the kids were. On my arrival they would step outside and did not want to come into the house. My parents tried to assure them: "This is your father. Don't be afraid." Everyone wanted them to accept me as their father but they were reluctant. After a long while the elder one started questioning me: "Are you our father? But what happened? How old were you when you left us?"

My wife was very worried. She wanted them to see and to understand me as their father. But she had a job in Port Elizabeth and the kids were still schooling there. We decided that she would stay in Port Elizabeth for the rest of that year and that she and the kids would join me in Mdantsane at the beginning of 1975. During the school holidays in June-July 1974 the children came to visit me. That was my wife's idea: "I want these kids to be with you for the holidays. They must get used to you too."

Later on they got used to me. The greatest difficulty for me was, however, to discipline them. My wife was always quarrelling with me that I was spoiling them. But I felt that I first had to convince them that I was their father. I would always just talk to them. You felt that you had been away for a long time and that it had taken time for the kids to know you. So, if you would discipline them, they might not like you.

You ask me if something stands out from all these experiences? Maybe there is this one thing which stuck in my mind and in my memory. During the first part of our stay we were often forced to strip naked so that we could be searched. It was common practice, this *Ukuthawuza*. We had to take off all our clothes so that they could see if we didn't have weapons or any other dangerous or forbidden thing with us. This was part of the procedure in prison. Criminals can of course be very dangerous, and they will use any opportunity to smuggle a knife or any other sharp object into the cells. But we always maintained that we were not criminals. We wanted to be treated as prisoners of war, with dignity. And to say that there was no dignity in *Ukuthawuza* was putting it far too mildly. It was a completely dehumanizing act—to be forced to strip and to show everything. What I will never forget, is the humiliation that we suffered, the filthy remarks made by the young warders, the feeling of complete helplessness. On those occasions I realized the true meaning of being delivered naked to my enemies.

4

Johnson Malcomess Mgabela: The Strategist

Born to Struggle

For me, life has always been a struggle for survival. My first few years on the farm in the Kwalera district is only a vague imprint in my memory. I was still small when my father came to East London to look for work. I was the only child and we settled in the Tsolo Location on the East Bank. Reading the history of the Border Region you will find that East London was the city where most incidents involving the pass laws took place. Many people from the rural areas came here and they were all expected to get passes even when they were only sleeping in the Location. At first we didn't have to pay a levy for this permit but we had to carry the permit with us. Later people coming to the Location from elsewhere had to pay—even just to sleep there for a short period. If you wanted to work, you had to have a pass. My first memories of living in the city coincide with this issue of obtaining and carrying a pass. The pass determined life for us. In 1944, when I was working in the harbor, I was already carrying a pass. Without it you couldn't work, you couldn't walk in the streets, you couldn't relax. So I grew up amidst this frantic scuffle for a pass. It was part of everyday life and almost accepted as normal.

I left school when I was twelve. I remember as a child I merely wanted a job, nothing more. But I was too young to work and for a few years I simply got caught up in the life of the Location. Maybe I was more conscious of the fact that my people were living a bad life, because when I started to grow up some of the older people insisted that I involve myself in politics. They said: "You should become an organizer for the Youth League because you are good. The people love you and you can talk."

For me it was enough to be a member of the ANC. I wanted nothing else. I didn't particularly want to be involved in more political discussions than was already taking place. An old man by the name of Mjo took me under his wing. He looked after me and forced me to think more about political issues. For weeks on end he would insist that I listen to political discussions. There seemed to be political talk on all the streets and in all the houses. I wanted to continue with my life, and getting a job meant a starting point for just that. By this time

51

Johnson Malcomess Mgabela in 1993

I was already carrying the membership ticket of the ANC but I was not anxious to involve myself in active politics.

The turning point in my life came in 1947. King George, King of England and also King of South Africa, came to visit East London. I was standing in Oxford Street, at the corner of the Belgrave Hotel, waiting for the King to pass by. Of course I was excited. It was the first time that I was to see a king. Some of us were pushing forward to get a better view. I wanted to see the King with my own eyes. I wanted to see him from as close as I could. It was then that the white policeman grabbed me behind my neck and pulled me back. Right in front of the King this policeman said, "Hey!" and caught me like this, like a dog. I turned around from the crowd and I went back to the Location. It was as if everything became clear to me that day. The whole situation here in East London and in the country is wrong. Everything is wrong because of the minority government. That is why the policeman treated me like this.

I was involved in politics from that day until today. And it was a full-scale involvement. The Youth League was already strong but we tried to motivate all the youth. As a young man I participated in the ANC Conference in 1949, shortly after the Nationalist Party took control of the country. At the very same time when the *Boere*-boys were passing laws emphasizing "a kaffir is a kaffir" we had our conference. Here in Bloemfontein we managed to get a new President for the ANC, Dr. Moroka, and we made it clear to all the leaders that the youth will be a new force within the ANC. We proclaimed the Defiance Campaign: Let everybody go to jail to show the government that the pass laws were wrong. Black people were afraid to go to jail, but we encouraged everyone to show the government that jail was nothing.

Defiance

Things became even worse when the mayor of East London introduced the two shillings tax. If you were from outside and you wanted to sleep here in the

Location, you have to pay two shillings. A mass demonstration rocked up from the Location, around the Location, into town, into Oxford Street, into Buffalo Street and back to the Location again. The issue of two shillings to stay over was thrown out.

The Youth League was gaining momentum now and people were getting more confidence in the Youth League. In 1951 we were organizing the Defiance Campaign in every street. Each and everyone had to join—men, women and the youth of sixteen and older. The people were organized in divisions and one by one the divisions went out without their passes. And as these divisions went out without carrying a pass, they were arrested: first division, second division, third division, fourth division ... up to the eleventh division. The jails were filling up. There was no place to seat the people, no space to sleep, no food to give them. Of the first division thirty-one were arrested, of the second there were a hundred and something, of the third division (which I was leading myself), 368 went to jail. The first division got fourteen days, the second division got fourteen days, but the third division up to the seventh division got a month or one and a half months. That was my first experience of prison.

When we got to the eleventh division, the ANC stopped the Defiance Campaign. We said we must try another thing now, we can't allow all the people to go to jail. But the government also took action. They banned all meetings. We as the Youth League then decided to inform the people: No more open meetings from now on in the Location. The government said that if you want to have a meeting you have to apply for permission to have it in the Town Hall. So we decided to tell the people at a meeting on Sunday 9 November 1952 that the government had banned all public meetings. We went to Bantu Square and as we were beginning to tell the people about the ban, the police arrived. But it was not the police that we had got to know. There was not a single familiar face—neither among the white policemen, nor the black policemen. They were all brought in from outside. It was clear that we were heading for trouble.

They gave us five minutes to disperse—but the huge crowd didn't want to yield to their demands. It was one argument after the other, and the minutes were ticking away. After five minutes they started to beat the people, and then the shooting began. Many people were killed—we never got to know the exact number. Among the victims was a white nun, Sister Aidan from the Roman Catholic Church, who was working at Frere Hospital. Sister Aidan arrived in the Location as the shooting continued. Eyewitnesses said she enquired: "Why are the police shooting these people?" To which the police answered: "You are white, you are not supposed to come here!" That day, when we lost Sister Aidan, we lost somebody who was very, very important in the Location. Her car was set alight; she was killed by the people.

The shooting continued throughout that Sunday night, and even on the Monday morning. The police were mowing our people. We tried to talk to the police. There were even efforts to contact the Minister of Justice, Charles Roberts Swart, but to no avail. Our people then turned on the whites in the Location.

Everything concerning whites in the Location was burnt down—the dairy, shops, everything. That Monday, the chap who was selling insurance, Vorster, was also killed by the mob whilst collecting premiums for policies.

After these tragic events my life changed forever. During the trial for the two people accused of murdering Sister Aidan, Vumile Nonxaba and Dumile Mquati, we visited Joe Slovo in the evenings to discuss new strategies. Slovo came down from Johannesburg to defend these two, and we had several meetings with him in the late hours of the night. The fact that the two accused were hanged because they killed a white person, but not a single person was prosecuted for the many killed by the police, made us very angry. We were not even allowed to bury in a proper way all those who died during the days of hell. At funerals only ten people were allowed; anything more than ten was regarded as an illegal meeting. At each and every funeral there was conflict, because nobody could keep the mourners away when the coffin was put onto the hearse.

The Defiance Campaign entered another phase after this. That phase was to try and boycott everything that was connected to the oppressor—brandy, cigarettes and other consumer goods. People were told not to buy from the white butcher here in the Location; we were not to go to anything that was the concern of whites. 1953 was a year when many things were put underground. The people were very angry and had very strong feelings. At the same time, the ANC got more momentum and confidence was growing. The politics of resistance which was planted in my heart by the old man, Mjo, took hold of me completely. In 1955 we adopted the Freedom Charter and we said to the government: "We want our own government. For that we will fight and for that we will go to jail." By the time they banned the ANC and the PAC, they realized that they were losing the battle. That is why they called a State of Emergency in 1960—not because of the shootings at Langa and at Sharpeville. No, it was because their Snyman Commission pointed out that the government was failing. By banning their enemies, the minority government couldn't see clearly who the leaders were. On 16 December 1961 the newly formed *Umkhonto weSizwe* (MK) started to carry out attacks against government installations.

For all the years since the beginning of the Defiance Campaign in the early fifties until the formation of MK, I was a Volunteer-in-Chief for almost ten years. I was organizing the cells of the ANC and I was teaching the people— giving instructions to the volunteers. Many people were involved as volunteers. All of them were prepared to go to jail and most of them were locked up at some time or another. But when they were released the ANC would use them again to carry out orders. I was in charge of this whole operation. We tried to pass on the message of what the ANC were saying and doing.

Going from house to house we spoke with the people and gave them some orders, trying to bring political understanding of what the ANC were doing. We had to organize small meetings because the government declared any meeting of more than ten people an illegal gathering. So we used the Mandela Plan:

going to a house; staying there with ten people; giving them an understanding of what the ANC was doing; giving them orders; going to the next house. We tried to give people a message of what the ANC stood for and what it plans of action were. You would tell people here, tell people there. You would even go to a public place like a shebeen or stand with a few people on a street corner. After a few days you would find that you had told a few hundred people about the policies and activities of the ANC. All of this was to be done underground. No name must be written down. Everything must be kept in secret. From the national level the instructions came to us through the leadership of the region. We had to take these instructions to the branches; the branches had to take it to the area committees and the area committees had to take it to the street committees.

All discussions had to take place in secret, but I was confident in what I was doing. For myself, I wasn't afraid. I knew I was doing the right thing. I knew what I was fighting for. Of course, there was always the possibility of someone acting as an informer for the regime. During my trial no fewer than 113 people gave evidence against me. But not one of these *iimpimpi* said that I had given him instructions. I had always given the instructions to a third person. That saved me from the gallows. We were five executives of the Border Region and we were all supposed to hang. But only accused number two was hanged. He was the only one who was found to have given instructions directly to ANC operatives to blow up installations and buildings.

Danger

Since the ANC went underground and since MK started to operate, I was Commander of MK. Actually I didn't know myself exactly when I was appointed to the Executive. At first the National Executive didn't put me in the Executive of the underground. People were asking: "Why is Mgabela not in the Executive?" But the National Executive said that they had special work for me. I became worried because my colleagues were in the Executive and I wasn't— I was loose. I didn't know what was taking place. But then I got a message to organize people to cross the borders into Bechuanaland. It was my first service as Commander. You can ask Joe Modise[1] : "Do you know Mgabela?" He will tell you: "Oh! I know him. He was my Commander!"

From 1961, when the ANC took the decision that MK was to be the son of the Convention, I started in the Border Region—organizing the people to go and do military training. I would recruit people from this area and from the Transkei and would send them to Johannesburg. From Johannesburg they would go across the border to Botswana. I myself never went outside the country—I was organizing from here. Mandela met with the first group who were recruited and who went for training to Tanzania when he visited there after going underground himself. I got my orders from my contact in the National Executive,

---

[1]Minister of Defense in the first democratic government.

Vuyisele Mini, who was later sentenced to death during our trial. Apart from organizing people to go for military training, I was also Commander for all acts of sabotage here in the Border. I was in charge on this side from Grahamstown to the Transkei and up to Queenstown.

We blew up power lines, post offices and beer halls. People were flocking to the beer halls where they were killing themselves drinking the foaming beer, Zimbamba, that affects the liver. This was part of the Apartheid regime's strategy to suppress our people. They gave them the beer halls so that they couldn't think. People didn't want to work either. So we wanted to blow that up. We wanted to destroy buildings of Native Affairs—where they planned and administered the practice of pass laws. Even today, when I see those offices that were used to run the pass system, I feel angry. We wanted to blow up those offices.

Our activities took place mainly during the night. We would first inspect the area—see if the police were around, check whether somebody was guarding there. Every little fact had to be recorded: how many policemen were around at any given time; when did the guard do his rounds; how long did it take for each individual act to take place? In all cases we had to think fast and we had to act fast. But the planning for a particular act could take a long time—sometimes as long as two weeks. We always planned our attacks for those times when there were no other people, except for the police. The government machinery must be attacked, but not innocent people. We were very strict on that—no school, no hotel, no hospital could be blown up. We knew that if we would blow up a hotel, people would run away from the organization and where would we get support then?

During all these years of active resistance and guerrilla warfare we had to deal with another enemy apart from the state and its operatives. The whole time there was the danger of informers. Some *iimpimpi* were prepared to sell information to the Security Police. But it was easy to catch *iimpimpi*—they usually made mistakes. *Iimpimpi* were unable to conceal their intentions. They would have a discussion with you and you would see that something was wrong. The moment you suspected something, you would tell that person: "Look, we are going to blow up this police station at 12 o'clock tonight." At 10 or 11 o'clock you would send someone to that police station and he would find the police planting people all around the police station. They were informed about this bombing. And you knew: "This *pampoen* was working for the police." We had no tolerance towards such a person.

Time and again we were taken in for questioning by the Security Police. They always suspected something, but couldn't really put their finger on it. We were often locked up for two or three or four days during which they were trying to crack us; question after question: "Look, I know you. You are in charge of MK. Pretoria know you are a member of MK because people who were arrested incriminated you. They told us you are a Commander of MK ...." Then I would answer: "No, it is easy to explain. People who want money will say anything because they are hungry. That is why they sat down with you, because you have money." To this the security policeman responded: "No, no, no! I am only working to feed my children." I would then say: "No! Government gave you money to come and interrogate me today. They want you to link me to MK because MK is the real opposition. I am not a member of MK. Ask me about the ANC and I will tell you about the ANC. But I know nothing about MK."

At no stage did anyone beat me or try to change my views. Maybe they were afraid of me, but most of the time it was more like a discussion. By the time of my arrest things had changed in the Security Police. The government took people with a good education and put them there. So when I sat down with a member of the Security Police and started to discuss things with him, I could see this chap is clever. He knew what he was asking me. And they were aware that it would not help to torture us. That was one thing about the Afrikaner: we knew where we stood with him. He would talk to me and we would have these long discussions. The whole time he would clearly state: "'n Kaffer is 'n kaffer." He would provoke you; would set traps. I always had to remind myself: Remember who it is you are talking to; and remember what it is he wants to extract from you.

Arrest and Trial

By February 1963 we could see that things were getting hot. The police started to move in on us. As Vuyisele Mini's lieutenant I had to follow him everywhere. We had to check what MK was doing in all these places. We were hiding in Port Elizabeth, East London, Cape Town—everywhere. On 31 July 1963 they got me. I was not afraid for myself because I was confident in what I was doing. I knew I was doing the right thing. But I had this heavy feeling inside myself: What is going to happen to my wife? What about my children?

For eleven months I was kept in detention before the trial. The first month was the worst. I was kept in a single cell, and heavy interrogations took place during this month. Sometimes, things got rough. My interrogators would get very cross because they thought I was laughing at them. They accused me of having had military training and invited me to show off my fighting skills. They became even more angry when I said: "I am not afraid. If you want to fight then you must fight. Don't ask me nonsense. I don't care what you do. If you think it is the best, take your gun and shoot me. But don't ask me nonsense. Let us discuss things politely. You can go to a thief and you can interrogate him and you can beat him. You can't do that to me. When you talk politics you have to talk softly and gently. Maybe then you will get information. If you try to get information by force and you come and push me, you will get nothing."

But apart from the Security Police's anxious attempts to get more information out of me, there were also moments during which I felt that we were actually having constructive discussions. Some men in the Special Branch were prepared to talk about the future of all the people in the country—not only the future of whites. We were tossing around ideas about the friction between the ANC and the Nationalist Party, about the need for the Nationalist Party to break down apartheid, about what it really means to come down to the level of the people, about what it is to be against humanity, about the hatred between people, about the feeling when you kill somebody. And as we were talking, we all knew that we were living abnormal lives in an abnormal society.

One of my interrogators was a young Captain Louis Geldenhuys—who later became a top officer. He managed to get hold of a leaflet written by MK. The leaflet stated that if the government would not change their ideas, then MK would change their ideas for them through the barrel of a gun. Geldenhuys would come to my cell and say: "Okay, let's sit down, Mgabela, let's discuss these things—it is a question of South Africa's future. What do you think of the National Party and of the ANC?" My answer: "You know, Captain, we can't discuss this thing because there is friction between the ANC and the National Party. If the National Party breaks down apartheid, then it will be easy to discuss this matter with you." The Captain responded: "Apartheid is not the problem. We are all equal." I could see that he was thinking about what I said when I reacted with vigour: "No, no, no! We are not equal. You come into my cell and talk to me as if I am a little boy. We are not talking like men. I am locked up here. When you go out of this prison building you go back to Afrikaners who govern this country by force. The mere fact that I am in here and you are free to go where you want, shows that we are not equal. But you can't stay forever on the wrong side."

When I was finally brought to court, the charge sheet read sixteen different counts. The main charge was sabotage—different counts of sabotage. Others were for furthering the aims of a banned organization, organizing meetings, collecting money, soliciting. Needless to say, there was no chance of getting out of this one. The prosecution knew of the South African justice's dependence on witnesses. They therefore brought 113 people to testify against me. All of them were giving evidence about what I did, where I was and what I said. In his judgment the judge referred to the one witness who recognized me by my white teeth at three o'clock in the morning when I put a petrol bomb in a house. I knew it would be useless to argue about this thing of seeing someone's teeth at three o'clock in the morning. I knew that thing because of the South African justice's dependence on witnesses. They will bring a witness—even if there is no witness. They had to prove that I was guilty. Even more. The state wanted to have me sent to the gallows—me and my four comrades.

Our trial was held in Queenstown, but towards the end of the lengthy proceedings we were taken to Grahamstown. I remember clearly—it was on Saturday 7 March 1964. On the way there the car in which some of us were travelling overturned. We were six in the car—two white policemen in the front. When the car came to a stop I realized that I was hurt. I could scarcely breathe. It was as if my chest was crushed. They took us away in an ambulance—still escorted by the police. We stayed in Settlers Hospital for a week. My whole chest was being put in plaster. It was painful to lie down, to sit up, to talk, to breathe. And, despite being in pain, the policemen on guard constantly taunted me by saying: "Why worry to get well? You will go to the gallows in any case!" All I could say was: "Thank God you are not the judge. You are only the police."

Two weeks later we found ourselves back in the Queenstown courtroom. Final judgment took place on 23 March 1964. Judge Cloete even gave the five of us who were tried together a chance to address the court. That was before he passed sentence. When it was my turn I said to the court: "I know the South African law. I can say anything in my defence—but because I am black I have to be guilty. Mr. Judge, I know that you have already found me guilty." Judge Cloete immediately responded: "No, no, no! You had better withdraw that. Your conclusion is wrong. I did not say that I will find you guilty. And I warn you: Nobody can say he has found you guilty until your case has been finished."

Then Justice Cloete started reading the verdict to the court—non-stop, from nine o'clock up until three o'clock that afternoon. No lunch, no break, no nothing. When he got to me, I had to stand. I hear his voice as if it was yesterday: "On count one I give you five years; count two—five years; count three— five years; on the main count for sabotage I give you eighteen years. A total of thirty-three years altogether, but running concurrently. You will stay in jail for eighteen years, because you are not supposed to be with the people. Your ideas, your influence, your words are very bad. And I myself, will look at you and pose a question. But before you answer that question you will smile. You are a dangerous person. You can thank God, because you should in fact be hanged."

On 6 April 1964 we got onto a truck, to be taken down to Robben Island. I was handcuffed to Galelekile Sitho and we were also leg-ironed together. Under normal circumstances a journey like this would be tough, but with my broken ribs and my chest in plaster it was sheer hell. Steve Tshwete was also on the back of the truck and he tried to cheer us up by saying: "Mgabela, you must be careful, we might roll again." Needless to say, I did not appreciate his joke.

My Prison "Home"

We stayed over in George and arrived at Cape Town harbor the next day. It was the longest journey of my life. Not only did I still have pain, but the whole time I was handcuffed to Sitho. If one of us wanted to relieve himself, the other one had to go along. Together, we crawled onto the truck, and stumbled onto the boat. Chained to each other, we stumbled and fell to the ground. When we set foot on the Island we realized that we were now in the hands of the warders. Dogs, sticks, everything! Then we were chased away to the water taps where we had to wash.

This first encounter with the warders was rough and brutal. But not all my experiences with them were negative. In a way I became attached to some of the warders. There was this one chap, Jordaan, who was also from East London, my hometown. One day the warders wanted to shoot us. A *bandiet,* a criminal, told one of the warders that we, the political prisoners, were planning a take-over. Maybe one of us said something about taking their guns and freeing ourselves, I don't know. But the warders were very angry. Especially the young warders came running to where we were gathered, shouting: "The *Poqos* want to get out!" Soon the whole area was surrounded by guns. There were even some trucks.

It was then that Jordaan stepped forward and said: "Hey! Hey! Hey! *Los dit! Los die bandiete!*" What a day it turned out to be! Jordaan continued, despite the noise and confusion and excitement: "I can take all these people and they will listen to me. I won't even carry a gun." He then turned to us and shouted: "Quarry *toe!*" We went to the quarry—quite a distance from there. When we reached the quarry I saw cars, police vans, the Colonel—all on the one side. Jordaan instructed us in Xhosa: "Take your tools and go to work!" We were working there for more than an hour. Then Jordaan spoke again: "Fall in! Let's go back to jail."

The Colonel did nothing to intervene when Jordaan took us back to the prison. But the following morning we all had to go to reception to have our names and addresses written down. Why, we were not told. All the warders were saying, was: "*Kyk hierso, dis Robben Eiland hierdie!*" And when we insisted on wanting to know what was going on, one of the warders said: "*God, die kaffers is dom!*"

Another warder that I got to like was Delport. Whew! He was a killer. He was a giant. He was tall. And he was always shouting: "*Haai! As daardie kruiwa nie loop nie, gaan ek julle moer!*" We knew Delport had a son, Gys, who was living with him on the Island. He was still a schoolboy. Sometimes Delport and I would talk, only briefly, but still: "*Oom* Dellie, one thing is wrong with you. You are not educated. These Afrikaners misuse you." "How do you mean they misuse me?" I explained to him that he will stay where he is because he didn't have higher schooling; that there was no future for his son whilst he only held a low rank. We agreed that he would come to the cells after hours and that we would organize him a teacher for each of his subjects—Afrikaans, English, Maths, History, everything. He came and he passed standard six. He did JC and passed JC. He did matric and passed matric.

It changed Delport's life. He became a kind man. He even spoke out against people who had a bad attitude which filled other people with hatred. When we were on a hunger strike it was Delport who would take us to the quarry and who suggested that we must go to the sea and collect food to eat. Occasionally some of us had to work in the village where the warders lived. When we worked at Delport's house his wife would give us something to eat. She would even give us a newspaper—and a paper was very special to us. Once I heard Delport saying to a prisoner who got a slice of bread from his wife: "Hey! Hey! Remember you are still in jail!" He said those words without hatred.

I started to work in the hospital in 1973, after nine years on the Island.

But the warder with whom I had the closest ties was a guy from the Transvaal, Schoeman, who was working in the hospital close to the communal cells. I started to work in the hospital in 1973, after nine years on the Island. Schoeman was different from the other warders. When other warders were around, he was trying to show that he was the jailer and we the prisoners. But when we were alone, I would fool around with him and would call him Schoentjie. He would react: "Hey! *Jy is'n bandiet hier. Moenie maak asof jy die baas is nie."* To this I would respond: *"Jy vloek my!* I am not a *bandiet.* Tomorrow I will be the boss and you will have to work for me."

Schoeman and I often discussed issues which came up on the Island. One such topic was the PAC. "What is wrong with these people? I can see that they don't like whites." "Listen, *Schoentjie*, they will take you into the sea when they take over. Fortunately for you, they don't have a chance. Otherwise there would be no place for you. Your people brought apartheid. The PAC want to break down apartheid but they want to take a black apartheid and put it in its place."

Sometimes my discussions with Schoeman helped me to understand better the situation of whites in our country. Once when we spoke about the PAC's intention to push all the whites into the sea, Schoeman said: "No, everybody is a citizen of South Africa. I don't know what these people think, these people who say we must go back to Holland. I don't even know where Holland is. I asked my father when I was on holiday and he told me he doesn't know where Holland is." For the ANC this was utter nonsense, this question that white people had to go back to Holland. And I told Schoeman that we thought it was nonsense. He seemed to agree with us when he said: "The ANC is right. We all have to live together in this country." But I could see his eyes look away when I responded: *"Schoentjie*, we can't live together. If I come and stay with you now, I will be arrested. It is against the law!"

The PAC seemed determined to chase whites into the sea. They often talked about it. My own reaction to this position was that by chasing the whites into the sea, a new form of apartheid would be practiced. The ANC did not want any form of apartheid. But the PAC stood by their view: "No, it is not apartheid to take the white man and put him in the sea." Sometimes the debate turned towards our situation on the Island. A PAC chap would say: "As long as you have whites around, you will have to complain to other whites about this white warder who treats us like dogs." My reply was: "That is nonsense. Do you think the whites outside are all like this warder? They are not all the same."

Working in the Hospital

Apart from the fact that I liked Schoeman, I also enjoyed working in the hospital. At first I had to take powdered milk to those who had high blood pressure. This low fat milk was part of their diet. So I got a *kruiwa* and I would go to the single cells in B Section where I would present the letter to the warder—authorizing me to hand out the milk. There would always be some joking as I was calling out the names: "Raymond Mhlaba, Nelson Mandela, Walter Sisulu, Ahmed Kathrada! Why don't you drink your milk? Why don't you see a doctor? I will cut your milk—I will do it today! You won't get milk. Kathrada, I warn you!" And from their side they would play along: "No, please, man, I will go to the doctor on Thursday. Please don't cut my milk. I promise."

Though I was in prison, I was still holding high office within *Umkhonto weSizwe* and I was regarded as somebody with authority. But I did not want to operate as a high ranking official of MK. The prison authorities had a lot of *iimpimpi* among the common-law prisoners and even among the PAC. I knew that if I acted as a high-ranking official I would be taken to B Section, the single cells, where Mandela and the other leaders stayed. And I didn't want to go there.

So I got a kruiwa *and I would go to the single cells in Section B, to hand out the milk.*

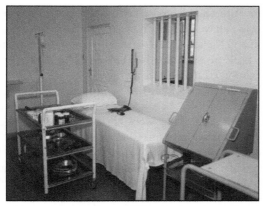

At the entrance to this section was the word Hospitaal *and we all referred to it as the hospital, but it was hardly more than a sick-bay—a few beds and some medicine.*

By the time I started to work in the hospital things had already improved a little. When we arrived on the Island there was no doctor. The person who was in charge of the hospital was some kind of a psychologist—not a doctor. He would ask you some questions, and instead of medicine, that man would give us some tablets. There was the one time when lots of prisoners flocked to the hospital, complaining about illness. This medical officer said: "Oh, there is nothing wrong. All of them are acting." A week later some of those people died. It went on like this. If you complained about a headache you were given Epsom salts—contrary to what your disease was. Later the psychologist was replaced, but the complaints continued. I often told my comrades: "No, man, that is not the medicine you are supposed to get." Not that the hospital on the Island was much of a hospital. At the entrance to this section was the word *Hospitaal* and we all referred to it as the hospital, but it was hardly more than a sick bay—a few beds and some medicine.

I was an *Ingcibi*

When I first came to work in the hospital, I felt happy. I wanted for quite some time to work there, because I was an *Ingcibi* when I was outside. An *Ingcibi* is the person who performs circumcision—cuts the boys, dresses their wounds, helps them to become men. Long before I started to work in the hospital one boy came to me. He knew that I did that work outside and he wanted me to circumcise him. But I was afraid that if they discovered that I did it, they would put me away for an extra two or three years. After this boy, other youngsters also approached me: "We are getting old here inside. And there are still more years because we are doing fifteen, seventeen, eighteen or twenty years. When we go home, we will be old and this thing must be done."

Shortly after starting to work in the hospital, this issue came up again. A fellow prisoner, Surish Nanaby, who was from Johannesburg, had to go to hospital in Cape Town to be circumcised. He had a serious problem and the only way to solve it was to have him circumcised by a Cape Town doctor. I was aware of this operation and Nanaby was aware of my knowledge of this kind of thing. When he came back from Cape Town he told Schoeman: "I know somebody who knows about this. Can he dress me inside the cell?"

They gave Nanaby the medicine that he needed and allowed him to go back to the cell. Then I fixed it up. I changed the dressing in the evening and again in the morning. By the end of that week his wound was healed and his problem was gone. Schoeman must have talked to others about this because, out of the blue, somebody gave me a message from one of the warders by the name of Fourie: "Fourie wants to see you!" When I arrived there, Fourie, who would normally never talk to a prisoner unless by barking out instructions and insults, said to me: "No, I didn't call you today to come and work. I want to discuss something with you."

He took me to the dispensary and, without explaining, he instructed: "Take out your thing!" I took it out and he glanced at it. Still without giving me any indication as to why he wanted the information, he asked: "Where did you get this, that you can cut and that you can dress somebody like this?" I told him: "This thing is a tradition among us. It is a very important thing. I was an *Ingcibi.*" Fourie then asked me so many questions: "What do you use to cut? What do you cut? Is there blood? Is there pain?" Finally, he said: "Dress in front of me!" Then I dressed in front of him.

Fourie watched me and after I had finished he stood there for a while before saying: "Look, I like this thing. You can do me a favor and do this circumcision to me." My first reaction was that Fourie was setting me a trap. I had to be careful. I was also afraid to do it to him because I had never done it to somebody outside of the bush and the ceremony of my people. To perform this on a white man never came up in my mind. To do it here on Robben Island to a warder was just unthinkable. I was confused. The *Ingcibi* was a man of standing, well respected. He was not a prisoner who was in the hands of the warder.

But by now it was clear. Fourie was serious. He wanted me to cut him. So when I told him no, a surgeon could do it, he insisted. It almost became a plea, although he was still the warder and I the prisoner. After a while I gave in: "The only thing I can do is try. Send your wife on a holiday; you need to be alone there in your house. Then I will cut you and I will dress you here—in the morning. By lunchtime you come and I will dress you again. Before you *tshayile* at five o'clock I will dress you for the night and you will go home. Then you come back in the morning. But your wife must not be there."

From then on, things happened very quickly. It was the middle of October of 1973 when Fourie took his wife to the mainland. I cut him one weekend and dressed his wound. I think it was on the Wednesday or the Thursday when Fourie got into trouble. They simply told him: "*Vat jou goed en weg hierso!*" The authorities gave him no chance. He had to take everything and go.

Fourie wanted to get hold of me, but it was very difficult. They were watching him. When he came to the hospital to pick up his things we got a small chance, almost a second, to talk: "Things are bad; information leaked out. I don't know where but some *iimpimpi* told them I got circumcision. But they will watch you now."

They sent Fourie away. I think they sent him to the Transvaal. A new warder came to work with Schoeman in the hospital. I remained there in the hospital, giving those who needed it, their milk, helping there. Schoeman and I afterwards spoke about the problem with Fourie. Although the authorities knew about this whole thing, I never got into any trouble.

In the meantime, some of the boys among us continued to demand: "You must cut us!" They even said: "You refuse to help!" I started to realize that these boys of the Western Cape, Transkei, Border and the Eastern Cape had a better chance now. And they would be old when they were released. After all, Schoeman was not too negative and the prison chiefs took no steps after Fourie had left. So the next year I started to circumcise. It was April/May 1974 that I started, right up until July and then I stopped. Then I started again in December. So many! Do you know how many altogether? Three hundred and sixty one— total number!

You see, after 1976 all these schoolboys were arrested; they were flocking to the Island. They all said that they wanted to go and be circumcised by me. By now they were openly asking for it. They even mentioned to the head of the jail, Mr. Hattingh, that they needed circumcision. His reply was: "Look we can send you to hospital." "No! No!" Later on, we accepted that the prison authorities would look the other way. They pulled up their shoulders and said that nobody should come and tell them that somebody else had cut him.

I circumcised even a few PAC boys—although the leader of the PAC did not like this idea and told the young PAC men: "This communist wants to circumcise you and after he has cut you he will organize you and will make you an ANC." The young PAC members did not like this interference and replied: "You can't tell us what to do with our bodies!" But the PAC leader was right. We did recruit many young PAC supporters as well as members of the Black Consciousness Movement. After circumcision we would be sympathetic and ask: "How do you feel?" They saw that the ANC had helped them and they became members of the ANC.

During all these years the prison authorities didn't know for sure that it was me who cut the boys. They probably suspected that it was me. The only chap that knew was Schoeman, the rest had some suspicions but they did not really know. Sometimes Schoeman would come to me: "Mgabela, stop this thing because there was a leak somewhere. I heard the others talking about this and about you. They say there is somebody there who cuts the others—circumcision." But to his colleagues Schoeman would say: "Stop talking this nonsense! There is no such thing. You've got nothing to do with it. I am working in the hospital, I know."

By the middle of 1981 Schoeman approached me again: "Hey! You must be careful. Somebody told the warders there is circumcision and they suspect you." But nobody came and said directly: "You are doing circumcision!" I then decided to stop cutting anybody because I was nearing the end of my term and I didn't want them to add another three years to my sentence. Because then I would be in for twenty-one years instead of eighteen. So I stopped. Until this chap from Swaziland started to beg me: "Please cut me, please." It continued until October and I finally said: "Okay, I will cut you."

This guy did not tell the warders nor informed on me in any way, but the day after I had cut him he went into a coma. He never told me that he was suffering from diabetes, and for somebody like this, a little cut means trouble. They struggled with him in the hospital and decided to take him to Cape Town. After a few days he recovered and the specialist in Cape Town said: "There was nothing wrong with the cut. It was something in his blood. He couldn't have got better treatment." The specialist turned to this guy: "When you get back on Robben Island you should say thank you to that man. He gave you the best treatment for your sugar-diabetes."

Everything came out because of this man. When he arrived back on the Island we were taken straight to the office of the prison commander. It was clear that the circumcision thing would now come out in full. Hattingh instructed me to write a report: "Put down everything!" I wrote that report and in it I made a strong statement. I had to explain to them why I did the circumcision. And I knew that they could put me away for some more years.

I was therefore very relieved when I noticed Hattingh's reaction to my report: "You are not supposed to cut anybody in jail. But I understand that there can be trouble between prisoners and warders when the prisoners do not subject themselves to discipline among themselves. The warders carry guns and the prisoners can be shot. That is why I want Pretoria to scrutinize your report. I want them to see this."

From his words it was clear that Hattingh agreed with what I wrote in my report. I wrote about my customs and about my culture. That the purpose of circumcision is to help us to subject ourselves to others. If a boy is not circumcised, he will not report to his seniors. By a certain time, when a boy reaches eighteen, he must be circumcised. It is the time now when he is supposed to be a man. If he is not circumcised he can't think correctly, he can't act like a grown up, he won't accept discipline.

After circumcision you sit down and you talk about this thing. You must change today. It is no longer a matter of a person growing up—now he is a man. He has to change in his mind; he should not do something wrong in the street; he should show respect. In my report I wrote down all these things. I also explained to them that in jail there is only one committee that can discipline the people and that is our own committee. There is no way in which parliament or the government can stop our own customs. That is why I told them I had to circumcise these boys—to put them into the correct line. The government can't put them in the correct line because they don't know that it is a question of circumcision. Furthermore, Pretoria will be in trouble when a warder is shooting people on Robben Island. All over the world South Africa is wrong in this and this and this. They can't allow the young prisoners to step out of line. But I can secure this danger in time.

I wrote down all these things and Hattingh submitted my report together with his own, to the prison authorities in Pretoria. In accordance with prison regulations there was an investigation into this issue; with me as accused, a prosecutor, Hattingh and the chap who was circumcised. They asked a few questions. Hattingh spoke briefly about his report and pointed out to the Committee of investigation: "The prisoner wanted to help the government, because if there is any shooting here, the government will be involved."

It didn't take the Committee long to reach a verdict. They found me guilty of having a knife in my possession. In prison one is not supposed to have a knife. But at no stage did they even ask for the knife. They knew I was working in the hospital and that I had contacts there. They knew that the warders in the hospital respected me. Without much further talking they announced my punishment: "You will miss two meals and you will stay for one night in the punishment cells."

After that I performed no more circumcisions. I was transferred to the kitchen where I worked until my release on 30 January 1982. I returned to East London, but it was only in December of that year that I started again to circumcise. But now it was different. Before I went to Robben Island I had to collect all my medicine myself—special plants and roots and leaves. Then I would go out to the *Abakhwetha*. After my release I would often go to the hospital and the clinic and speak to the nurses. They would give me some special gauze to dress the wounds.

Out of Prison but Still Underground

Committed to the struggle, I remained in East London until December 1985— still working underground for the ANC. From here to Lesotho, to Zambia and even to Hungary where I had to receive medical treatment. Back from Hungary I stayed a short time in Zambia, then went to Angola for further military training, and back again to Zambia.

On various occasions after my release I had contact with Security Police members. No longer did I fear them. It was possible for me to deal with them confidently. On one of my return journeys from Lesotho a captain in the South African Police, Spyker Van Wyk, arrested me in the Ciskei. We sat down and he took his coffee saying: *"Die troos van die boere—soet koffie."* To which I replied: "You are still young, my boy." "Yes, I am still young but I am a captain." My response to this was: "Yes, you are a captain but who is the person, Spyker Van Wyk? I want to know who he is because I want to know who is in charge of security. I don't want any policeman to relax and I don't want anyone in security to relax. You must work hard. I will make sure that you do your work."

I met this same Captain Spyker Van Wyk again when returning from Lesotho at a later stage. He knew I had come from Lesotho and threatened: "Look here, I will confiscate your passport!" "You can take my passport but then you won't even know that I went to Lesotho. With a passport I use the front gate. Without a passport I use the underground gate." He did not answer to this but asked: "Why did you go to Lesotho?" "My wife has passed away and I want a white girl from Lesotho." He asked: "Why Lesotho? There are so many white women here in South Africa." "No, apartheid won't allow me to be involved with a white woman." I could see from his reply that he was irritated: *"Nee, kak, man!"* But I did not let go: "No, you must not talk like that. For one, you are a child. I am your senior, politically and otherwise. And secondly, you must talk constructively."

Spyker Van Wyk realized that he would get nothing out of me by heavy interrogation or by torture. He changed his line of questioning: "Why do you make cells in Mdantsane?" My reply took him by surprise: "No, you can't talk like that. You can't ask me about cells. The ANC can ask me that question, not you. You are a policeman. You can arrest me if I make cells of the underground movement. That is your duty. If you find people operating within a cell, arrest them. Take those people and put them inside and take me and put me inside. But don't ask me why I make cells." All that he could say was: "Jesus! You are the only person who is not afraid to tell us what you think." His reply gave me more confidence and I went a little further: "You are still young, you know nothing. The fact that you can take me and that you can lock me up, doesn't mean that you don't have to have respect."

I was in jail for eighteen years. Nobody can tell me what is jail. Both my parents died while I was on Robben Island. My father passed away in 1965 when I had only been on the Island for a year. This made me very angry and frustrated. As the only child I was supposed to arrange the funeral and to look after my mother. But there was nothing that I could do. My mother passed away in 1974 when I was still in jail. The same anger and frustration got hold of me. I was not able to perform my duties and pay respects—and there would never be an opportunity to make up for this.

Personally, I am opposed to putting people in jail for political purposes. I don't think that can be a right thing. It is the duty of the government to teach people—to convince them politically. But they will not teach and convince them by putting them in prison.

5

Monde Colin Mkunqwana: The Analyst

From Botha Road to the Township

Both my parents were domestic workers. During the early part of my child-hood my father was working for the George family of 22 Botha Road, Selbourne, here in East London. We lived in the servant's quarters in the back yard, but I remember being treated almost as a son in the household. I never experienced prejudice or any other negative attitude. Mr. and Mrs. . George had two sons, far older than me, but they allowed me to play with their toys and to ride their bicycles. It was in particular with the younger son, Brian, that I had a close relationship—a relationship that continues until today. Although our family income was very meagre, we had shelter and food. That gratified my father because it was his main mission to provide food and shelter for his family. And as a sign of his gratification my father gave me the name Colin as a second name—after one of the George's cousins who lived in what was then Rhodesia. This shows the special relationship with this family; a relationship that lasts until this very day.

I grew up like a white child, there in the posh suburb. Yes, there were differ-ences. I was not sleeping in the main house. And in the mornings the Lewis twins that I grew up with, who lived next door, would go to Selbourne Primary School and I would go to the Moravian Church on the border between the townships and the white urban areas. My parents would often say: "No, this does not belong to us; it belongs to them." I could see there was a difference between me and the white kids. But after school we would sit together, play together. It was only the school and the house.

Mrs. George was an artist and she once made a portrait of me. This portrait was exhibited with her other work at the Anne Bryant Gallery here in East London. In those early years I never had a problem at school with finance. Mr. George had passed away by that time but Mrs. George supported me in all respects. She liked me a lot. There was even a stage when she wanted me to go and live with her sister, Mrs. Grace Davis, in Northern Rhodesia (now Zambia). The Davis family were well-off and had business interests in the copper mines of Kitwe and Ndola. They were prepared to take me with them to Northern

Rhodesia so that I could get a better education. Mrs. George was very much in favor of this idea. She knew the political situation in South Africa and thought that it would have been better for me to go there for my schooling. But my parents wouldn't agree with this plan and I remained in Botha Road.

But then the Group Areas Act was passed and enforced and we had to move out of Selbourne into the township. That was a major turning point in my life. In Selbourne I felt as if I had everything. When we went to live in the township, I realized that there was a great difference. I could feel it: the small houses, the dusty streets and the noise. Especially the noise annoyed me a lot. Up to now I cannot stand noise; going back to those days. In Selbourne we children had to be indoors by early evening. By six in the afternoon we were in the yard at home and by seven we were inside. In the township it was different. At nine or ten in the evening children of my age were still outside.

The townships were in turmoil. The Defiance Campaign of 1952 caused serious riots. Even as a twelve/thirteen year old I attended meetings—public meetings on Bantu Square at East Bank. Invariably we were affected by these big gatherings. I listened to the accounts of injustices; I read the documentation. One of my father's friends was seriously injured during one of the riots. There was no way in which one could avoid becoming involved. This, of course, brought the beginning of consciousness of what was going on. Why were these people beaten up? Why were they shot at? Whether you belonged to a political organization or not, you could see that there was something going on.

Drawn into the Organization

Right in the very same street where we lived was an ANC office run by Malcomess Mgabela and others. They also played a part in building my consciousness about the struggle of my people. Quite often they would request us as young people to scatter pamphlets around the township and that activity alone had an impact on us. It really opened our minds. The atmosphere of political involvement was all around me. Also, what the South African government under the Nationalist Party then did—the laws of the country—made people become aware of who they are and what they want. In 1958 I was formally inaugurated into the ANC. Not only me, but a bunch of youngsters at Welsh High School.

The general strategy of the ANC at that stage was not really different from the strategy employed by churches when going on a salvation or preaching mission. That was not strange because the very same members of the ANC were often prominent members in their own churches. As if it were on an evangelizing mission, the ANC would move through the township. Sometimes volunteers would go from door to door, sometimes a group would be marching in the streets singing and chanting. The words of the songs always carried a message. After the introduction of the pass laws a frequent refrain was: "We are tired of the passes; we are tired." Often the marching group would chant: "*Vukani, vukani*! Wake up, wake up!"

Monde Colin Mkunqwana in 1958

A lot of our frustration was against the pass laws and the way in which these laws were applied in East London. Because of East London's position—close to the Transkei—the pass laws were very vicious. Although I was born and bred in East London I wasn't allowed in the urban area unless I was registered by an employer. And there was the Two Bob Permit. This permit would allow me to stay over in East London for seventy-two hours. You had to pay two shillings for this permit and after the expiry of the seventy-two hours you had to leave.

The East London Municipality had a Municipal Police Force led by a man called Mangxe. His real surname was Ntutu and he was originally from Peddie. We all knew about the actions of the Municipal Police Force. They would knock at the doors at any time of night, even as early as four o'clock in the morning. Often they would bundle the adult members of a family into the van. The children would be left without anybody to take care of them. You would have to pay a fine at the municipal office and be deported back to where you came from—back to the rural areas.

We often got material to read and we attended meetings—in East London, but also in Port Elizabeth. These two places in particular had been the pots of the African National Congress: cooking political cadres. One could not escape that atmosphere. Apart from it being fashionable to be politically aware and active, the very circumstances themselves made us become aware of what was going on. There was also the issue of our manhood pride. After all, it had something to do with our nation and our integrity. Our national integrity had been degraded, run down. By joining the organization which was challenging the granite, one was picking up the pieces and integrating them.

Later we had to go underground. We could see the repercussion; it was a sacrifice. But we were proud of ourselves. We thought of those who died in 1952 during the Defiance Campaign, those shot by the police, those protesting against the pass laws. The Sharpeville incident of 1960 had a direct bearing on our minds. We knew that we were getting into war and that we might not come back. It was also mixed with adventure. We had the plan drawn up by Mandela, called the "M-plan," to evade or to minimize security risks. The ANC was a mass organization but it had to change its stance after it was banned. We couldn't operate on a great scale. A selected number of members had to go underground to direct things from there. The aim was still to have support from the masses but only a few cadres would be operating. Our meetings were cut down to seven persons a meeting and the area would be divided into zones and streets. A Volunteer-in-Chief would take charge of the whole area and you would only communicate with one other individual. The other six in your cell would not even know whom you are communicating with. The Volunteer-in-Chief would take all the messages so that the rest of the people did not know. The plan itself was very, very security conscious, although it had some weaknesses. The weaknesses were caused by individuals—but the plan worked well.

The Cape Province was divided into two areas. We operated in the Port Elizabeth/East London/Transkei area. Malcomess Mgabela was our volunteer-in-chief who was the link between the different cells. He reported to the co-ordinating leader for the Cape Province, Comrade Vuyisile Mini, who was later executed in 1964. Our connection with National Office was Comrade Govan Mbeki. Life changed completely for all of us. It changed in particular for those of us whose involvement was no longer only a political involvement. Once we were nominated to serve in the *Umkhonto weSizwe* wing, the struggle took over all aspects of our lives.

When the Sabotage Act was passed around 1962—empowering the state to detain you for 90 days without trial—things changed. It was then that we realized: man, some of us must leave the country and others must remain. Those who remain will have to be in hiding or semi-hiding. By 1963 about 90 percent of us were in hiding. We resigned from our workplaces and went underground. Some even left the region. I was working as a petrol attendant then, having left school after standard eight.

You know, once you become involved politically, you are drawn deeper into your mission. You want to liberate your country. There is always that urge to organize more people, to make others aware that the country is in turmoil. That becomes a motivating factor. You develop some determination. But there was no coercion. You were driven by the realization that the conditions in the country had to be changed. The more you learned about the political situation, the more you realized that you had to commit yourself. It was not as if you had joined a club from which you could resign when you wanted to. It was also not as if you could jump from one club to the other. You simply knew: here it is a lifetime commitment. Who else but you could change the situation? You are aware of the dangers you are operating under but it is nothing. What is important is for your people to know that the country is in turmoil, for them to know about the force causing the turmoil.

My Arrest

I was arrested on 17 July 1963, in East London, in the early hours of the morning—at two o'clock. For almost six months I knew that we were being hunted down. It was a very difficult period in my life. Sometimes we slept under a tree, other days we were luckier and would sleep in a friend's house. Those were the days of the pass laws and I didn't even have a pass. Though I was born here in East London, grew up here and so on, I had to carry a permit to be in this area. The Municipal Police would raid houses, arresting those without a lodger's permit. We had to avoid them. We also had to run away from the uniformed police and we had to avoid the Security Branch. Always on the run!

For the first six weeks I was kept in the West Bank Police Station; alone in solitary confinement. Under the provisions of the ninety-day detention bill we were not allowed to see a lawyer. We were not allowed to see anyone—no parents, no relatives, no friends, nobody. The law only made provision for a magistrate to visit the detainees. But we had no trust in the magistrate who occasionally came around. You would try to complain that you were assaulted but they would simply bang the door in your face, mumbling: "Oh, we'll see tomorrow." We had no recourse at all. Later, when we had access to a lawyer, we discovered that the good lawyers were not interested in taking our cases. The few good lawyers who were prepared to stand up against the system were either arrested or they had left the country or they had withdrawn from political cases. In the end we were left with those who would largely be singing the tune of the government.

There were lots of interrogations at any time of the day, and in particular very early in the morning. Sometimes when you were taken back into the cell you wouldn't have any idea of what time it was. No wonder, because they were using crude methods to try and extract information from us. Most of the time they would handcuff you behind your back. The most popular method was simply to hit you. Hitting your head against the wall. This big policeman, with his big hands, holding your forehead and hitting your head to and fro against the wall. Another method involved them taking a wet towel, wringing it around your neck and policemen on both sides of you choking you with the towel by twisting it tightly. After three or four minutes you lost consciousness. What was also popular was the wheel. They handcuffed and blindfolded you, brought your handcuffed hands over your bent knees and then they would shove a stick behind your knees and in front of your forearms. Bundled up like this they would pick you up by the two ends of the stick. The two ends would go onto two tables about a metre apart and then they would spin you. Rotating like a wheel, still blindfolded, you lost all sense of contact with the ground.

There were no sophisticated methods. They wouldn't put you there on the other side of the table and converse with you, trying to convince you, working your mind, offering you perhaps some deal. No, there was no sophistication whatsoever. Plain, crude methods of assault: take it or leave it. They had one belief, that if you want to extract information and truth from a black man you must hit him.

Under those circumstances it was only natural to fear for your life. But that was not the main concern. Once they touched you, you started thinking of what other comrades could say about you. Only then did you realize how important it is that particular comrades would not be arrested. Sometimes you became despondent and your mind stopped functioning. You became angry. You resigned yourself to the fact that you were arrested now; all along you knew what you were doing. There was nobody to be blamed but yourself.

My parents were very, very supportive. And even my father's employers, the Georges, came to visit me once. Brian George, the younger son, took good care of my father—in particular when he fell ill and couldn't work shortly before his death. One of the cruellest parts of detention was the absence of communication. The only regular sound that you would hear is the sound of the approaching keys turning in the locks as they came closer to your cell. Any approach with that "skitchy, skitchy, sketchy" sound was tormenting. You were always expecting them to come and fetch you, thinking: They must have received fresh information. This suspense remained until we were transferred to the West Bank Prison. The mere fact of being now with five others in a cell brought more normality to our lives. It brought at least some relief because we were able to talk freely to others. During exercise time we could at least talk to those in other cells, although very briefly, about our interrogations.

The Trial

You know, it was very difficult to get proper defence at that time. The apartheid laws were so devastating, it permeated every aspect of life. For us blacks it completely destroyed the judiciary. Very few lawyers would take political cases those days and we had to take *pro deo,* state appointed lawyers. There was no proper defence because the organization also had a problem in raising sufficient funds for our defence. The organization was underground; we were in disarray; there was no proper structure. Close to 60 people were tried in the same group as me, with 136 state witnesses. All of this took place in Queenstown—far from our homes.

If it was just an ordinary criminal trial, it could have been described as a fair trail. We had done all the things they accused us of. We committed those acts of sabotage. We organized people. But the question for us was: Were we wrong in doing these things—morally and politically? We strongly believed we were not wrong in doing it. For us it was not a fair trial. We were not supposed to have been arrested.

Furthermore, what was very disturbing was to stand there and listen to all the false testimony. To me that was an emotional aspect and it affected me to listen to them, denying that they had assaulted me and declaring that I had made all those statements of my own free will. There was the police cover-up. There was the state witnesses exaggerating some of the things in the evidence against us and portraying us as nothing else but weird people with no vision—fit to languish in jail. I had the feeling that it was just a matter of formality that we had to stand there. There was no fair trial. They had already decided we were guilty; we had to be punished. To be portrayed in this way as criminals just added to our misery.

Being tried with a large group of comrades did, on the other hand, help us to deal with this experience. We realized the seriousness of the charges and we also felt betrayed by some of our former comrades who turned state witnesses. But within myself I realized that I could change none of this. Standing there with my other loyal comrades, this feeling within myself started to strengthen me. My emotions turned from negative to positive. It became clear to me: no matter what happens, I do not care, because the only truth is the suppression of my people. I knew that the only option to escape the consequences of my actions was to sell out my people. A strong positive feeling came over me when I pledged anew to myself that I would never do this. I was involved in a war. Wars come in various forms and a courtroom can also become a battlefield. If you have to be one of the victims in the battle, let it be so. What matters in the end is: who wins the war?

But even with all this positive thinking we were fully aware of the seriousness of our situation. So when the judge had to pass judgment we were very tense and afraid. There had been a possibility of the death sentence—the state argued for this, the maximum. But Justice Janet soon indicated in his summary that he would not sentence us to death. He started off by using language such as: "You are not supposed to be in such a position as this one; you are too young; you should have been at school." I am not trying to whitewash the judge. He might have been more unreasonable in some other instances. But the fact of the matter is that other comrades were sentenced to death in cases similar to ours. My own sentence was eleven years on one count and eleven years on another—with eight years of the one running concurrently with the other. Effectively, it was fourteen years. The sentence was passed on 25 March 1964. The following day we were taken back to East London and on 8 April we were moved to Robben Island.

Welcome to Robben Island

It was late afternoon on 10 April 1964 when we arrived on the Island. With the sun setting, the feeling gripped me: Now the chips are down. Having left the mainland behind, we realized that we were now thrown on our own resources. This feeling started when we were met in Cape Town docks by a Lieutenant Kilian. I remember him clearly. He had a stoutish body, short and very, very brown. Hey! This had an impact on us: It must be very hot on that side because this guy had lots of sun!

Later that day we were initiated by Rheeder and his men. They chased us around the yard next to the cell, hitting us with their batons.

When we arrived on the Island they took off our handcuffs and manacles. At the kitchen a common-law prisoner dished out some food. Without caring about your hands you had to grab a piping hot metal plate. *"Kom jong! Kom jong!"* They didn't give us any spoons or forks. We had to eat with two fingers whilst the warders were shouting instructions: *"Sit! Sit! Sit!"; "Eet gou, jong!"; "Ons wil toesluit!"* From there we were bundled into a cell. We were separated from the rest of the prisoners because we were not yet admitted into the prison. In the morning we were the last to be locked out. They took us to the reception where they gave each one an identity card with his name and number: "You must never lose this card! At any time a warder can ask you for your card and you must hand it to him."

At lunchtime we received a brisk command: *"Kom eet!"* We were still busy eating when the next command came: "Alright! *Val in!*" The chief of the prison wanted to address us. It was clear that he was in charge. This big man, Theron, grew up in the prison community. He had adopted all the tricks and he knew how to work with prisoners. In an authoritative way he barked out: "This is not East London West Bank Prison and this is not Port Elizabeth *Rooihel* Prison! You are now on Robben Island, surrounded by water. You are going to do as I tell you and abide by all the rules in this prison." After Theron the head warder, Rheeder, spoke. He was very fluent in Xhosa and sounded like a very sympathetic man—but that was only in front of Theron.

Later that day we were initiated by Rheeder and his men. They chased us around the yard next to the cell, hitting us with their batons. I overheard one guy coming in saying: *"Ek het nog nie 'n hou ingekry nie. Ek wil ook slaan!"* To which his colleague answered: *"Kom aan, man, jy gaan te laat wees! Waar is jou stok?"* This ordeal took about fifteen minutes. They ordered us to the bathroom—if one could call it a bathroom: two open, cold showers and two

The bathroom : two open, cold showers; two concrete washing troughs; two toilets.

concrete washing troughs. One of the common-law criminals stood at the entrance and smeared a splash of liquid soap onto your head. They gave us no time to rinse off the soap properly. And when we complained, one warder shouted: "Hey! It is not our problem. You didn't wash properly. By the way, why do you want to wash in prison? You never washed the whole of your life; you don't even know water!"

Prison Brutality

The humiliation experienced on arrival was only the beginning. It continued in several other ways and coincided with a great degree of brutality. The brutality of the warders was clearly meant to instil the idea that the white man is superior. Only white warders did duty on Robben Island; only white men interrogated us before and during our trials. The language that they used further instilled this brutality. Most of the time they would call us *bandiete*. And when we objected to this name, they took it even further and explained with malicious joy that a *bandiet* is just a thing: *"Julle is bandiete, en bandiete is niks anders as goed nie!"* You are nothing else, you are lower than wood. This was a concerted effort to suppress our dignity. The way in which they instructed us to line up, to fetch our food, to sit in rows on our heels whilst eating, not giving us a proper spoon because they said we would stab each other, to be rushed to finish eating—all of this was brutality of the worst kind.

All the warders were Afrikaans-speaking. But it was not only a matter of them speaking the same language. It was clear that some of them had extreme views. They tried to instil fear in us, to conduct some kind of reign of terror. There was this one warder, Van Rensburg, who had a swastika tattooed on his hand, and who often said: "I am here to crush you!" At a later stage, some of them confessed to us they were told by their superiors and by their leaders that we wanted to take the country to the Russians, the Communists. They said that these very same people told them that we wanted to sleep with their sisters and their wives. One of the warders told us: "I was born on a farm. The only black people that I knew were the blacks working on the farm. Later I heard stories that some of the blacks own big houses and smart cars, but I have never seen one who lives like that. The only blacks that I knew were the ones working on my father's farm. And I couldn't care less for them."

When we arrived on the Island there were incidents of physical assault, but that stopped later on. We fought against these assaults through our lawyers, and the Prison Services realized that they had to drop these assaults. I remember one incident in particular. Comrade Henry Fazi from Port Elizabeth, who had been trained in Ethiopia and who was one of the first ANC guerillas to be arrested in what was then Rhodesia, was a strong, hefty chap. *Here,* man! One warder by the name Van den Berg singled out Comrade Fazi that day. It was straightforward provocation, straightforward vindictiveness. We were just moving along in the passage—it was raining that day—when Van den Berg confronted Fazi: *"Nou is jy parmantig, nê?"* He gave him claps—both sides; this side and that side; slapping him; provoking him. Fazi could do nothing, because if he dared to fight with Van den Berg the whole prison force was ready to crush and assault him. So he suppressed his anger and he endured all those slappings. They knew about Fazi's training and it was clearly a case of a show of supremacy: *"Hier kan jy niks doen nie. Ek is die baas."* Comrade Fazi of course felt very humiliated and very angry. And so were all of us—very, very angry. But what could we do?

Although the physical assaults later stopped, other forms of assault continued. We complained about these. One day in our cell we told the Chief of Robben Island, Theron: "The warders assault us." "In what way? Where? *Binnein julle koppe?* Let me see your heads. Do you have any gashes in your heads?" I was the one who tried to explain to him that by insulting a person, one is assaulting him: by upsetting somebody's brain, one is causing physical assault because the brain is physical.

General conditions also illustrated the brutality of the warders, not only the assaults and the insults. The food and the clothing itself represented brutality. We were scantily clad there. We were given short pants and a pair of sandals—sometimes no sandals. And no socks; socks were only meant for coloreds, Indians and whites—black prisoners were not allowed to wear socks. That was brutality. If they find a pair of socks, you were charged; taken to the main office. Those socks were regarded as stolen if you were found having them in your possession, because you were a black prisoner. You had to forfeit three meals or go on a spare diet, because of having stolen prison property—socks.

Robben Island is a cold place, almost throughout the year. We would be given jerseys around April; by September they took it away, because they said it was summer. When we complained they said: *"Man, dis somer! Hoe kan jy 'n trui dra in die somer?"*

Initially we were not allowed to take sandals and shoes inside the cell. Before entering you had to take off your shoes and park them there, outside, next to the door along the wall. You would get your shoes again in the morning. We had to do that whether it was raining or not. Then in the morning they would rush you to such an extent that you take anybody's shoes—size ten this side and size six that side. You became so confused, and in the process all that you could do was to keep those shoes or those sandals, hanging them over your shoulder. The warders would then shout at each other: "Hey, look at them. They don't know shoes from outside. Look, this is exactly what they do outside: they go into the shoe shop, they only point out the shoe that they want, without considering the size. *Hulle ken nie skoene nie. Kyk hoe loop hulle; kyk hoe dra hulle hul skoene!*" You know, that was humiliation. That was brutality, because those words permeated into your innermost parts. It broke down your dignity.

And blankets? During weekends on Saturdays and Sundays, whether it is winter or summer, at half past eight—after eating—blankets were called out. Each of us had to fold his three or four blankets in the prison way. The blankets were then thrown outside the cell. That was torture.

Coming to correspondence: they wanted to break us so that we would lose our resistance. On arrival we were classified as D Group—with hardly any privileges. We could receive one letter in six months, but this letter was usually heavily censored. If they didn't want you to see a sentence, they would cut it out with a blade. Most of the time they would cut into other sentences and in the end the letter would be so porous and damaged that you couldn't make sense of what is said in the letter. What can be more brutal than to sit with the only letter that was allowed for six months, not being able to make out what one's loved ones wanted to say?

And medical care? Medical care was almost non-existent. The orderly of the prison hospital was a warder himself, not a doctor. I witnessed the occasion when a PAC comrade, Mountain Lang-Ben, was treated for the last time in the hospital. He was very ill—had cancer of the oesophagus—when he was ordered out one cold morning: "You are stinking, man! Wake up; go and wash!" Two of the prisoners who worked there in the hospital took him to the shower to wash. Later that day he was discharged and shortly thereafter he died in the cell. Of course he was not buried on the Island. No, they had that semblance of sympathy or decency. They would inform the people so that they could come to collect the body in Cape Town. If they couldn't bear the cost to collect the body, you would get a pauper's burial in Cape Town.

Another part of the brutality was the way in which we were exposed to manual labor. We were people with high aspirations and with a mission. They knew that and they wanted to break these aspirations. One way in which they could do it, was to give us work that was a waste of our labor. We had to go around the Island, clearing the sea bamboo. Where have you ever seen people cleaning the sea? The sea bamboo was there naturally. You clean there today, tomorrow there is a big pile like this. We also had to work in the stone quarry. On the side of the Island that is facing Namibia and Angola, there is blue stone. We used to mine it, to crush the stones. Every day we would go to the stone quarry, sitting with a hammer and a big stone in front of you and a piece of rubber with which to control the piece of stone which you are crushing. Not only was it a form of labor, but it was also a form of torture. You had to fulfil your quota every day. By the afternoon the warder would bring a triangular-shaped piece of wood and if your heap didn't touch the peak of the triangle, then you hadn't done your work and you were liable for punishment. Hundreds of us would go without food every weekend because of this. Later we discussed the issue with the PAC and resisted the idea of piecework in prison. We went on a go-slow and some even refused to work at all. Later they did away with the quota, and other things changed as well. Some of us got engaged in more constructive work like carpentry, tailoring, bricklaying and plastering.

Reacting to the Brutality

We often discussed this issue of brutality and how we should react to it. At no stage did we accept this brutality. We fought against all forms of assault, insult and cruelty. And we often spoke about the human reaction to all these things. When somebody inflicts this kind of pain on you, you want to react. It is only human to take a position and to become bitter. During our political discussion sessions we spoke about this human element.

But we also spoke about what we would like to see in a democratic South Africa. The radical changes would only come through pain and suffering. Should we subject other human beings to the same conditions of pain and suffering when our struggle brought us to victory? Would it not be a betrayal of our convictions if we harbored a grudge? Should we not strive for a peaceful society where we won't do to our enemies what they did to us? Could revenge have a place in a society with opportunities for everyone? These questions came up in our discussions but it was very difficult to discuss them objectively. From the moment we arrived on Robben Island we were confronted by a reality which made it very difficult to deal with these questions in the objective way one should have dealt with them. Although it was only human to think about revenge, we soon realized that we would destroy our ideals and make our life on the Island unbearable if we harbored grudges. The blueprint of our organization, the Freedom Charter, right at its end, says: "We will not rule with vengeance."

Politics was part of our daily life and we discussed whatever aspect of international relations could be seen as an example to our case. One of these topics was the history of Nazism. We reminded ourselves that not all the followers of Hitler were persecuted. Only a few leaders were brought to trial in the Nuremberg trials. We agreed that although apartheid was nothing but a progeny of Nazism, and although some white South Africans were sympathetic to the Nazi cause during the Second World War, we could not put whites on trial for this.

Uplifting Ourselves

Sometimes we became despondent. We knew that our organization was in disarray—especially within the country. In order to conduct effective propaganda against the government you need a structure that is working. But the ANC was in trouble during those years—especially during the sixties. Sometimes there was that feeling: okay, if I die, I die; perhaps my people will at least bury me. Other times we became aware of the intensification of the struggle internationally. We picked up small bits of information by bribing some common-law prisoners. Some of us had money—small amounts, but enough to buy toothpaste and bath soaps like Lux. The common-law prisoners didn't have money, but they sometimes worked in the gardens of the prison warders who lived in the village on the Island. We would bargain: "Look, man, bring me a newspaper and you can have toothpaste." Then they would do it and we would analyse the news, any news that was remotely relevant to our incarceration. Especially news about the United Nations kept our hopes alive. We often said to each other that one day we would be liberated; maybe after ten years or fifteen years, but it would happen.

Many of our comrades were illiterate—couldn't read or write. Early on, right at the outset, we devised a system whereby if you have standard eight, then you must teach standard six—up to standard one or sub A. Each one teach another. The prison authorities never had a hand in helping us. During that time there was another section that was being built. We used to take those cement pockets and convert them into books. Very skilful people among us would bind sheets of brown paper together in book form. We started on the floor. Sometimes we did not sweep the floor; we needed the dust. And when the sun shone into the

Many were illiterate. Early on, we devised a system whereby each one would teach another. We started on the floor. Sometimes we did not sweep the floor; we needed the dust to write on the floor.

cell by late afternoon, the starters would write the five vowels—a e i o u—and the others must read. Later we started the technique of writing—also in the dust on the floor.

We really helped each other in terms of education. I myself went into prison with a standard eight. I passed matric there and I started with a degree—through UNISA. I finally got my degree from Fort Hare, here outside, after my release. I taught English, commerce and bookkeeping. Everyone who could teach, had to do it. If you had standard ten you had to teach standard eight; if you had standard eight you had to teach standard six. We even had an Education Committee—some of the comrades were qualified teachers with lots of teaching experience. We had to spend so much time in each other's company that it was no wonder that we often went further than the syllabus. As a result, most of us managed to grapple with the work. Before I studied through UNISA, I shared books and study guides with others. I would do assignments like any other registered student, in spite of the fact that I was not registered. By the time I was a registered student, I already had an idea of the work. This was general practice—many of us did it this way. Because of this, the pass rate was high.

When locked in after five in the afternoon, we got a short time to prepare ourselves. The starters would soon clap their hands, signalling that the classes should start: the standard one group over there, the matric and JC groups over here. It was necessary to organize these classes. We were roughly fifty-five to a cell but the cell could sometimes take as many as 70 prisoners. After an hour it was time for a short break, whereafter it was news time—discussing the current news. Over weekends we usually had political discussions. These discussions were organized by the ANC. Representatives from the sixteen cells (one from each of the sixteen cells) formed the Political Committee and this Committee was responsible for organizing and running political education on the Island.

Political education was very important. We would discuss any topic. Of course, the history of our own struggle took up a high position. But we also focussed on the history of Europe and how important this history was for the colonial struggle in South Africa. We would interpret the colonial wars which took place in Russia, in England, the Napoleonic wars, all of those. We dealt with topics such as the emergence of the Dutch East India Company, the interests of England in the Balkan States. We even looked at the history of China under Mao Tse Tung, and the Korean War, asking ourselves what that meant for us. We tried to relate all of these to our own anti-colonial struggle. Most of the time the discussions would come back to our own situation: political organizations before the ANC was born; the rise of Afrikaner Nationalism; the role of the English in bringing Afrikaner Nationalism and our own Nationalism into conflict. In dealing with our own Nationalism, we of course had to deal with issues such as the birth of *Umkhonto weSizwe*—the Spear of the Nation. We asked ourselves to what extent was MK different from or the same as military wings of political organizations all over the world.

The political education included learning about Marxism—the dialectical; the dialectics of nature. It was of course not an ordinary individual who could fully expound or interpret Marxism. It must have been somebody who had been trained by the Communist Party itself. We had people like Harry Gwala, for instance, and they introduced the discussions. What was the role played by Marxists within the ANC? What was the effect of the alliance between the South African Communist Party and the ANC? What is the ANC? What is our attitude to religion? Are we anti-Christian because we have communists in our midst? Are we anti-Hindu? We often said to ourselves that we were a bus-like organization: as a liberation movement we took everybody on board. On the opposite side of the Marxists we had our own Nationalists such as Comrade Ntsangani and Comrade Zola Nene. Now, they were strong Nationalists—solely focussing on national politics, not on the working class. Often these discussions led to the question: where do working class and national politics meet?

Sessions for political education were often mixed with the discussions of those news items from newspapers that we could lay our hands on. Whenever we read about the war in Mozambique or the war in Angola or the war in Rhodesia, we asked ourselves what these wars meant for us. Often we would come back to the question: How far are we from being liberated? During these discussions we encouraged each other by saying that the winds that were blowing throughout Southern Africa would soon also move our situation. The encouragement that we got from telling one another that freedom would soon come, kept us going. We always related events from the north of our borders to our coming liberation. It helped us during those times.

The type of education that I got on Robben Island was unique—nowhere else in the world could I get a better education. Before being sentenced to Robben Island, most of us were constantly on the run. We hardly ever had time to sit down and to discuss issues—we were always on the move. But on Robben Island we had time to analyse where we had stumbled, what is our future, how to deal with issues.

Political discussions and political education undoubtedly played an enormous role on Robben Island. But it was these very same discussions and education which emphasized more often the divide between the ANC and the PAC. On the surface, relationships were not bad; most of us had friends in the other camp. But it was a daily-bread exercise among the PAC to attack us—on our policies in general, on our acceptance of whites into the organization, on our allowing whites into leadership positions. They often proclaimed that they were anti-communist and that we were colluding with the communists.

Shortly after arriving on the Island it was already clear that we were not seeing eye to eye. It became clear that we will not be able to convince them or change their views. We said to ourselves that we had come to an understanding as an organization, as the ANC, and that we were not to answer anything to them. It developed the way that, were we to discuss political issues with them—

that is, if we were forced into a discussion—then we would just do it as a matter of exercise. We would just talk shop rather than trying to convince them. After about six years even these talks stopped and we had very little common ground. At times we would conduct campaigns against prison conditions and although they were affected by these same issues, they would be lukewarm in supporting us. Because of our political standing, they wouldn't want to support us too openly. It even went beyond political issues. When organized recreation was introduced on the Island around the mid-sixties and we were allowed to form soccer clubs to compete against each other, the PAC formed their own clubs along political affiliation. However, this did not last for long and we supported the idea that the soccer teams should be mixed. But at the beginning this political division ran through most aspects of life on the Island.

The ANC and the PAC were the two main political organizations. At a later stage, especially around the 1976 Soweto uprising, the Black Consciousness Movement also arrived on the Island. Some of these youngsters from the Black Consciousness Movement joined the PAC, some joined the ANC. The present Minister of Defence, Mosiuoa Lekota, for example, was not a member of the ANC when he got to the Island. But we organized some of them into our structures. This was done through political discussions.

Almost every day we started at five o'clock with education. Later in the evening we continued with our discussion groups: ANC one side, PAC the other side. Each group would have its own discussions: What will be happening the next day? What news has found its way into prison? Was there any political announcement from Madiba's[1] side? What does the Disciplinary Committee want us to discuss? We didn't know the members of the DC and we didn't know how they were selected. But we knew that the DC existed. It was part of the leadership of the ANC.

The DC organized political education and it supported the question of education in general. The political committee was under the wing of the DC and would draw up the political syllabus. There was hardly a day without political discussion and the discussions continued over weekends—in particular on Sundays. Saturdays were busy days. There was sport and we usually did our washing on a Saturday. But on Sundays we would sit around and for about three hours it was just politics. After that we would sing freedom songs. These things kept us disciplined.

Looking Back

The years of imprisonment had a direct effect on my life. I can only guess as to where I would have been without my years on the Island. When I got there I had a standard eight qualification; when I left I was studying towards a degree.

---

[1]Honorific/clan name for Mandela.

Robben Island was for me a well of education. And that was apart from the political education and the growth in political awareness. We had so many learned men among us: teachers, medical doctors, philosophers. During the later years we had study rights and we could get books from the State Library or from UNISA's library. We had study groups during this time and we could discuss our study material.

It went broader than formal study. I had the opportunity to study speech and drama, serious art and also music. We focussed on the interpretation of art itself; we looked at art in relation to our own social condition; we analysed art with regard to our political convictions. This entailed themes such as "South African arts under apartheid" and "Arts from a Marxist point of view."

We performed various plays on the Island. I once acted as Che Guevara in a play *Long Live Che Guevara* and I remember that our present Deputy President, Jacob Zuma, was one of the lieutenants who chased Che Guevara. He was a brilliant artist: he could sing; he could dance the traditional Zulu dance; he could act. Another play was "The echoes of the old Congo." We even adapted some plays such as *Miss Julie* by Strindberg. But that was only at a later stage when we were allowed to get books from a library. We performed these plays for the other prisoners—most often in December. But throughout the year some of us would be reading poetry, and some would be playing musical instruments. In fact, I was the vocalist of a band. We even did our own musical arrangements.

Just as a matter of interest: you know, the PAC had their own interpretation of art. There was more of an emphasis on Africanism. Our perspective was more international and more linked to the ANC's approach to the struggle. For the

Monde Colin Mkunqwana in 2001

PAC, many things in the way they approached art were connected to a fear of the "wrath of the ancestors." One of the PAC inmates, Neville Ncube, for instance, wrote a play in which he portrayed the destruction of African values by colonialism. This kind of theme reflected the PAC thinking. But when you look at plays written by ANC people, you will find that they often wrote about the working class or the broad, national struggle.

So when I look back, I can say: Robben Island made me a total person. I can honestly say that in a psychological sense I hadn't been affected by my incarceration. In fact, I had become very proud of my Robben Island days. Should I die today, I know that I fought for the betterment of my people and this betterment has been realized. We got the vote. Now we are busy with the second stage of our struggle, namely, nation-building. This stage will have its own teething problems. We have to be patient because Rome was not built in a day. As a matter of fact, I do not bear any animosity, none at all. I wish that reconciliation should succeed. I bear nobody a grudge.

What we went through was all part of a war. Our organization was forced to move from a non-violent to a violent one. I personally think that the violent part was the most effective one. Our war was unlike those fought in other Southern African countries. The guerrilla warfare in Mozambique and in Angola differed from ours in that they had managed to control large parts of their countries. We were mainly operating in the cities. Through significant acts of war we made an impact. If it wasn't for this, the South African government would not have started to talk with us.

You want to know what I think about imprisoning those with whom you disagree? In our present situation in South Africa there is no room for political imprisonment. I state it personally and categorically: there is no ground for imprisoning people politically. That would be like turning back the clock.

6

The Context of the Czech Narratives

"In Every Czech there is a Drop of Hussite Blood"

The place was the former Czechoslovakia, and the time just after World War II, when the world seemed to hold its breath as old ideologies breathed their last, and new ones gathered strength. As the Nazi tanks and uniforms disappeared from the streets of towns and villages, those of the Red Army took their place. For many, the Slav brothers from the East were hailed as liberators who would help the besieged Czechoslovakians ensure that the hated Germans never again set foot on their soil.

But for many others, there was a deep sense of unease at the presence of the Russians, a foreign force whose culture and history were perceived as backward and alien, and whose ideology—communism—seemed to clash with the deeply cherished ideal of every Czech: democracy. For a country whose collective memory has engraved on it occupation, persecution, and forced removals, and whose landscape is scored with the tracks of occupying powers—from the Turks in the first millennium, to the Holy Roman Empire, Polish kings, the Hapsburgs, the Austria-Hungarian Empire, the Third Reich and the Soviet Union in the second millennium—self-determination has been an elusive goal.

The struggles for nationhood in the Czech Republic go back to Jan Hus in the fifteenth century. The establishment of the Republic at the dawn of the third millennium also seems to vindicate Hus's appeal, "Defend truth till death." The popular saying, "In every Czech there is a drop of Hussite blood" may explain a national tradition of dissent against foreign ideologies that do not accord with the Czech ideal of "truth." But the price of "truth" was, in the case of Hus, martyrdom. The memory of the fire to which he was eventually consigned may be lodged as deeply in the memory of the Czech national consciousness as the memory of his heroism. Over time, a sense of spiritual superiority in the absence of physical might, developed, and with it, those characteristics that have come to be seen as germane to the Czech consciousness: consensus, rationality and intellectual independence.

The Role of Humanism, Nazism and Communism

In order to understand the role of the Soviet Union in contemporary Czech history, it is necessary to glance back briefly at the early twentieth century. The event that precipitated the declaration of Czechoslovakia as an independent state in 1918 was World War I, in whose aftermath came the collapse of the Hapsburg Empire. Exiled revolutionary leaders Tomáš Masaryk and Eduard Beneš formed the Czechoslovak National Council in Paris in 1915, which eventually formed the basis of the Czechoslovak Republic in 1918 with Masaryk as President.

A tradition of "Czech humanism" was established, whose influence was to withstand the onslaught of powerful antagonistic forces as the century unfolded. At the same time, however, Masaryk attacked the passivity that seemed to characterize his countrymen. In rejecting martyrdom, he saw resistance as the only answer to tyranny, and for him, humanitarianism did not imply passivity.

Masaryk felt strongly that the materialist analysis of Marxism was incompatible with Czech ethicism, creativity and spirituality: "Socialism will either be humanistic or it will not be at all." He saw the values of Czechoslovakia as being compatible with those of Western humanism. The Germanic influence, for all its negative impact, had also left a cultural legacy that raised levels of thinking and contributed to that intellectual awareness as well as analytic logic and rationality that are attributed to the Czech national character. It may be claimed that Czech interaction with its Western European neighbours resulted in the development of a national awareness based on humanism which persists into the twenty-first century. This humanism expressed itself in laws such as the Land Reform Act of 1919 whereby large agricultural properties were confiscated in order to prevent manipulation, profiteering or speculation. This law, according to Masaryk, gave the people the hope of acquiring land.

Throughout the difficult period of the world depression of the 1930s, farmers were represented by the Agrarian Party. This party resisted the revolutionary tide that swept through the highly politicized and organized workforce, which, influenced by Marxist teaching, identified with the Communist Party that was formed in 1921. Masaryk rejected bolshevism as a communism of misery and degradation, and espoused, instead, social democracy which was, he said, the goal of real socialism. Determined to make the words of the Constitution live, the government embarked on a huge adult education programme, and illiteracy rates dropped to 4 percent. During this time left-wing radicals were instructed to wage a revolutionary struggle and unite with comrades among the German and Hungarian minorities. Under the leadership of Klement Gottwald, the Communist Party of Czechoslovakia (CPC) branded Czechoslovakia a jailhouse of nations where Germans, Hungarians, Ukrainians and other minorities could not be free. However, faced with Nazi expansionism and the rise of fascism, the CPC changed its strategy, supporting the Popular Front and thereby also the territorial integrity of Czechoslovakia.

Ethnically heterogeneous, 22 percent of Czechoslovakia's population were Germans—economically the most significant group. The German parties in Czechoslovakia adopted an increasingly violent stance after the Nazi victory in Germany, and, though banned in 1933, they re-emerged in the form of the Sudeten German Party. Notwithstanding the Party's Nazism, and its demands to become part of the Reich, Masaryk nevertheless tolerated its existence.

1938-1939: Betrayal and Nazi Occupation

At the time, Britain did not want to enter a war with Germany for the sake of a far-away country and a people of which it knew very little. At the same time, France reneged on a formal treaty to assist Czechoslovakia in the case of unprovoked aggression from Germany. Both countries put pressure on Prague to cede Sudeten territory to Germany, even though the majority of the population (1,116,000) were Czechs and would soon be displaced refugees. After protesting to Britain that the nation of St. Wenceslaw, Jan Hus, and Tomáš Masaryk would not be a nation of slaves, Beneš was soon forced to capitulate to the 1938 Munich diktat. Czech territory that provided raw materials and a substantial industrial base was surrendered to Hitler so as to avoid war with Germany. With confidence in Europe eroded, there was, after the Munich ultimatum, a rise in sympathy for communism.

By March 1939 the German army had completed their bloodless occupation. Answering criticism that the country had been given away, Beneš said that, alone and encircled on all sides, there was no other option if Czechoslovakia hoped to survive. But, as history was to show, capitulation did not guarantee survival: the Nazi occupation destroyed everything that had been built up since 1918. Prague became the puppet of Berlin, Jews were ousted from government and the Republic was forced to withdraw from the League of Nations. The Communist Party was banned and the Social Democrats fused with the National Socialists to become the National Labor Party, while smaller parties were joined to form the Party of National Unity. Hitler attempted to solve the "Czech problem" by a combination of Germanization (those who were deemed to be anthropologically "suitable" would form the core of a labor force), forced migration and extermination.

"Everybody hated the Germans," says Jiří Mesicki in his prison narrative in these pages. Underground activities were consolidated in the Central Committee for Home Resistance (ÚVOD) in 1940, which kept contact with exiled dissidents in London. Left-wing intellectuals, in collaboration with workers, formulated an underground anti-Nazi programme. And then, in 1942, the *Reichsprotector*, Reinhard Heydrich, was assassinated. As a result, Nazi persecution and reprisals intensified as 23,000 Czechs were executed. An entire village, Lidice, was destroyed, its male population of 193 executed, and the women and children deported to extermination camps.

1945: Reconstruction

There was a massive swing to the left after the War throughout the country, but particularly in the Czech lands. This was the result of factors such as Nazi anti-Soviet propaganda and the anti-capitalist mood after the world economic recession of the 1930s. During this period, Beneš—ever the pragmatist—forged stronger links with the Soviet Union, hoping to stave off future attempts at interfering in his country's affairs, and developing a foreign policy that faced both "East and West." He also discussed with Moscow future policies for Czechoslovakia, including land reform and the nationalization of key industries. Though he had signed a non-intervention pact with Moscow in 1945, he accepted a detailed programme devised by Moscow which formed the basis of negotiation between the political parties. The communists secured seven of the twenty-five government positions, including the strategically important Ministries of the Interior, Information and Agriculture. Klement Gottwald, Communist Party of Czechoslovakia (CPC) leader, was one of five deputy prime ministers.

While national liberation had been achieved in 1918, national reconstruction, i.e. full social liberation, was now the aim. The Košice programme embodied plans for a mixed economy, with small privately owned enterprises, small peasant farms supported by co-operatives, the nationalization of heavy industries, and insurance and bank credit under a democratic central plan. Political and social equality were redefined, and the populace assured of basic civil liberties such as freedom of assembly and expression. A cultural renaissance occurred. Intellectuals reinstated the old ideals of humanity and truth and envisaged a synthesis of individualism and collectivism. At the same time, organizations regarded as fascist—including the Agrarian Party—were outlawed, and National Committees took administrative control at local level.

A shadow, however, was falling between the idea of democracy and its reality. The attempted institutionalization of democracy in the context of an industrial society gradually gave way to a communist dictatorship. The expulsion of the Sudeten Germans was followed by a mass migration of Czech peasants, whose resettlement was controlled by the communist Ministries of Agriculture and the Interior. Party supporters were given preference, and workers in nationalized industries were promised privileges.

As properties were confiscated and individuals denounced, a psychosis of fear began to develop. The strategies of democrats and communists were irreconcilable, and tensions emerged. Divisions between "Muscovite" and "Londoner" emigrés and Eastern and Western army officers developed. There was general social fragmentation, and support for the new government fell away. In the general mood of disillusionment, people joined organizations and resistance movements.

Many opportunists joined the CPC, which relentlessly extended its influence. The Ministry of Information controlled the media and promoted Communist publications, and the secret police and armed forces were infiltrated. Key positions in industry were given to Party loyalists, many of whom were not, however, up to the task. At the same time, the CPC abandoned its old strategy of resistance, and participated in the nation-building exercises of the National Front. The tactic of revolution was inappropriate to the moment and was, temporarily, shelved. Instead, the strategy of cooperating with the democratic parties and professing support for parliamentary democracy was adopted.

1946: Elections

The 1946 elections once again saw the old enemies ranked against each other: pluralism and totalitarianism; democracy and a one-party state. Eduard Beneš was President, and CPC leader, Klement Gottwald, Prime Minister. Through its control of the media, the CPC hid its real intentions behind the rhetoric of "democracy" and "personal liberty." Those who had been associated with the Nazi regime were pressurized into supporting the CPC with carrots and sticks: promises of reward and veiled threats. The loyalty of many farmers was bought by providing them with farms in the Sudetenland.

A large number of Czechs voted for the Communists in the hope of getting aid, jobs, houses and land. The Party was seen as a benevolent provider that would open up a new world and break the shackles of tradition. It also promised certainty and a simple, understandable system. Its greatest appeal was to the rootless and marginalized sector of society, who saw the Party as a means of getting even with those who had formerly humiliated them.

Though the democratic parties won 59 percent of the total vote, they did not have a coherent plan, however, and lacked unity. The CPC, on the other hand, was united and well organized, and retained the key Ministries of the Interior, Information and Agriculture. Democracy was further undermined because the government of national unity—the National Front—lacked an opposition, and party leaders, rather than elected representatives, took decisions.

Nevertheless, a social transformation programme was embarked upon, which entailed the equitable redistribution of the nation's wealth. Arable land and properties were allocated to peasants and workers who received state aid in the form of free use of implements, goods and easy credit. Forest land was distributed to the state, communities and cooperatives. Industries, including the banking and insurance sectors, were nationalized.

1948: Communist Putsch

The crisis of 1948 was the result of a complex interplay of events. After the 1946 elections, the Cold War intensified, with a deepening divide between East and West. Locally, the CPC tried to regain support it had lost, particularly among students and the intelligentsia, by making a number of popular proposals. These included the "millionaire tax" on properties above a certain value, the extension of health insurance to all citizens, and new land reform proposals. These appealed to peasants, many of whom, particularly in Slovakia, lived in appalling conditions in one-room log cabins that accommodated up to fourteen people, which they shared with chickens, pigs, and other livestock.

The *coup d'état* coincided with a continuing egalitarian revolution—the support of the lower strata for a system which bestowed privileges and advantages on them. Indeed, eventually about 250,000 workers ascended to the party elite. In the absence of a nobility and an upper bourgeoisie, egalitarianism is deeply rooted in Czech consciousness. This, coupled with the fact that egalitarianism is a cherished value in most societies threatened by poverty, would explain the popular support for the *coup*. The poor and disadvantaged were to become the beneficiaries of an anti-meritocratic system. However, history had to prove whether this would in fact be the case.

An infiltrated police force spread intimidation and violence, and democratic leaders were accused of being reactionaries, of distributing weapons and mobilizing trade unions. The Communist Party—having taken all the leading posts in government, parliament and public institutions—also controlled the army and the committee for interior safety. On 17 February 1948 the CPC mobilized its members, and masses of workers—all armed—went out into the streets. These workers were prepared to take power by force, if necessary. Three days later, twelve ministers representing the democratic parties, resigned in order to voice their protest against the unconstitutional acts of the CPC. Klement Gottwald put President Beneš under considerable pressure to accept the resignations which, he said, constituted a plot against the state. Beneš bowed to expediency and confirmed the new government—a government consisting mainly of CPC members. This moment signals the beginning of a system of totalitarianism in Czechoslovakia which was to last for forty years.

Gottwald, as Prime Minister, declared a state of emergency and ordered the police and army to search and arrest. All the religious orders of the Catholic Church were disbanded and churches put under government supervision. The most vehement opponents of the communist regime were young people between the ages of fifteen and twenty-five who resented the restrictions imposed on them, particularly the removal of freedom of expression.

Democracy was, once again, destroyed, and with it values such as trust, tolerance, order and justice. Beneš resigned soon after when he refused to sign the communist-drawn constitution which guaranteed human rights—but only insofar as they did not contradict the laws established by the Party. His resignation deeply affected the morale of the ordinary citizenry. Antonín Zápotocký, head of the trade union movement, was then appointed Prime Minister, with Gottwald as President.

Descent into Darkness

Almost immediately, foreign newspapers and non-communist publications from the West disappeared from the streets. A statement was issued preventing the "partisan misuse of the press" and recommending that it "devote itself fully to creative criticism." Communist publications threatened "reactionaries" and hinted at purges that would rid the country of the "Western bourgeois capitalistic mentality"—thus targeting the majority of Czechs and fuelling fears of personal safety.

Middle class families who were lucky enough to have an extra room in their houses were threatened that it would be taken away from them—and they soon realized that the only way to stop harassment and threats was to join the Party. Some 250,000 politically active Party workers were promoted to leadership positions formerly occupied by specialists, managers, professors, scientists, etc. who were forced to enter the ranks of the working class. Thus, education, qualification and specialized knowledge were ignored, with disastrous results both politically and economically.

A new class, the *nomenklatura*, emerged. These were cadres who had an extensive bureaucratic background, and formed a political elite that gained undeserved economic privileges. This group, about 15,000 strong, governed lower party and state bureaucrats in an authoritarian manner—a dictatorship with proletarian origins which soon, however, became alienated from broader society.

The army, air force and police were purged, thus becoming lethal organs of the state, while the ubiquitous Action Committees monitored the activities of ordinary people. Surveillance became the order of the day, as the number of plainclothes policemen more than doubled, and spot censorship of mail and telephone eavesdropping became part of daily life. Every block of houses was organized with a communist block leader who kept a file on each inhabitant, monitoring his activities, and ascertaining what his political beliefs were. Conspiracy was widespread, forcing everyone, as the Czechs cynically said, to have two faces. There was no *habeas corpus*, and people did not have the right to a trial. Criticism of the authorities was forbidden, and even a mild Marta Gottwaldová joke could result in arrest. Vigilance against underground movements increased.

From 1948 to 1956, CPC bureaucrats attempted to remake Czechoslovakia in the image of the Soviet Union. This was particularly evident in schools, whose Marxist-Leninist content and authoritarian style mimicked those of the USSR. Workers' children were given preference at schools and universities. In 1960 the Czechoslovak Communist Party officially declared in a "New Constitution" that the country had reached the stage of socialism. A command economy had been introduced, with centralized planning, controls and pricing. Agriculture was fully collectivized, and increased nationalization eventually resulted in 96 percent of the workforce being employed in state enterprises which included mines, industries, trade, banking, etc. However, many of these were heavily bureaucratized and managed by underqualified people whose party membership guaranteed them jobs. There was a general shift from self-employment to wage-dependency. Markets switched from the West to the East. Feeling secure in their power, and riding the swell of the wave of de-Stalinization, the Party granted amnesty to 11,000 political prisoners. There were, in this period, certain advances, for example, in the science of medicine. Also, as general employment figures improved, so did the economic lot of the proletariat.

But the Third Five Year Plan of 1961 had to be abandoned as it soon became obvious that the economy was failing. People's living conditions had deteriorated. New apartment block developments were utilitarian and ugly. Families lived in cramped conditions in rooms comprising a combination living-dining-bedroom, with one or two small bedrooms, a tiny kitchen and an even tinier bathroom. Other families shared apartments that had been divided up, with each being allocated two small rooms, a tiny bathroom and a kitchen. Most of the former large middle-class apartments were "proletarianized," i.e., partitioned for families to share. The general impression in towns and villages was one of shabbiness, overcrowding and poverty.

The Party's admission of failure allowed intellectuals to come to the fore during the second half of the sixties, thus opening the door to change. Forced industrialization and the collectivization of agriculture had failed, and new thinking was needed. By 1962, economic stagnation demanded that "scientific socialism" be reviewed. Recognition of the need for flexibility in planning, marketing and production ushered in a process of reform. The idea of "socialism with a human face" was promoted by Alexander Dubček, first secretary of the Communist Party of Slovakia. The liberalization that occurred in the Party had deep roots in an underground that had persisted in the Party from before 1948.

Reforms were introduced, including freedom of expression and freedom of movement, as visits abroad were slowly allowed. Artisans who had been placed under state control were allowed to resume their private practices, and places in schools and universities were once again opened to the children of the middle classes. A cultural renaissance ensued as people turned to their cultural past, rediscovering Franz Kafka, Gustav Mahler and Tomáš Masaryk. The Jan Hus heritage was also revived, and people spoke openly of the democratic freedoms that had existed between the two world wars.

1968: A Brief Spring

By the beginning of 1968 there was a general cry for personal freedom: freedom from arbitrary arrest, from intimidation, from compulsion to obey a power that was neither respected nor welcome. People wanted to be free to travel, to speak, to shape a new society where there would be autonomy, dignity and decent housing for all, where people would be freed of their political enslavement. It is estimated that those who ushered in the quiet revolution numbered no more than 40,000—an underground that had survived the dark years of repression.

An Action Plan was drawn up in April 1968 by intellectuals and members of the Party's Central Committee. It aimed at rehabilitating socialism by means of a new constitution. Freedom of expression flowered and real democracy began to bloom. The economy introduced flexible market mechanisms; the trade unions were reoriented to serve the interests of workers rather than the Party. The broad effects of all this were soon felt both in the National Assembly and in the courts.

A seminal document, the *2 000 Words*, was published in June. Signed by 150 persons drawn from all social strata, it attacked the past practices of the CPC and called for the resignation of corrupt members. It also demanded many reforms, including the reinstatement of relations with Western Europe, and equal status within the Warsaw Pact. Many of those who had previously been punished unjustly for political crimes organized themselves into "Club 231"—thus named after the paragraph in the penal code under which they had been imprisoned. As the reforms gathered momentum, intellectuals demanded: We want democracy, not democratization!

In reaction to all this, Party leader Novotný was replaced by a man generally considered to be Stalin's lapdog, Ludvík Svoboda. For pragmatic reasons, it was decided that the CPC would effectively remain the single governing party, playing a leading role in the National Front. Despite attempts to block the movement for change, however, the CPC was swept by the tide of reform. Its eventual statement, "The construction of socialism ... is our internal affair," resulted in criticism from Moscow, who condemned the "counter-revolution" and called for solidarity. It argued that socialism could only be defended within "the collective security of the socialist countries."

But Dubček—now accused of betrayal—and his colleagues refused to capitulate. Indeed, the hypocrisy of the Soviet Union's call for "fraternal mutual aid and solidarity" was exposed when, in August 1968, some 600,000 Russian, Polish, German, Hungarian and Bulgarian troops invaded Czechoslovakia, surrounding the radio and television stations and Hradčany Castle, the home and offices of the President, General Svoboda. Of these, 85,000 remained to enforce the will of the Soviets, effectively withering the brief Prague Spring.

The Return of Repression

After protestations, Svoboda and Dubček eventually capitulated to Soviet pressure by signing a dictated military treaty with the Soviet leadership authorizing the military occupation. Soviet ideological influence which had been so powerful in 1948 was now almost nil. It was replaced by military occupation. In exchange for a gradual withdrawal of troops, press censorship was renewed, the media was purged, newspapers were closed down, non-communist political parties were disbanded, liberals were gradually removed from office, and Soviet administrative, police and military control increased. Though 165,000 people were dismissed from work for political convictions which, months earlier in 1968, had accorded with those of the Party, the mood of defiance persisted amid the vast human tragedy unfolding. Once again, professors and other members of the intelligentsia were forced into street cleaning, sewage disposal and window washing.

The old bonds between the Czechs and the Soviets—their erstwhile Slav brothers—were by now nothing more than a memory. Censorship and bannings of "anti-Socialist" organizations took place. And again, the ghost of Munich arose as Czech leaders decided to sign documents of capitulation in Moscow rather than resort to armed defence. Once more, the world witnessed the tragedy of the small nation's futile struggle for humane ideals. Anti-Soviet demonstrations—at home and abroad—came to nought as Czechoslovakia stood alone and betrayed, just as it had in 1938.

Economic problems arose as a result of external factors: the price of crude oil and raw materials rose and Czech products lost their competitive edge on European markets because of their shoddy quality. Also, internal power supplies were vulnerable. Anti-Russian sentiments were pervasive. Pupils refused to attend classes in the Russian language, and refused to read Russian journals and books. They regarded it as a language that isolated them from the West, and had little scholarly value. Russian films and other cultural products were also boycotted. Many young people regarded membership of the Communist Party as shameful.

More than 100,000 people emigrated illegally immediately after 1968, and by 1989 the number of legal and illegal emigrants rose to 565,000—thus delivering a serious blow to the intelligentsia. In 1979 Václav Havel and other "Charter 77" cultural dissidents were arrested. Charter 77 was dedicated to "the respect of civil and human rights." Thus began the last decade of repression, a period from 1948 that saw more than 250,000 people sentenced in one way or another. But the monolithic power of the Soviet Union was fast eroding, and the centre could no longer hold. The satellite countries were soon to be released to find their own orbit in a post-Soviet world.

The Czechoslovakian Tales

There is a new democratic dispensation in today's Czech Republic. But the three people who tell their stories of resistance against oppression in the pages that follow remain somewhat sceptical, of its advantages. Almost a decade after the establishment of this new Republic Jiří Mesicki remarks: "Nothing has really changed very much." Lola Škodová is deeply cynical about the value of the personal contribution she made to the new democracy, and laments the lack of reparation: "I have lost everything I had. No, I would never do it all again."

The stories that follow are those of two young men and a young woman who stood up against the anti-democratic forces in their country after the Second World War, and gave up everything in the process. They exchanged the security and comfort of family and home for a grim prison existence, for life in work camps and cold prison barracks. Their motivation was simple: they experienced shame and anger at the events of 1948, and wanted nothing more, and nothing less, than freedom both for themselves and for their country.

When the state retaliated, the three were moved from one prison to the next, as prison authorities used every means to prevent them from experiencing a sense of home or community with their fellow inmates. Denied the status of political prisoners, they were thrown together with murderers and prostitutes, as a systematic programme of abuse both physical and emotional, was embarked on. They languished in excruciating circumstances, frequently in solitary confinement, knowing that their families were being victimized. Haunted by the persecution her mother suffered, and taking full responsibility for her actions, Lola Škodová, for example, remarks: "I will never forgive myself for what I did to my mother."

Each of the three emerges from the experience of imprisonment distinctly disillusioned, yet each story tells of a deep and lasting wisdom that developed within the grim confines of the prison walls. While the feelings of hatred and revenge were so strong that one confesses, "If we ever get out of here, we'll even shoot the geese on the pond," the anger gave way, over the years, to a sense of pride, stoicism and courage as the limits of self-knowledge were explored, and a realization gained that the "*mukl*" is transcended by one's own humanity.

7

Jiří Mesicki: The "Mukl"

Recollections of Russia

It's hard, now, to make sense of it all. What was it that set me on the path to political imprisonment? My clearest recollection is the persistent unease I felt, the disturbing sense of the wrongness of things as I listened and looked—a boy caught up in turbulent times. And then, in the aftermath of 1945, I witnessed the political manoeuvres in post-war Czechoslovakia and felt a fundamental opposition to it all. I didn't trust Russia. I didn't trust Moscow. Like the Nazis before them, the Russians were doing their best to get Czechoslovakia under their rule. I was afraid—and angry. If a Third World War broke out, I didn't want to live under Russian occupation. I didn't want to fight in the Bolshevik army.

You ask why? Well, it all goes back a long way, to my childhood, in fact. I was very well informed as to what the Russian Revolution was really like. I knew this from my father who was actually there, you know—he had spent three years in the Austrian-Hungarian army during the First World War. So when the trouble in Russia started in 1917—this my father later told me—he sold his uniform and travelled from one country place to another, teaching children French, religion, and so forth. He was a Serb, you see, and considered the Russians to be a friendly nation. But always, when the Bolsheviks or the Revolutionary Armies approached, he left the place he was at, and moved on.

I remember my father's tales about coming home from the Russian front in 1920. When he arrived home in Vršac—a little town in Vojvodina which became part of Yugoslavia after World War I—he had a long beard, he was dirty and full of lice, he stank and he was terribly thin. And, as he later told me, he was unable to speak—he just stared—when he saw his mother again. No one at home recognized him, and it was only when the dog in the yard leapt up at him, wagging its tail wildly, that his mother said, "Oh, Branco, Branco, it is you!"

After a while my father found himself drawn to that new state, that new country in the centre of Europe—to Czechoslovakia. He decided against studying in Switzerland because, he thought, "Well, the Swiss people are Germans too, so I will rather go to a Slavonic country." There was a broad Panslavist movement after World War I, and my father wanted to be part of it. He travelled

Jiří Mesicki as young man

to Prague and enrolled at Charles University. To make some money he was privately teaching Serbian and among his students was my mother, who was Czech. After getting married here, in Prague, they returned to Yugoslavia, to Vršac, where I was born. But because conditions there were very, very difficult, and a boy from a poor family couldn't study there, we returned to Prague in 1928—or was it 1929?

When I was a child, he would tell me many stories about Russia, and he would tell me about the ignorance of the Russian soldiers. Do you know, that during the time he spent in Russia, he used a menu card from a French hotel as a passport! Because nobody could read, the soldiers—whether Communist, Red Guard, or Whites—just looked in bewilderment at the letters of the Roman alphabet, and after turning the card around a few times, would say, "Let him go." My father told me much about the Russian Revolution. He didn't like the Soviets. He knew that they cheated and lied and robbed. And he had witnessed murders. The same things that Solzhenitsyn wrote about in his *Gulag Archipelago*—my father saw this with his own eyes—lorries filled with murdered bodies. So he didn't trust the Russian soldiers at all.

Genghis Khan Invades the Twentieth Century

When, many years later in 1945, I witnessed the so-called Liberation Red Army enter Prague, I had sharp recollections of my father's stories. You have to understand—the soldiers of the Red Army were like the hordes of Genghis Khan invading the twentieth century when they entered Prague. I could not tolerate them because they were of quite a different mentality. They were primitive, they were wild, aggressive.

I remember one day when three or four Russian soldiers knocked on the door—I was alone at home. They had several bottles of wine or some kind of spirits—it stank awfully. When I invited them in, they insisted on sitting in the kitchen, and, when one of them wanted to wash his hands, I showed him the sink with the hot water tap. He said, *"Nyet voda ... nyet voda"* (But there is no water). He was surprised when I turned the tap on, and then sheepishly said "Oh yes, this is the same like we have in our country—the very same—I have only forgotten because of the war, but it is the same thing." Then he washed his hands, wiping them on some rag he took out of his pocket—and then he took the sink and almost tore it from the wall. He wanted to throw the water out, but I stopped him—"Don't do that," I said—and pulled the plug out. He looked on in astonishment as the water disappeared down the drain. These soldiers had no idea about the twentieth century—they were so primitive, it was incomprehensible to us in Central Europe. And, when they left, two of our watches disappeared with them—as we later discovered.

But you couldn't hate the Bolsheviks—not like the Nazis who came in 1939. You merely detested them. They were everywhere, like bugs, and it was awful having them among us, telling us what to do, because we were much more advanced. They had rather peasant-like attitudes—do you know, when my father tried to strike up a conversation with them, the Russian soldiers simply ignored him—they saw him as a typical bourgeois. We were part of Europe, and they were part of Asia—not even a very developed Asia. We learnt about the Russians and their revolution at elementary school—which at that time taught us about democracy and about President Masaryk. We also heard about the Russians from legionaries who had been in Russia, France and Italy, and who wrote books about their experiences.

1939: The Arrival of the *Übermenschen*

But let us go back a few years, to 1939. Before the Bolsheviks arrived, there were the Germans! Everybody hated the Germans. They were nasty. They were authoritative, they had elegant uniforms, they thought they were *Übermenschen*. So I also hated them. I was fourteen at the time, and we were all against the Germans, against the Nazis—all of us. We hated them because they were totalitarians—just like the Communists. There is no difference. Hitler liquidated about seven or eight million people in concentration camps. And how many millions were liquidated by Stalin in Siberian concentration camps from 1920? Many, many more. It was an awful time.

During World War II, most of the men in my family were in prison. An uncle of mine, a professor in Yugoslavia, was in a camp in Yesenowatz. Another, an officer in the Yugoslav army, was a prisoner of war in Hamelsburg. My Czech uncle, who had worked in the presidential office of President Masaryk, was arrested in 1943, and executed a year later. And years later, when I was in Pankrác prison, I was with a man, Jaromír Panenka, who was also eventually executed as a collaborator—he had worked with another of my uncles in the resistance. There was also my mother's cousin who had been in Terezín concentration camp, a fortress north of Prague. We were all against the Germans.

During World War II I witnessed many acts of resistance—I saw the bravery of my relatives as well as that of my school friends' parents. I saw people being arrested and taken away, and I knew that somewhere executions were taking place. I remember the impotent anger I felt, the bewildered rage that engulfed me. I wanted to join the army. I had wanted to join the army from the time I was six. I remember seeing pictures in newspapers in 1931 of the Moegden incident in China. I remember also how disappointed I was in about 1935 to read in a newspaper that the underground in Prague would be unlikely to emerge before 1940—what a long time that was for a ten-year-old boy to wait! I had known about Hitler and the Nazis since 1933—people visiting my parents would speak about politics. You could say I was different from many of my friends—as a thirteen-year-old boy I felt—so strongly—the imminent danger when the Germans occupied first the Rhine valley, and then Austria—and then the Sudetenland. I remember saying, "Well, we are lost!"

I had seen the Nazi army invade Prague on 15 March 1939—it was very depressing, very, very sad. I was attending a grammar school at that time. In the morning when we went to school, we still had a Republic. But we had heard on the radio, early that morning, that the Nazis were crossing the border. Everybody was very depressed—even us, boys of fourteen. During a lesson, at about nine in the morning, a boy looked out of the window, and said: "Look—they are here." We saw an army car with a swastika parked in the street below. When we left school later that day, the streets were full of German soldiers. They occupied every street, every bridge, even the post offices—it was a full military occupation.

When we arrived at school the next day, we saw it was surrounded by barbed wire—the German army had turned our school into a barracks, which they occupied for two weeks. From then on, there was a secret bond between teachers and pupils—they knew that we knew and we knew that they knew and we were all outraged, and in this thing we were united. The Director of the Grammar School was soon fired by the Germans—it is not surprising that in 1948 he was fired by the communists again.

But, you know, we were anti-German even before the occupation—with their arrogant ways they annoyed us all. When I was a child, there were many Sudeten Germans studying in Prague at the German Technical School. They wore a sort of national costume: leather shorts, white socks, and a green hat—the white socks especially made us terribly angry. When we saw a group of them, we would squirt their socks with ink. I remember them, long before the occupation, greeting each other in the streets of Prague with a "Heil, Hitler" salute.

We can never forget what led to the Nazi invasion: the infamous Munich Treaty. We were terribly disappointed by the attitude of France and England—the French said that if we did not agree to the Treaty, France would join the Germans and compel us to respect the Treaty. This was the occupation of the

Sudetenland. It was not long after this that they occupied the rest of the country—just as we had feared. Our only hope was war, for we continued to believe that the Western powers would declare war on Germany—and this happened on the first of September 1939.

I was on vacation with my parents at the time, not far from Prague. I remember meeting my mother when returning from a walk in the woods one evening. She was in a state, and spanked me, "We must leave at once for Prague—the war has started!." On our way home, I bought a "Masaryk's cap," a peaked cap with a tricolor, which was soon worn all over Prague. The air was thick—I could feel the emotion, and a demonstration commemorating the founding of the Republic on 28th October 1918 was held in Prague, and the crowd shouted, "Down with Hitler! Long live Beneš and freedom and London and Paris!" Communists who shouted "Long live Red Prague!" were beaten up.

And so, history took its course, and at the threshold of adulthood I found I was *eingesetz*—conscripted to work in a printing plant in Prague—where I discovered that the workers adopted the symbol of the Soviet Union—the hammer and sickle. It was only after the War that I passed my matriculation examination and enrolled in the Faculty of Law at the University. However, I never finished, because of what happened to us again in 1948—the year of the Communist *putsch*, which I will return to later.

1945: The Changing of the Guard

The war took its bloody course and in 1945, on the fifth of May, the uprising in Prague against the Germans started. The mood was reckless and defiant—and the radio started to broadcast only in Czech. I happened at the time to be in the broadcast building on Vinohradská Street. We were well supplied with food and ammunition—but on the 7th they bombed us. A German aeroplane dropped a bomb through a window and it exploded in the cellar. The inside of the building was badly damaged, and we were forced to stop broadcasting. We had suffered such bad losses that I didn't care if our liberators came from the East or from the West. Surrounded by destruction, we soon ran out of water—we were very hungry, but hunger is not as bad as thirst. So several times a day, for about fifteen days, I made an expedition to find food and water.

During one such attempt, I saw up Balbínova Street in Vinohrady a strange green vehicle—a jeep, though I didn't realize it at the time—with two soldiers wearing white helmets and white belts. They had an American flag, and smoked cigarettes. I ran to them and in my broken English—school English—I asked them: "Oh! You are here. So we are freed. We are liberated." But they explained, "No, we are just on reconnaissance. We aren't allowed to come to Prague because the Russians are coming here. We have to return to Plzeň." I asked, "Why?" and they said, "This was the agreement." I thought that the road might have been blocked by an SS Pantzer Division in Benešov, but the soldiers said, "No, no, it isn't blocked, it's free, but it was decided that the Russians will come to this section." I was very disappointed because, though I had never met the Russians, I had of course heard all about them when I was a kid. Later, I was even more disappointed at the reaction of my father when I returned from the broadcast building. He spanked me, and said, "I was four years in the war and I didn't shoot a shot. And in just five bloody days, you had to join the revolution and the resistance, and cause such shit!" The next day, I saw my first Russian soldiers.

The Soviet army—the hordes of Genghis Khan—arrived on the 9th of May. You cannot imagine what it was like. Let me tell you, the Russian Army that came in 1968 was elite compared with these hordes. The peace treaty had been signed on the 8th, so they did not in fact liberate anybody. But immediately, local communists who had remained silent during the Nazi occupation filled the streets and decorated themselves with red flags and red banners, you know, and everybody was for the Soviet Union. As for me, I believed that the so-called liberation by the Russians was just the beginning of the invasion of Western Europe—which later political events confirmed in France and Italy, where governments were undermined by the Russian fifth column. Let me say again, that while I hated the Germans, I despised the communists—they were like bugs, like ants, spreading everywhere. Communism is dangerous, it infects you, and goes everywhere. Of course, I hated those individuals who committed crimes, who killed and murdered and tortured people—but communism as such, I just despised.

Here, in Czechoslovakia, the Communists very soon infiltrated each of the permitted political parties—the National Socialist Party, Popular Party and Social Democratic Party. They had also formed the new Communist Party. This wasn't real democracy at all, of course, it was only a partial democracy. The Agrarian Party, which had been the strongest party before the war, was banned. The Soviet influence was very strong, and very few people resisted it. They infiltrated not only the official administration but all organizations, all clubs, the army—everything. They were, I must admit, very diligent, very persistent. Soon they had leading positions in all organizations—including the Ministry of Information. They had people everywhere—you never knew who exactly you were speaking to.

There was, in fact, a new occupation, a new tyranny. As soon as the Soviets came, they arrested many people, including Russian immigrants who had fled the 1917 revolution. These asylum-seekers simply disappeared—nobody ever saw them again. Then, in 1946, the Communists won the elections, getting 38 percent of the vote. And then it all began in earnest—they insisted that they had more rights than any other party. It was clear that a putsch was being planned, but other members of the government believed that the Communists would not risk this, because of the popularity of President Beneš with Western countries.

I would like to say at this point that our resistance against the Communists was very easy for many of us, because of our involvement in the resistance against the Germans. I, in fact, had joined the resistance against the Germans at an early age by helping my mother smuggle letters from prisoners at Pankrác to their families.

But, you know, in 1945 I was the only member of my family—I was twenty at the time—who was against this new regime. My family didn't believe me when I spoke to them of my fears. I decided I would escape to the West with two of my friends, though we were afraid that we might be sent back by the Americans for seeming to flee without any reason. So we waited for an opportune moment. And as things developed, it became clear to me that you cannot use democratic methods in fighting against totalitarianism. Violence was the only way. And because the Americans had the atomic bomb, I thought World War III would soon follow—the Americans had to ensure that the Russians did not get the atomic bomb

1948: A New Tyranny

The Communists in the Soviet Union, in Moscow, had started preparing for the overthrow of democracy here in Czechoslovakia from the time President Beneš flew from London to Moscow for discussions with Stalin in1943. Beneš sold out to Stalin! We were merely part of a larger plan that included Rumania, Bulgaria, Hungary and Poland in 1947. It was now our turn, and this happened in February 1948—it was only with the *coup d'état* that my mother, like many other people, opened her eyes for the first time.

But I had been suspicious of Beneš's negotiations right from the start. The man was an opportunist—he was not material for a president. He wanted to make Czechoslovakia a bridge between the East and the West, but how could this be possible with Stalin in control? Roosevelt had also been duped at Yalta in 1945, when Europe was divided. I felt awful, awful—I had known since 1945 that the Communists would take power here. My mother, however, trusted Beneš, and even went to greet him on his return from Moscow in 1945. When my parents asked if I would join them, I refused, saying, "I don't care for Beneš." Even at my trial, I admitted to being willing to overthrow Beneš—I was very strongly against him.

The National Front was absolute nonsense. It consisted of three parties forming the Socialistic Bloc: the Communist Party, Social Democrats and National Socialists. The only party that perhaps tried for democracy was the Popular Party, which was led by two priests—but even so, in 1946 it dismissed one of its own members of parliament, Dr. Helena Koželuhová, for her anti-socialist leanings. Those few ministers and members of parliament who wanted to resist the Communists were practically helpless because, from the time of the end of the war, Russian agents who spoke good Czech began to penetrate the state apparatus and public life.

I would never have approved of the National Front, even if there had been no Communists, because it included only socialist and left-wing parties that had been penetrated by the communists. In any case, look at what had already happened: innocent people were thrown into jail as Nazi collaborators and their factories nationalized; banks and mines and big farms went the same way, and later even craftsmen—barbers, smiths, tailors—had their businesses nationalized. And anyone who wasn't a hot communist sympathizer—or who refused to pretend to be one—was arrested, put in a camp, and sent to work in the new uranium mines. Everybody was afraid, and pretended to sympathize with the regime, with the Soviet Union.

There were many bans on everything, and everywhere there were collaborators directed by the NKVD, the Soviet Secret Police. It had gone so far that later on, at the University, I saw communist students in the student organization, Všehrd, in the Faculty of Law, bring in an adviser, an older man—he was certainly no student!—with a shaven, bald head, wearing a winter coat. He came into the room and they all tried to hide him by screening him from us with their bodies. Every time a communist student made a speech, he first went to this adviser, and talked with him. It was like this everywhere. The Soviet influence was very, very strong.

To get us on their side, they used the tactic of whips and carrots—except that the carrots offered to the beaten donkey were very small. Soon, workers were doing the minimum. There was a kind of silent treaty: the government paid them—but not very much, and the people worked—but not very much. Also, people were becoming aware of the dirty means the Communists were using to gain power, and a spirit of resistance began to develop quite spontaneously as people feared the end of democracy and the loss of freedom—I mean political freedom. People started leaving Czechoslovakia. The door was still half open, and I knew that it would soon close altogether. Before it closed, I wanted to get out. But instead of crossing the border as soon as I could in 1948, I told my two friends, "Go alone without me. I will leave the country too. But before I leave, I must do something against despotism. I must answer somehow because what they have done with us is such a dirty business—I must respond."

Resistance and Arrest

After our experience of the Nazis, it was natural for us to resist this new tyranny—this communistic tyranny. But still, what deep motive was it that drove us? Many years later, when I was in prison, I would often ask my co-prisoners, "What made you join the resistance?" Some said, "I love my country. I love the nation." But I said, "Well, I cannot say that I have some special attachment to this country or to the nation. What I have done I would have done in any other country. I was against totalitarianism. I fought for democracy because of my strong convictions. I don't care for any nation or for any country." I was inspired by Tomáš Masaryk—and also by my imprisoned relatives in Yugoslavia.

When, in 1948, President Beneš accepted the resignation of ministers of the National Socialists and Popular Front, there was nothing left but for anti-communists to leave the country—illegally, of course, because they had started to guard the border. Our last gesture of resistance against the Bolsheviks was on the 25th of February 1948 when everything was already lost. A large crowd of students gathered at Charles Square and marched towards Hradčany, wanting an audience with the President. But we didn't get further than Nerudova Street, a steep, narrow street leading to the Castle. We were met by police with machine guns behind a barricade—strong, cruel police blocking the way to the Castle who beat us back to Malostranské Square, badly wounding two students. But we were defiant: "Let them shoot! Look! Czech police are shooting Czech students!" I decided then that I would cross the frontier to the West. Before leaving the country, though, I decided I had to fight back against this dirty business, to hit them back in a very painful place. It was all so swinish, you know—I had to do something, so I did.

There were, at the time, many illegal groups who had illegal stores of arms for sabotage purposes. The aim was the violent overthrow of the regime. The first of many attempts was made in 1949—but all these attempts failed because Soviet and even Czech espionage was so effective. They always succeeded in infiltrating illegal organizations. But their methods were subtle: they didn't arrest people immediately, they let them carry on, and after six months or even a year they would arrest the whole group—and so, many, many people were removed.

But I never worked in big groups, especially after my experiences in World War II—that was the easiest way to go to prison. Instead, I worked in a small group of five friends, four boys and one girl, all students in the Faculty of Law. At the time, I had access, through a friend, an old school mate whom I had known since I was thirteen, to important military documents concerning the Czechoslovak army. His father held a high position in the army. I then copied the documents and passed them on to another friend who was supposed to smuggle them out of the country. The problem—though I didn't know it then—was that he was part of a large illegal group. Rather naively, I suppose, I wasn't afraid at the time because I trusted them. And because I had been visiting them for years, there seemed to be no reason for the authorities to suspect our meetings.

One of the members of the larger group that my friend was working with was a student, Milan Choc. He was later accused of shooting Major Šram of the Cominform, who had very close connections with the Soviet Centrum in Prague. There was a strong backlash, and 300 people were arrested in one night. But, to continue with my own activities, at first I supplied information via this friend, but later I found a direct contact through the embassy. All went without incident until the 10th of May, when two agents of the CIA were arrested in Železná Ruda, and they found my documents on one of them. I later realized that this was not surprising, because these documents were not in fact being smuggled to the West—they were instead being copied and given to various members of the organization.

Then, on the 27th of May, Major Šram was assassinated and on the 1st of June Choc was arrested, and they found the same information on him. I had no idea at the time how this happened, though much later, when newspapers were un-censored, I discovered that there had been an informant, and that one of our group of five had spoken to someone else about our activities. Of course, I knew that I was being spied on, and I suspected it was because, through her daughter, Martha, I was in touch with Helena Koželuhová, the woman who had been fired from the Popular Party.

There was, as I had already discovered, no place to hide from the Secret Police. You see, the previous year, in 1947, I had visited my friend, Milan Herben, grandson of Dr. Jan Herben, a writer and newspaper editor, who was a personal friend of Tomáš Masaryk. Milan and I were talking, when he invited me to his father's library to show me a new make of cigarette that had been given to his father. When he tried to open the drawer of the writing desk, he found it was locked. But later, while the family was away over New Year, the desk was broken into. I was then called in to give evidence that the drawer had indeed been locked before the theft. And in another instance, I had direct contact with them. In February 1948—just before we were at our most active—the Secret Police approached me to work for them. They told me that my studies would be much easier, and they said: "We need people like you because you are a member of an opposition group, and we need information about them." But I merely looked at them, and said nothing in response. I didn't say yes. I didn't say no. I simply left, and I never saw the person again.

It was always my intention to make as much trouble as I could, and then leave the country. But my plan to cross the border at Šumava on 1st of June with a friend didn't materialize. He needed to stay in the border zone for two or three days as he had a task to complete. Since I didn't have the necessary permission to stay in the zone, I decided to leave later, on the 4th of June. My friend had promised to wait for me in Plzeň, at the railway station, at twelve o'clock on Friday morning. We planned to cross the frontier the next night. But, as I had feared all along, the authorities arrested all 300 members of the big resistance organization he was working with. Even though I had been very careful—for I had had experience of resistance against the Nazi regime—I was also arrested. At home, in bed. At half-past two in the morning. It was the 3rd of June 1948.

They took us to the police station in Bartolomějská Street, and Major Pokorný handcuffed me. I noticed the word *Gestapo* on the handcuffs, which were de-signed to tighten a click each time you moved your wrist. They told me I was under arrest for espionage, under a 1923 law for the defence of the Republic—though of course I would never have needed to do what I did in a democratic country with normal channels of legal opposition. That year—either in Spring or Winter—a new law, number 231, dealing with espionage and resistance, was passed. Anyway, Major Pokorný said, "Come here! Kneel here! Here! What? You don't want to kneel?" He hit me hard then, so I had to kneel, and they began to interrogate me, and Pokorný smoked a pipe all the while. I was questioned for fifteen hours at a time, day and night, over a period of many days. Some people said that Pokorný kicked them while they kneeled, and hit them in the face with a big bunch of keys, and even hit his pipe hard on their heads to clean the ash out.

Though I was allowed a visit from my family, the conditions at the station cells were very bad. There were about thirty-five of us, including many Ukrainian and Russian army deserters, as well as Bulgarians and Poles, and we were allowed only one shower a week. The food was very bad. In the morning we got black coffee—but it wasn't coffee at all, it was some liquid, bitter and black—in cups made from old tins. At noon we had half a tin cup of vegetable soup and potatoes with gravy. Once or twice a week we had a piece of meat, or a dumpling with gravy. In the evening we had mainly soup. But we got through this because we were allowed to receive weekly parcels from home.

At the beginning of July I was moved to Pankrác prison, where we were detained for six months. We were imprisoned at first in the basement, in the new Department A4 for so-called hard-core political detainees. A couple of weeks later we were moved upstairs, and put under the Ministry of Law. Before the Communist putsch the Minister of Law was a National Socialist and many people in his Ministry were tolerant to us. At least we were no longer under the communist dogs—the police guards—as the guards upstairs included many ex-soldiers and legionaries from World War I. But later, however, swine—young people from the militia—took over from these retirees.

We got the same food as the condemned prisoners: black coffee in the morning, and slightly better soup and potatoes, though the gravy was terrible. We used old German tins. The onion soup stank terribly, and so did the fish sauce. Oh! It stank! All the food stank! On Fridays, we got a *buchta* (cake), which was

Pankrác Prison in Praque

very good. We looked forward to the parcel from home we were allowed once a fortnight. There was so little to break the boredom. We were forbidden to smoke in the cells—only in the yard during our one-hour daily walk, which was usually in fact only three-quarters of an hour.

I was in solitary confinement all this time, and for several weeks I was quite alone. I remember Cell 77 in Section A3. Milan Choc was three or four cells away, in number 79 or 80—a death-row prisoner of my own age: twenty-three. I felt that I already had a foot in the grave, I felt very low, very depressed. I had a bad experience in August—I think they had planned a way to get rid of me. They fetched me for one last hearing and took me to the top floor of the police station at Bartolomìjská Street, to the last office along the corridor, where they asked me a few questions.

Here, an official, Rybin, took out a pistol, looked to see if it was loaded, and then put it in the drawer of his writing desk. Without closing the drawer, he left the room, leaving the door slightly ajar. This was, I think, the worst moment during the whole time of my hearings. I knew what they expected—that I would take the gun and try to escape. And they were waiting there. I was perspiring. I didn't move at all—for how long I don't know, five minutes, a quarter of an hour, I don't know. I just sat there, in front of the desk, thinking that the tension was worse than the beatings during interrogations—but this was before the arrival of Soviet advisers in the fifties, before they started using brutal methods like electric shock treatment.

After this incident I was transferred to Section B2 at Pankrác where I was put in solitary with two others. One of these was Jaromír Panenka, the ex-police Commissar who, as I mentioned before, had known my uncle. He was accused of collaboration with the Nazis, and in October Mr. Panenka was executed. The night before the last day of his trial, the guard kept coming round every half hour and he would switch the light on to check if he was all right. I remember, clearly, the dogs that night. The dogs were howling outside—always, outside in the yard, the dogs howled when a man was to be executed. It was always at night. Each evening, you see, the dogs were brought to the yards—there were several yards in the prison, and in each yard there was one guard dog who, the whole night long, would run along the length of the fence, with his collar tied to a piece of wire attached to the fence, all night the dog was running, howling. Without fail, before an execution, the dogs howled, always. No doubt they felt something was wrong. They felt it. They had to feel it—the atmosphere was thick with the sense of death—it was as if everything in nature was shouting against injustice. And so, when the dogs howled, we knew that someone—one of us—was going to be executed.

Trial and Sentence

Eventually, on the 15th and 16th of December 1948 we were tried—in secret, of course. No one was admitted until the end, when our parents could enter the courtroom. We were not allowed to have our own lawyers and had to be content with *pro deo* lawyers—who were acceptable to the Communist Party. The court—their court—was told that our espionage had caused damage to the Czechoslovakian Republic of 300 million crowns because they had to change their mobilization plan. It satisfied me enormously that such a small group of students could have been so successful! But there were really bad moments during the trial. Like the day an intelligence expert took me aside, and said: "You. It doesn't matter how it will turn out with you. But you can be glad you got to the court. Because people like you disappear."

The night before my sentence was passed, the guards switched the light on in my cell and kept it burning all night—and I remembered Mr. Panenka, and knew that I would soon be hanged too. That was a very bad feeling. When they took us to the trial the next day the passage was full of guards. It was very strange. Everyone was nice, they were all polite. They kept us from the rail and the stairs and took us to the ground floor. We were told to face the wall. Everything was polite, everything was nice. You knew then that it was pretty serious for you. In the moments before the trial I was very stressed because it was obvious that the whole business was reaching a definite end—and I had no illusions as to what the outcome of the trial would be. It was all over for me. Once, during the fifteen-minute monthly visit allowed parents and friends, my girlfriend said, "I will wait for you till you come back." But all I could say was, "No. Don't wait. I will be hanged," and I saw her turn pale. Later on, she married, of course.

My friends and I pretended at the trial that we were merry, but of course we were not, because it was pretty bad. Three of us were, in fact, sentenced to death. It was such a relief, though, when two of our sentences were later changed to life, and the third to twenty-eight years' hard labor. The fourth boy got nine years, and the girl got three years. But nobody was hanged, and so in a strange way we were happy to be sent to Bory, to prison, where we would spend the rest of our lives.

Two days after the trial they cut our hair and gave us prison suits. My jacket, which had been that of a German policeman, was too small, and the trousers were far too big. So we looked like clowns, you know, in these clothes, with our shaven heads. And though it was awful, we joked about it and didn't care. The main thing was that we were alive. And we were optimistic—we believed that in 1949 things would change. We knew that there were many groups planning the overthrow of the Communist regime. And we believed that the Western countries would start a war and stop Soviet expansion before the Russians developed their own atomic bomb—though I was afraid that they hadn't much time. We hoped that America would win and then release us—but we were also afraid that we might be murdered in our cells before this could happen.

Prison Experiences: Bory, Libkovice, Jiřetín, and Most

After three more days, about twenty of us were woken up early and given civilian suits again—and dirty coffee. Chains were put on our wrists, and we

Jiří Mesicki in 2001

were taken to the main station in Prague where we were put on the express to Linz in Austria, that went via Plzeň. We joked when we saw the carriage: "So, they are taking us to Linz—that's fine!" We were not bound during the three-hour journey, though there were guards. We were even allowed to eat and smoke. From Plzeň, we were put in a windowless car and brought to Bory—but we didn't care at all. We were still in very high spirits because we were sentenced to life and no longer faced execution.

At Bory they gave us grey-brown prison suits from the time of the First Republic—there was a shortage of cloth during the War. The suits had been mended many times and they looked terrible. Our shoes also looked awful—but still, we didn't care. We were told by the Super Inspector—a very nice guy, an old legionnaire from World War I—what the rules were. Each of us had a file—I saw mine, with a hand-written phrase "Sentenced to ... death," and below, written in small letters "Altered to life-term." My prison number was 8912.

We were put in solitaries again, and there were two prisoners in each cell. I was transferred to the common cells: DI. An old school mate, Radim, was in a nearby cell. We were not allowed to smoke, and, though the quantities were the same, the food at Bory was different to what we had at Pankrác. At Bory the cabbage was blue, while at Pankrác it had been green.

The hard reality of prison soon hit us: there is nothing to do. Nothing. You are in solitary. For breakfast you get a piece of bread and some coffee. You get your lunch: a few unpeeled potatoes with gravy. And in the evening, soup. Day in, day out, it is the same. There is never enough food. Twice or three times a week they take you out for a walk. You walk with your hands behind your back. You walk around the yard for about twenty or twenty-five minutes. That is all.

When I was told that I had been expelled from the University I was not disappointed because my mother had already told me this on a visit to me. In any case, I had other things to worry about now. We soon saw that our families were suffering bitterly. Many families of arrested people were moved from their homes to places far away, in very bad conditions, where the children had to walk almost ten kilometers to school. Where there was no chance for the wife to get a job. So they practically starved, many of them. And they were bitterly persecuted. My own parents were allowed to stay on in the same apartment, but my father's small pension of 630 crowns a month was not enough for living— and too much for dying. And when other people saw this kind of thing they were afraid to resist. They pretended they were peaceful inhabitants of the country, and that they sympathized with the Soviet Union.

After a few days I was transferred to the communal cell, D3, a big room with fifteen beds. Nobody was there at first. When other prisoners later arrived I discovered that none of them spoke Czech. They were all Germans. When I spoke to them they started to tease me: "Well, we have a new one here. Look, look. What are you? Who are you?" I said: "I am a Czech student." "Oh! A student—and condemned. So, you didn't like us, and now you are here among us, and you will go with us to the mine because everyone who passes through this room goes to the mine. You will dig coal with us." I said: "Well, I wasn't satisfied with the Nazi tyranny and I am not satisfied with Communist tyranny. Just as I was in the resistance against the Communists, I was in the resistance against the Nazis."

During my stay in D3 I got a parcel from my mother. While the other prisoners were at work, I divided its contents into fifteen portions. The piece of sausage, the piece of cheese—I divided it all into fifteen parts, and when they came back I took the box and went from one to the other, offering each of them a piece. They were surprised, they didn't expect this, and after this they changed, they became more friendly towards me. In the time I was there, each one tried to explain to me personally why he was a Nazi. But one, Hubert Oesser, wasn't a Nazi at all—he was Danish, just a *Wehrmacht* man, an ordinary soldier that had been running from the Eastern Front. He didn't want to be taken by the Russians, so he threw away his uniform and stole civilian clothes. But because he couldn't speak Czech and could only speak German, they arrested him and he was sentenced to fifteen years.

I stayed with the Nazis for about a fortnight and then they transferred me to Libkovice prison camp where the prisoners stayed in wooden barracks and worked in a coal pit. We were there for only a fortnight, luckily, as it was terrible. Terrible. I was the last prisoner to arrive in the barracks and the only bed left was next to the door. And it was winter. They used to put our rationed food in the open doorway and hand it out there, so all the cold and the snow got into my bed. The nights were terrible. My mattress had hardly any straw in it— I was practically lying on wooden boards.

From Libkovice we went to Jiřétín, which was better as the barracks was divided into single rooms in each of which about twelve men slept. Again, we worked in the coal pits. But in March 1949 we made plans to escape, because we saw that things were rather lax in the camp. They took us to the pit every day in two lorries, and we decided to disarm the guards in the rear lorry and then overtake the first one, which we would stop. We would then all cross the mountains to Germany. But as often happened, one of the group announced the plan to the guards. Fifteen of us were taken to Most prison before being taken back to Bory. They bound us in twos, and I remember being hit hard in the face during the journey—I flew over the passage and pulled the other guy with me. I almost lost consciousness, and when we started to move again, I felt myself wetting my pants—and I was unable to stop.

When we got to Most I was put into a cell with a broken window. I was alone. It was March, and snowing outside, and we had no bedding—nothing. So I lay on the floor, and it was so cold. Ha! I howled so much that I woke myself up! But the next night they took us to Bory, and put me into solitary for three months. Here at least we were allowed to go for a half-hour walk a day, though no one was allowed to walk closer than six steps behind the next prisoner, and we were forbidden to speak at all.

I didn't mind being in solitary. I missed decent food, and a newspaper or radio—but nothing else. By lucky chance, a friend who was condemned with me was in the next room, and after three months he asked the guard if we could be put together. So, for some time we were together, in the one solitary—until they found out that we were involved in the same case.

Every day, we plucked feathers—an awful job because they kept increasing the quota. It peaked at three-quarters of a kilo a day, and to reach the quota we got up at half past four in the morning and plucked until nine in the evening. It was terrible—the feathers stank so, they were dirty, and everything smelled of napthalene, which was kept in big sacks. We slept in the same room as the feathers, and lived there all the time. Once they found a dead rat in a sack—you can imagine the stink. It almost drove us crazy.

So much so, in fact, that once, when we were in a defiant mood—we would show them that we weren't afraid of them, and, just for fun you understand—about fifteen of us who had been sitting at a table all day, plucking, plucking—we decided that when we did our weekly report to the prison Commander we would tell them that we were on strike. We refused to pluck any more feathers. Yes, believe it or not, we did this just for fun—we asked to be transferred to new solitaries, to the worst place in the entire prison. And I was terribly afraid of it, of course. But just imagine: fifteen thin and wrecked men parading in front of the prison Commander, asking to be transferred to the very worst—the strictest—department in the worst, most oppressive prison in Czechoslovakia! And, do you know, for some reason, they did nothing to punish us.

As luck had it, I was transferred on the 15th of September to the workshop common rooms where we worked on weaving machines. I came across several friends here, people I had met during the daily walks in Pankrác and Bory. But we suffered physically with the machines. You had to stand on your left leg all day long because, with your right leg, you had to stand on the weaving machine while both hands were engaged in the weaving. The workshop was in a room separate from that of the guard, so we felt almost free there. Our quotas were low, and the food was better: dumplings with meat and gravy, and as much bread as we wanted, because, of course, we had to be strong enough to work. And each week we got five extra sausages. We were no longer allowed parcels, but we got by with the prison food which was better than before.

One day—in the Bory Prison in Plzeň on the 3ʳᵈ of December 1951, I remember—we were returning from the workshop when a prisoner whispered in my ear, "You are going to be transported." About a half an hour later, a guard came and told me that I had to get ready to leave the camp the next day. This was easy—all I had to do was fetch from the store a paper bag containing a piece of bread, a toothbrush and toothpaste, and a piece of soap—that was all.

Early the next day, we did not go back to the workshop. They brought us to the solitary cells and we gathered in rows on the ground floor. I whispered to the man on my left: "How many years?" He said, "Life term." And then I turned to the man on my right, "How many years?" "Life term." The man in front of me had twenty-five years, the man behind me had twenty years. And they asked me, "And how many do you have?" I said, "Life term." So, this was really going to be something! We saw on the right, through a big open hall, in the common DI, that they were calling generals and high-standing people—members of the Czechoslovakian hockey team, General Janoušek, General Mrázek.

We all hoped that we were going to a prison camp, because life in the labor camps seemed to be more free: at least you were allowed to move around in a camp, and the food was so much better. But instead, they pushed us into solitaries and left us there without food for two days. There were 126, perhaps 127 of us, and they needed buses and an armoured vehicle. On the night of the 5ᵗʰ of December, St Nicholas Day, we could hear beyond the prison walls the sounds of children laughing and crying out as they celebrated the day. In my mind's eye, I could see them mischievously running from place to place, dressed up as angels and devils. They were the guards' children and suddenly they reminded me of my own childhood. But I had a grim feeling that I was going to go to another hell. So eventually, very early on the 6ᵗʰ of December, we were put into three buses and, accompanied by a panzer with a machine gun, we moved on. It was obvious that we were not going to a camp but to another prison.

We travelled east, along side roads, and had no idea of where we were going. Someone thought we were going to Brno, but we passed Brno. It was night already, and we arrived in Bratislava, and Stěpán Gavenda, who was sitting behind me, smiled and whispered in my ear, "I need to get over the border to my CIA boss because in the Third World War prisoners need to be transported to Bratislava and put on ships on the Danube to be evacuated to the Black Sea." Ha! Ha! I really laughed at this. And he said, with a kind of mock-seriousness "If any of us survive, maybe we won't be under arrest for long."

Life-in-Death at Leopoldov

We emerged from the buses into the cold night—the huge old fortress of Leopoldov looming against the clouds. My life in this notorious prison began on the night of the 6th of December, 1951. But my imagination had not prepared me for what I found—the place was beyond description. To say it was awful gives no clue at all to the reality of Leopoldov—a reality that hemmed me in on all sides and in all ways. It blocked out light and freedom and, young man that I was, I recoiled at the bleakness that seemed to stretch ahead of me interminably. At that time, Leopoldov was the worst prison in the whole of Czechoslovakia.

The prison building dates from the time of Kaiser Leopold, and architecturally it is similar to Terežin. We were put in the "new solitaries," a five-storey building built in the time of the First Republic as a military prison for hardened offenders. Those in the upper level were told they were lucky because they were "nearer to heaven." At least we had water taps, even if they only had cold water, and lavatories in the cells—not those buckets we had in Bory. In that way it was better. At the beginning, the food also seemed to be better—but only at the beginning. We were given a brush to scrub the floor, and every day, in summer and freezing winter, I had a cold shower, and scrubbed myself with the floor-brush, scrubbing hard in winter to keep myself warm.

It soon became clear just how bleak and comfortless our lives were to be, as things soon slid into a monotonous sameness that was worsened by the fact that we had no walks, and no work. There was nothing. About ten days after our arrival, they took us—no matter how old we were—to work on the battlements of this fortress. This was in December 1951, and, oh, it was bloody cold out there. Working behind me was a very old gentleman, Vladimír Sýs, a famous anthropologist, who had spent twenty years in Senegal, in Africa, and spoke several African languages. He had a walking stick in one hand and in the other a little axe. I don't know why he had the axe—he just had it. There was another white-haired gentleman who walked with both hands in his pockets and with a shovel stuck through his crooked elbows behind his back. This was General Karel Palečîk.

We were certain that those of us who had life terms—men who faced twenty or twenty-five years in solitaries—had been brought to Leopoldov so that they could eliminate us. We worked on the battlements all day long, in a cold that I will never forget. Though nobody drove us to work hard, we did. You had to move all the time, because if you didn't, you would freeze. The prison clothes were so thin that you could only keep warm by working. We worked like this until the end of December. We worked until four o'clock in the afternoon, and came back to our cells, frozen. I would then undress, and sit under the tap, and scrub myself until I felt warm.

On the 2nd of January, 1952, I managed to get into a group that was cleaning a big factory hall inside the fortress. It was wonderful, because I was warm. I was under the roof, heated by a stove, and just had to move a little cart along. We got home at about four o'clock, before the people working out on the battlements. We waited for them to return but after more than an hour the guards called us downstairs, to the ground floor. There they had a roll call and we discovered that six men had escaped: Štěpán Gavenda, Pravomil Reichel, Josef Heřmanský, John Hvasta (an American citizen) and two others whose names I can't remember. After half a year of hiding, Hvasta succeeded in getting to Prague, to the U.S. Embassy, where he stayed for two years before they allowed him to leave the country. Reichel and two others managed to get over the border to Germany, but Gavenda and Heřmanský decided to stay in Czechoslovakia and to join the resistance again. They were soon caught and Gavenda was executed in Prague. Heřmanský was later brought back to Leopoldov. He could not walk, he could not speak—the result of the interrogations. They took him to the prison hospital where other prisoners had to feed and wash him. His condition saved his life, because they could not hang him, but his life changed forever.

And then, by chance, I became a barber. We had been transported to Leopoldov from Plzeň according to an alphabetical list. The name that came after mine was Molenkovič: Mesicki, Molenkovič, and so on. So, when we arrived at Leopoldov they put me together in a cell with Molenkovič. And the next day, because we were not working, not going out, nothing, Molenkovič told me: "Don't worry, I am the only barber here, and after a few days the men will start growing beards, and they will ask if there is a barber here. I am the only one. So they will take me out to shave the men, and, after a while, I'll tell them that the men aren't soaping themselves properly and that I need someone to help me soap them, and in this way I will help to get you out of solitaries." And, do you know, this really happened! Later on, we also succeeded in getting a soaping job for Milan, a friend of mine in a cell across the hall. This Molenkovič, a professional, was the prison barber, and we were his assistants.

But, after a while, a minor disaster arose because Molenkovič was summoned to be the barber in the guards' barbershop. We two assistants were now forced to choose: we either had to do the shaving ourselves, or go back to solitaries. Well, I had had some practice many years before as a thirteen-year-old, when I secretly shaved myself with my father's razor. I remember how he used to swear: "What has happened to my shaving blade—it's blunt again!" He soon bought me my own razor and some Gillettes. But I hadn't held a razor in my hand since that time—and now I had to start shaving other people! It didn't take too long, though, and after a fortnight or so, Milan and I were shaving the men quite well—almost like professionals. But long afterwards—to this day, in fact, when I meet old friends, they point to their faces and say, "Do you see this scar? You did it, Jura!"

During this time, from 1949, we were cut off from all connections with the world. We weren't allowed to write for a year—my family knew nothing about me at all, and they had no information from the Ministry of Law or from the police. They didn't know where I was, or whether I was alive. Unlike Pankrác and Bory, there were no opportunities at Leopoldov for getting news to the outside world.

Eventually, when visits were allowed—these happened twice yearly—we were forbidden to discuss politics. So, while my parents told me how they were living, they couldn't give me details, because, of course, they were living in very bad conditions. But I couldn't help noticing their shabbiness. My mother— I saw, for instance, that her winter coat was worn out and they couldn't afford to buy another one. My father was shabbily dressed—I could see very, very clearly that they were living in really poor conditions.

For three years, we lived in hope—hope that something would happen, that the regime would fall, that the situation would change, that the Communists would be forced to leave the government. But nothing happened, and gradually we saw that we would have to stay in prison a long time. Those who were married, who had children, were very depressed of course because they were not allowed to see their children—after the age of fifteen, children were not allowed visits. I shared a cell with a captain of the Czech Army who had been imprisoned three days after his wedding. And after nine months, he had news that his wife had had a baby. And he never saw that baby. And he had in fact done nothing—he had simply met another officer who told him that he had deserted the Army, gone to Germany, worked for the CIA, and returned. And all the captain had said was, "Oh, goodbye," because he was afraid to continue talking to him. The other officer was arrested, and he admitted to talking to him. So, he got about fifteen years, too.

We saw that there wasn't any hope, there wasn't any hope for us. I had a life-term, and I worried about many things. My parents were not young. If they died, what would happen to the apartment, to the furniture? What would I do if I ever got out? Where would I live? Because there were no answers, you give up after a while, you no longer bother. You realize that you can't beat the system. It was getting stronger and stronger. There were conflicts all over the world—for instance the communists later won the Korean War in 1953. And the West was very lenient towards communists, and also very naive—very naive. When you came to terms with all this, with the sheer strength of the system, you just began to live from one day to the next.

The older, married prisoners were allowed to have photographs of their families, and in the evenings, they would put the photographs of their wives and children on their beds and look at them. The evenings were very emotional times, especially in winter when it got dark very early. But for the rest of us there was nothing. We were not allowed to play chess or gamble, nothing. We were allowed one book each per week from the prison library, but these books were terrible. There was only Marxism and Marxist novels. We hated them. We didn't read them. This situation was horrible for all of us, and especially so, I would say, for the intelligentsia. And remember, Leopoldov was a special prison where bishops and cardinals, university professors and scientists were put so that the intellectual class could slowly be liquidated by starvation.

In solitaries in Leopoldov we were forbidden to read anything. When I was alone, most of the time I had no books, nothing. So, what was there to do? It depended on your imagination. I imagined, for instance, myself in the time of old Egypt, or in the time of the Thirty Years War. Or I imagined the situation in some other historical period—and I tried to visualize what it must have been like. I would try to remember the past—though I didn't do this very often. I tried not to because remembering the past made one weak. It was better to concentrate on the present—on resisting the present situation. It is very difficult to explain—it all depended on your personal attitude to the situation. Some people tried to commit suicide. They had simply gone mad being alone.

But I thought of the old monks from the middle ages, and I tried to understand what it was that made it possible for them to live cloistered lives—quite apart from the world—studying the Bible and writing holy texts. In Leopoldov I said the Rosary three times a day. This took about an hour each time—it is strange, you know, but when you have been in solitary for a long time, your way of thinking, your mental world, alters somehow.

I realized that I would have to find some kind of equilibrium, some way of coming to terms with the present situation. There was no point in asking how long it would last. And it was no good thinking about the past, about your family, because this would weaken you. So, whenever the cell door opens, you have to stand firm, resisting your fears, not being anxious about what might happen. Not being afraid of what they might tell you or what they might do to you. Because you live in a continual state of not knowing your fate, of having no control over what happens to you. You never know when you will be transferred or where you might be transferred.

And yet always, when I was in solitaries, I would have an intuition, a sense of what they were up to, when they examined my file in the office—and you know, several times after I had these feelings, it would happen that after a week or maybe a fortnight, I was transferred somewhere else. It was very strange, and I still don't really understand how it was that I had a sense that something was going on—though I never knew quite what this was, of course.

It was very difficult to block the past out of my mind. I was still a young man as you know, and it was very difficult to put out of one's mind the girls one had met before. It was better altogether not to think about the past. I realized this during my first three-month solitary in 1949, when they brought me from the coal-pit.

I knew it was a question of mind over matter, of gaining mastery over physical desire. As a result, I had no trouble with these things in all the eight years I was in prison. I never, in all that time, had an erection. You see, for me, women faded from my mind and were no longer part of my mental landscape. Because of my efforts at overcoming my sexual longing, my mental powers had evolved, and I managed to block women out of my mind completely. They simply didn't exist. Desire died in me.

Some people might think that this breaking down of normal physical impulses and desires was a degradation of the self. But this was not the case at all—well, not for me, at least. I saw degradation differently. Let me explain: there were people I had known in civilian life who were important, who sat in offices, elegantly dressed, with a secretary and all the symbols of power, and everybody was polite to them. But when, after a few years, I saw them again—in prison—with their heads shaven, dressed in rags begging for a cigarette butt, or, "Have you a piece of bread, or something, anything"—well, it made me think about the real meaning of degradation and humiliation.

I realized that these men were broken because the centre of their lives was that office, the secretaries, the elegant clothes, the environment they lived in. And when they got to this bad environment in prison, they somehow collapsed mentally. Their mental life was in tatters. Their lives were nothing but debris. They themselves were nothing. More than anything, I resolved that I would not end up like them. By conquering my inner self, I would gain power and mastery over the temptations of the world, over the outward symbols of power, and in this way achieve a kind of integrity.

Since the whole of the Czechoslovakian elite, you could say, was imprisoned in Leopoldov, there was the opportunity to learn, to study. Some intellectuals even gave lectures in the common rooms—just as they did in the camps, where we were not bound to one room but could walk from one barracks to another, almost as if we were students attending different classes on a campus. But this was all done in secret, of course. The teaching was all illegal—but still, you could do a lot of learning in this way. University professors lectured about philosophy, about physics and chemistry. Many of us started to learn foreign languages—English, French, German and Spanish because there were people who spoke several languages. Prison life makes one ingenious—it forces one to be inventive.

We devised a way of making books, for instance. We were allowed to smoke, and we rolled our own cigarettes. So, we used the cigarette papers to write on, and with needle and thread, we sewed these together into copy books. And to write in these miniature "books," we used small, sharp, hard pieces of lead from pencils. We worked out ways to teach one another languages such as Spanish, French and German. One man—but he was extraordinary—managed to learn thirteen languages! The clergymen were particularly eager to share their learning. They baptized many prisoners—secretly of course—who wished to join the Church. And for the more ordinary among us, it gave us a great deal of moral support to know that we were not alone—that important people, people with status before men and God—shared our fate.

We were all in the same boat—bishops, generals, students, workers and craftsmen—and because we felt that we were together in this, we all helped one another. Those who were without education tried to study something. We studied literature and many other things besides. I remember—in 1955 when I was removed from Leopoldov—finding in the transport room on a pile of things that had been confiscated from prisoners, a small book made of cigarette papers. It contained information on nuclear physics! So I took it and rolled cigarettes from it while I was being transported back to Prague.

It was often difficult having discussions with fellow prisoners, because these could only really take place in the common rooms. Also, you didn't always find a suitable partner. For instance, if you were among former officers, they tended to speak about the war, about their experiences during World War II. And again, if you were among—I don't know—say, entrepreneurs, they spoke about business, and even then, not very much because they were wary of speaking about these things. Maybe it reminded them of the past. You see, you had to be in a common room with a professor, or some member of the intelligentsia. And I was fortunate, because I had many opportunities to discuss with intellectuals—even in solitaries.

I managed to teach several friends English. I wrote simple notes on English grammar on three or four pieces of toilet paper: the present tense, the past tense, perfect and imperfect, the conditional form and such things. In fact, when I was in the common rooms and we were plucking feathers, we all learnt English together. I remember the bricklayer, Rudla Mašata, who had plucked feathers with me—he wore a roll of toilet paper on the back of his shirt, which was full of English irregular verbs. Each morning, before we started, we would meet and repeat the verbs written on it. We used to start the day by repeating all these English words. And once—I forget the details—a piece of brown paper fell from a parcel that someone or other had received, and on this piece of paper were printed the words: "On the service of Her Majesty the Queen." We kept this, and read it daily for about three weeks before they removed it.

But we had one overwhelming problem—and therefore only one real interest: food. The punishments made this worse. We would, for instance, be forced to do hard exercise on half rations for a whole month, every hour, from six in the morning to ten at night. With our arms stretched out in front of us, we had to go down on our haunches, and up again: I once had to do fifty sit-ups, sit down-and-up—just believe it!—fifty every hour for a whole month, on half rations. They tried to threaten us. Once, they had asked me to become, an informant. Since I was a barber, and was therefore the only person those in solitaries saw every week, the authorities wanted me to denounce my fellow-prisoners. They thought they could tempt me with better conditions because in solitaries there was no work, no exercise—nothing. Of course, I refused.

So, they put me in solitaries, and for a month I got half-rations. After a fortnight all I could manage was thirty-five sit-ups, and then I collapsed. But they couldn't break me. They could kill me, but I would not allow them to bend me and shape me as they liked. No! Never—even though they tortured us by never giving us enough to eat. Because, as I said, we were never full, never satisfied—we thought about food and cigarettes all the time, all the time. At that stage, I weighed less than fifty kilos. We looked like the skeletal inmates of concentration camps. Our ribs stuck out, and our ankles and legs swelled—full of water. Awful, awful!

The only sad thought I had, really, was for my parents. When I remembered them, I thought about how sorry and depressed they would be to get the news that their son, their only son, had died in prison. That was the only thing I really cared about. Because gradually, we became dull, we became primitive. We no longer cared about anything—except food, as I said. All we cared about was survival. But how can you survive when you are in solitary, quite alone, and there is not even a crumb of bread? For breakfast, you got about eight spoonfuls of coffee, of that black dirt. Then you got two and a half potatoes with a handful of some kind of gravy. And in the evening you got about twelve spoonfuls of soup. How do you think we looked, after enduring this?

But in 1953 things changed slightly—for the better I am pleased to say, as food was no longer so strictly rationed. From then on, for lunch we got watery soup, some potatoes with cabbage, and once a week a dumpling with some gravy and a piece—a very small, tough piece—of beef. The beef lasted until the next meal—you could chew it all afternoon, until supper. And we had no other vegetables, and no fruit—nothing like that. Just dumplings, potatoes, some noodles—never rice—sometimes beans, and that was all. But later things really improved when a master chef from Prague was appointed as the prison's chief cook. He had worked at a big café, called Phoenix, and he was a good cook. The food was excellent, really tasty, but in a strange way this aggravated the situation because we were limited to the small prison portions—though we might long for a morsel more, there was no possibility at all that we would be given it.

We had very little opportunity to discuss political issues with one another. When we were in the common rooms, we did, but just hypothetically, because we didn't know what was going on outside. We could only speculate on what might be happening outside. It was very difficult to discuss anything, really, apart from the memories we had. We were, in a sense, living in a frozen past, with little access to the present, and therefore we could not really speculate on the future. We discussed the history of politics. But though we had no news of the outside world, there were, as you can imagine, many whisperings.

I never felt that I was part of a group, because I was in solitary. We could communicate from one cell to another only by knocking on the walls. There were no walks. You couldn't get out for a walk in the yard. The only exercise we had was the seven steps we walked, over and over again, the seven steps from the door to the window, and the same seven steps from the window back to the door. The door opened once a week only, and that was when the barber came to shave you and cut your hair—that was all. Our food was given to us through a small window in the door—and that was all.

Only once did I feel anything like a feeling of solidarity. This was when I had to go to the doctor, once, for some reason that I can't remember, and Bishop Gojdič, who was in the cell next to mine, went with me. He used to say to me, whenever we passed each other on our way to our cells, that I should pray. And so, I said to him, during our visit to the doctor, "I want to tell you that I do pray. I kneel in a corner three times a day, and say the Rosary—even though I don't have much faith that we will get out of here alive." And he told me then, "I feel it when you pray. Yes, I know, I feel it."

But prayer did not fill me with forgiveness for my persecutors. You see we were filled with hatred. I am sorry to say this, but in the solitaries at Leopoldov things were so bad that I heard the prisoners saying: "If we ever get out of here, we'll even shoot the geese on the pond." The hatred I felt—and it was deep and powerful—was for the system. But I cannot say that I hated the guards—rather, I despised them. It's hard to generalize about how prisoners felt towards the guards, but it's probably true that our feelings were specific to each individual. And I'm sure that there were many prisoners who would have liked to kill them—to kill the guards.

You know, if the gates of Leopoldov had ever been opened and we were allowed to escape into the world outside, it would have been terrible. There would have been bloodshed. I remember coming out of hospital, towards the end of my imprisonment, and feeling that I hated every civilian because I saw each one of them as an enemy, responsible for my fate. I remember the anger I felt when I saw them, "You kept your mouth shut, and you lived here peacefully while we were suffering in hell in that place. And there are still thousands, thousands, who continue to suffer—and you don't know about it, and you don't care, and you are living peacefully—getting married, having children, going to work and earning money." How could they be so indifferent, so cruel, I thought.

My aversion towards the system grew as I witnessed its workings. I remember escapes—several cases when escaping prisoners attacked the guards. Yes, they beat them up and bound them, but there were no killings. During attempts to cross the border, there was perhaps some shooting and maybe, even, guards were killed. This was the case in the escape of the Mašín brothers—who now live in Florida and Canada. They killed six people here in Czechoslovakia and in Germany while trying to escape abroad. And they have never returned, they are still afraid of what could happen as public opinion is against them—they are still called murderers. But you know, if I had been on the run with a gun in my hand, I would have done the same. I would have killed anyone—anyone—who stood in my way. I would not have hesitated. When you're on the run, you have no alternative but to kill.

Mukls: Men Destined for Liquidation

After about three years, the civilian in us all—the human being—began to evaporate somehow. It disappeared because of the terrible monotony of our lives. We were just part of a mass, called *mukls*. We were *mukls*—men destined for liquidation. Our brains had leaked from our heads. We were brain-dead. We didn't care for health, we didn't care for life. We were merely creatures destined for liquidation. We were not allowed to enquire about our fates, to speak about our lives, our futures. The only chance we had was when we went to the doctor. We would ask, "What's new? Any chance of change?" And the answer would be, "It's forever." The question was always, "What's new?"—and the answer, always, "It's forever." After five or six years, we had no hope at all. We saw, with the little information we got from outside, that the West's attitude towards the Soviet Union was changing. There was no hope that World War III would start. At that stage we believed that only a new war could lead to our freedom. So we were not sure that we would ever leave prison, that we would survive.

Through all this, however, I was never emotional. I am a beast of a man, you know. I was never sentimental. I realized in Leopoldov that I would have to make an account of my life because I saw that I was going to die there. I hadn't even the will to survive because conditions were so bad—I no longer cared for life. I prayed often, and asked God to forgive me. I was preparing to die, because I looked back on my previous life and realized I had much to atone for.

I had wasted time with frivolous things, got involved in nonsense—I had gone to parties and many balls, I had been drunk many times, and I had lived the high life. All of this was worthless, unnecessary activity. I now saw that in death I would be alone if I didn't trust in God. When a child is born, he is not alone, he has the company of his mother. But when you die, you are either alone, or with God. I even began to see the fabled tunnel through which those who are about to die travel. I saw this tunnel in Leopoldov. I was slowly entering the tunnel. I wasn't ill—only so undernourished that I was already dying.

And yet, strangely—paradoxically, even—considering our conditions, we were proud to be prisoners, proud to be *mukls*. I remember once, seeing Count Esterházy, who shared a cell with me, standing to attention in his tattered underwear, with bare feet, in front of a guard. And the guard was shouting and swearing at him. And Count Esterházy said, with a bare tone of defiance in his voice that I will never forget, "Mr Commander, I have been in prison for too many years—I am too old a *mukl* for your tricks. You can say or do what you like to me."

You see, he belonged to this mass of unknown, unnamed men who together formed one mass where the individual meant nothing. He wasn't proud of being a Count, he was proud of being a *mukl*. For this is something more, you know. We felt that we were on a higher level than the people living outside, because we had resisted and they did not. And we continued to resist—there was something in us that made us decide that we would resist to the end. It was as if we had reached a higher level of consciousness.

Once, for instance, fifteen prisoners refused to work in the uranium mines at Jáchymov and Příbram, and as a result they died in the bunker. Also, at Leopoldov, there were about 2,000 political prisoners, and of these, about forty or fifty cooperated secretly with the guards. We called these traitors *bonzaks*. Sometimes it was very difficult to find out who these *bonzaks*, these secret collaborators, were. But once we thought we had identified one, one of us would volunteer to befriend him and plan an escape. And, of course, in the final phase that *bonzak*, that traitor, would denounce you. Then it was obvious who the traitor was, because while you were sent to correction, to the prison within the prison, he was not.

It was revealed, after 1989, that about 400 former political prisoners who had survived the hell of places like Leopoldov—honest, tough men—became secret collaborators with the police after their release. But this is easy to explain. Whilst in prison, their mental attitude to life, to the world, to everything was completely different from the mental attitude of normal, free people. They were just a little wheel in the system, part of a big group of *mukls*, opposing the oppression by the guards. Within one year of their release they became "normal" people—having a job, earning money, getting married, looking after a family. So when two men in leather coats came around and threatened them that if they didn't sign the secret treaty, the agreement to co-operate and to spy on other people, they would be arrested again, they broke down mentally. They simply agreed to do what was demanded.

A very good friend of mine did this. He had been caught smuggling foreign newspapers, and was told: "Either you will sign, or you will go back to prison." So, he signed. He never betrayed anybody. But, once a fortnight, he had to report to a secret policeman. And then, in 1965 he fled to Switzerland with his wife and baby son during a trip to Yugoslavia. He was afraid of being forced into betrayal. I remember, also, someone with two children who was warned: "Either you sign, or something will happen to your children. Be careful!" He refused to sign, and some time afterwards, one of his children was run over by a car. The kid was dead—murdered. That's what it was: murder. So, to save the other child, he signed co-operation with the Secret Police. Mothers were also targets. They were frequently warned: "If you do not sign, we will take your children and put them in an orphanage because you don't educate them in the proper socialistic way." These people were not *mukls*, so what else could they do, but sign?

In 1953—August it was—I was transferred to a prison camp, Bitýz, near Příbram. Here, we worked in uranium mines. Of course, my physical condition after the solitaries of Leopoldov didn't really equip me to become a miner, particularly in a radioactive environment. At this stage, most of us had tuberculosis. Though I was only diagnosed in January 1956, I suspect that I had a high level of tuberculosis long before that. I must have had it in the work camp at Příbram where, every day, I climbed 150 metres from the pit to the surface of the mine—and this with a lit cigarette in my mouth! As I later found out, the main reason that I had been sent to Příbram was because I was born in Yugoslavia, and they wanted to negotiate with us to send us back. But I refused, since I was a Czech citizen. So, I remained in solitaries at Příbram before being taken back to Leopoldov.

Though little changed in the years that followed and our fates seemed bleak, the spirit of resistance somehow prevailed. We were determined to show the prison authorities that we were impervious to their abuse: though we might die, they would never break us. We were what we had been before. And then, throughout 1955 there were hunger strikes in the prisons and prison camps. The instigators were all put on trial, their sentences increased, and they were then brought to Leopoldov. Old friends—strong opponents of the regime—were coming to join us, so we said, "Well, now that they will be here, we'll make a real stand. We'll organize a hunger strike in the worst prison in Czechoslovakia!" And we did it! For a week, 2,000 prisoners did not work. Many went on strike for two, and some even for three weeks. The authorities struck back and stopped the strike by unleashing unmuzzled dogs into the cells, and then beating us up— brutally.

I was put into the correctional—the prison within the prison—for about ten days. Here I got only bread for two days—200 grams, the size of a piece of cake, much less than the 350 grams allowed in the Jewish ghettos in Lodž, for example. Each third day I got half rations—without meat, and without fat. Because of our *mukl* mentality, we were not afraid, however. We simply didn't care about our lives. A *mukl* sees himself as being just one little wheel in a big machine, and this big machine was all the prisoners. You yourself are nothing—just one of thousands and thousands. You knew everyone because prisoners were continually being moved from the camps to the prisons to the camps, and back again. There was this one and that one and so on, and I saw him and I waved to him. You knew more or less where everyone was, and it didn't matter if you got information about different people only once a year, or once every two years. Time didn't play a role at all, because you had all the time in the world—to the end of your days. You don't care if you die or live, whether you are put in the prison of the prison, or if you are an ordinary prison worker somewhere—you are simply a part of a big machine.

The Warders

I should say something about the warders—they were so much part of our daily lives. At each prison, the situation was different. And, so, yes, there were some good warders—especially in Plzeň, in Bory, in 1950. Here, a number of warders were themselves arrested and terribly treated. They were terribly beaten and condemned to long sentences because they helped prisoners by bringing them food, or letters, and that kind of thing. At Plzeň, in Bory, where I worked in the weaving department, there were two excellent warders. One of them was from the Western army and had served in the British army during the War. The other I don't know anything about. Anyway, we gradually made a connection with the outside world through the civilian for whom we were doing the weaving. Since he was allowed to come into the prison we were able to arrange with him to smuggle letters for us. He also brought food and medicine and was even prepared to bring a radio transmitter for my friend until I said, "You are an absolute idiot. You would transmit twice, or maybe three times, and then they will get you, and hang us both!"

But at Leopoldov—here it was quite different. No warder risked being friendly with the prisoners. It was very strict. The warders were young people, and most of them were Communists. They behaved very badly. They were sadists, you know, and they did really bad things to us. And then there were the gypsies, who were also very cruel. You need to understand that they are people with a *Minderwertigkeitsgefuhl*, and now, suddenly they were masters of prisoners whom they knew were members of the intelligentsia—professors, priests, generals and important politicians. They beat us. They shot at us. In Bory, twice a week we heard terrible beating and yelling in correction—the special prison within the prison, a basement area where prisoners were punished. Those who had tried to escape, for instance, wore leg-irons weighing eight kg. for three months or more. After a second escape attempt, the weight of the chains was increased to fifteen kg.—and on a third escape attempt prisoners were punished with chains of twenty-five kg. Not only this—they were beaten senseless twice a week—beaten until they lost consciousness.

But almost worse than this, at Leopoldov we were subjected to psychological torture. The guards never tired of telling us that the only way we would leave Leopoldov was feet first. And, of course, we knew we were in terrible physical condition, and could see that they really were out to destroy us by starving us. The effects of solitary confinement eroded our sense of who and what we were. The meaning of our lives seemed lost and often I felt that I no longer understood why we were there.

All we had to look forward to was the weekly visit of the barber. The only time we were allowed to open the little cell door windows was once in the morning, once at noon, and once at night. That was all. Can you imagine this? Can you? We were like rats in a dark cage, starving rats. We were worse off even than rats, because rats couldn't be psychologically abused in the way we were. They found all kinds of reasons to punish us—we were punished for not being disciplined even when we were perfectly obedient. For instance, every day we had to wash the floor. And if the guard came after the floor had already dried, he accused us of not washing it, shouting at us that the floor was dirty. They didn't need to beat or assault us. They killed our minds and bodies off slowly, starving us. We were at their mercy. Sometimes a guard would walk into my cell with something in his hand, dust or something—I could see he had something, you know—and he would put his hand under the heater or the bed, then point and say, "What is this filth? You will have half-rations!" The deprivation, the sense of impotence—it was awful.

But the warders never succeeded in totally breaking us down, in annihilating us. They oppressed us, but never succeeded in making us change our minds. We resolved, "Either we will leave together, or we will die together, here in prison." So they gave up attempts to make us change our opinions. For we were *mukls*. We did not suffer alone.

Illness and Amnesty

Things really deteriorated after the hunger strike. Shortly afterwards, they took me to a transport cell and brought me back to Pankrác, and asked me again if I wanted to go to Yugoslavia. When they discovered that I had tuberculosis, there was a big fuss. However, they made a mistake—for three days they left me with two Yugoslav citizens on the transport from Leopoldov to Pankrác. One was Professor Spiro Vrcej, a mathematician. I told him about my illness and asked him to contact my relatives in Belgrade. After he visited my uncle a campaign for my release began as my uncle went from the Ministry of Foreign Affairs in Yugoslavia to the Ministry of Czechoslovakian Foreign Affairs, to the Ministry of the Interior, and so on.

When the transport department found out that a prisoner who was supposed to leave Czechoslovakia had tuberculosis and was in a desperate condition, there was consternation. The result of all this was that my imprisonment was interrupted for six months after I was diagnosed in 1956. I stayed in the prison hospital first at Pankrác and then Mírov, another prison fortress in Moravia. I had stopped eating—I simply couldn't bear the food. Though the doctor came once a week and gave me pills, I perspired all night long, and once, when my temperature was taken, it was over 40 degrees. I was then taken for X-rays, and, at the age of thirty-one, found to be in a hopeless situation with dispersed TB in three cavities. From here an ambulance took me to Prague, to the Thomayerova Nemocnice Hospital, a civilian virus hospital, where I stayed from July 1956 to December 1957. You see, they didn't think I would survive more than six months, and they didn't want the embarrassment of me dying in prison because I was due to be transported to Yugoslavia, and the secretary of the Ambassador of Yugoslavia had himself come to speak with me.

When my parents heard about my illness, they requested that I be treated for another six months. So I stayed in hospital, but I had no word from the authorities, and nothing happened to change my status. I wasn't pardoned, nothing. In fact, I lived in the hospital illegally for about three or four weeks because officially I was supposed to go back to prison. But what did they expect me to do? Did they think I would knock at the prison gate and say, "Please let me in, I have come back for sixteen or seventeen more years." You could say I wasn't in the mood anymore. So I just waited, wondering what they would do with me.

After three or four weeks of this, my father arrived one day and told me that I had been given amnesty from the President on condition that for five years I would not commit a political crime. It was over. Suddenly, it was all behind me—from being a *mukl* I would be a man again. The amnesty granted to me was much better than those granted in 1960 and 1962, because those were conditional on no crime of any sort being committed for ten years. So, for example, you might go to a pub, where someone might insult you, and if you hit him in the face, you were back in jail for twenty-five years. So, I had it much better.

An Enchained Freedom

In the summer of 1957, during my illness at Thomayerova Nemocnice Hospital, I was pardoned by President Zápotocký. I was granted amnesty—individual amnesty. But though I was free, I was unable to work. I remained under medical supervision, and for three years, I went to the hospital every month to be examined. I found it very difficult to adapt to civilian life after my ordeal. It was very bad. Everything made me anxious, nervous. Even little things, like my parents offering me a meal, and pressing me to have some of this and have some of that while we were sitting at the table. It made me mad, because for years I had struggled for food, and now I was being told to eat a variety of things, and to eat more.

Big things didn't really worry me, but trivial things would make me very angry. I remember looking for something once—I don't recall what exactly it was—and when I couldn't find it, I became very upset and angry because I wasn't used to living in an environment where it was possible for things to be mislaid. You see, I had lived in a prison cell all those years where all I had was a table with one drawer, and perhaps a piece of bread, and a bed with two blankets. And now, suddenly, I was faced with confusion—I found myself in a room where there was a lot of furniture—many drawers, rows of books, many, many things that I had to keep in mind. Being surrounded by so many things disturbed me.

Life outside the prison walls continued to be difficult. I was living with my parents in very cramped, poor conditions. I couldn't get a job because the employer always wanted me to be examined, and the doctor always said, "He mustn't do hard work, he mustn't work at night, he mustn't work in a dusty environment, or in a cold or wet environment," and so on. Or they would say, "You have passed your matriculation examination, so we can employ you in the office, but for that you need to be 'clean'." Of course, I was an ex-political prisoner, and when I showed them my papers they shook their heads and said, "We are sorry."

But eventually I succeeded in getting a job in a factory in Prague. Afterwards I changed jobs and worked in a boiler room for three winters, but after some time I found it too hot. Then, for about twelve or thirteen years I worked at the Geological Investigations with a pick and shovel, out in the countryside. When my back gave in I was unable to carry on doing physical work. So they allowed me to work in an office at a firm of undertakers, on Old Town Square.

You ask what I think now about the eight years I spent in prison. Well, it was the worst time of my life, not only for me, but also for my parents. And yet, I am not sorry for it. It taught me one thing. You cannot value yourself until you reach two limits: there is the lowest limit when you are in the worst situation, and there is the top limit when you are in a high position: rich, competent. I have seen members of former governments at both ends: I saw them at the top of their careers, and I saw them defeated, pressed down to the level of the floor. So, it is very difficult. You see, nobody can really say that he knows himself unless he explores these two limits in himself.

And what did I learn about myself? I discovered that I am very pig-headed. Let me tell you about an incident in section D at Leopoldov—you remember, the section that is "close to heaven." On one occasion, when we were all being driven down the stairs by the guards, I happened to speak to a fellow prisoner. A guard saw me doing this. That evening, after roll call, everyone was told to go back to their cells, except for Mesicki, Štěpánek and Deči, a former National Socialist member of parliament who had picked up a cigarette butt that had been dropped on the staircase by a guard. They gave him three days of half rations.

There were about six or seven guards present, and they then confronted Štěpanek and me. But we had already decided that we would not admit to anything. No. So, when they asked, "Mesicki, what did you say to Štěpanek?" I said, "Nothing." "But you spoke with him—we saw you!" I stared at them and said again, "I did not speak with him." We were given half rations for twenty days, and every hour we had to do sit-ups, from six in the morning till ten at night. And twice a week, the guard who had seen us speaking came to my cell. "So, what did you speak about with Štěpanek?" "Nothing," I said. "Tell me what you were saying, or admit that you were speaking, and I will pardon you." "We did not speak." And so it went on, he kept coming, even at night. I would admit nothing. He eventually went on vacation, and one fine August day, a prisoner came and brought me an army pot, full to the brim with soup, and said, "The guard sends it to you." But, of course, this was a different guard. And so I survived the rest of the month, even though I nearly lost consciousness at times. I had decided that rather than giving in, I would die of starvation—death by hunger is not so terrible, you know, you just slowly fade out.

But there is another thing. I am a Christian. I was a baptized Christian before I went to prison, and, as a boy, I attended Catholic as well as Orthodox catechism. As I have said, all the members of my father's family live in Yugoslavia—they are Serbian Orthodox. When I was at school in Yugoslavia in the first and second class, I also attended Catholic catechism. So, for five years I listened to Catholic teaching at school, and at the same time, once a week I attended two hours of Orthodox catechism with a Mr. Petříček.

When I was an awaiting-trial prisoner, I prayed every night, as I had done all my life, and at Leopoldov in 1952, when I was in the solitaries and forced to do fifty up-and-downs an hour, my faith strengthened. I felt it was the end of my life, and I would have to account for my life because I was going to die there, and there was no way out. I can say that I have always trusted in God. But since that time I have been a deeply believing person, a deeply believing Christian. But the faith that grew in me can never be appreciated by someone who has never been imprisoned. There is an old proverb: "A man who has not been at sea cannot pray." I would change it in this way: "A man who has never been in prison cannot pray"—because you never pray in civilian life the way you pray in prison. The eight years in prison brought me to the deepest faith in God. If I hadn't gone through those eight years, I might not be such a convinced Christian today. So I thank God that it was given to me, and that I was not alone.

There were many more like me—and many people who were baptized illegally in prison by fellow-prisoners who were bishops and members of the clergy. You could say that these baptisms were the high point of many peoples' lives. Just yesterday, in the afternoon, I met an old friend of mine who was also arrested in 1948, and who was also involved in our escape attempt in March 1949. He is a deep believer, Christian, Catholic. And he said to me, many times, "I remember those years spent in the prison with pleasure, with pleasure. Because, you see, if I had not been there, I would not be a Christian today." He told me that he regularly goes to church. He reads books about Christianity, about Christian philosophy, and so on—and he said he would continue to do so for the rest of his life.

When I look back on the physical stress I suffered, I wonder how it is possible that I survived, and how it has been possible for me to reach this age—I am now in my seventies. I think that if these things happened to me today—all the hunger and maltreatment—I couldn't bear it as I was able to when I was twenty-five or twenty-seven years old. Mentally, I believe I think in much the same way as I did then, though I have matured in some ways. My thoughts and beliefs are far more complex now. But my time in prison altered my character and perhaps even my way of life. For instance, because my wife works, I do my own cooking. And sometimes, believe it or not, I even make food that is similar to the prison food we had—except, of course, in larger quantities!

I live a quiet life today, and I have little contact with society. I didn't try to get back into society, because when I was released, most of my friends were still in prison, and the rest had gone abroad—they had fled the country. And, you know, I have troubles with my co-prisoners now. When we meet, I recognize their faces because I used to see them in prison almost every day. But I no longer remember all their names. They still call me Jura because that is what I was called in prison. But I don't remember many of them—it is as if I lived, how shall I say, among their faces in prison. I know they were prisoners, but often I don't even remember the prison where I met them.

Today, all of us are civilians—we have lost our *mukl* mentality. We no longer see ourselves as destined for liquidation. Some of us have joined political parties, some have grandchildren, some are retired, and some save money to support their grandchildren. Some are well off—but these are just a handful. But many of us still don't know what is proper behaviour in civilian society. Recently, for instance, there was a luncheon reception for about 500 ex-prisoners in the Spanish Hall in the Castle, and it was interesting to see how people dressed. Some just wore sweaters, and one man wore full evening dress at noon, at half-past twelve. He was a lawyer who wanted to show off, so he came in a tuxedo—at noon! But, as I said, I do not seek society. My life is not like that of other people, other civilians. I don't need society, I don't go to pubs, or to restaurants. I don't drink any alcohol. I live simply. I am not ambitious. I read the Bible. The main task of a human life is, I believe, to live in accordance with God's commandments.

But perhaps, in my own way, I did gradually start to live a more normal life among civilians. I got a job, I met a woman and I got married, and today I have two sons. I can now say that I am a happy man on a personal, private level. But politically, I do not feel happy. I feel much as I did after being released, when I lost all hope that political change would come to Czechoslovakia. It was as if the people had a silent treaty with the government. The government paid them a sum of money, not very much, and they did their work—which was also not very much. But it was a system of peaceful co-existence. Even those who were released were sucked into the system. Because, of course, when they got back to civilian life many of the young ex-prisoners got married and had children. And they began to have difficulties earning money and feeding their families. Many, many of the 400 I have mentioned who began to cooperate with the regime, with the Communists, did so because they had no choice—whether willingly or unwillingly, they simply had to.

And so, it was no surprise in 1968 when Dubček's movement began. Because many, many communists—people who were hot communists in my time, in 1945, '46, and '47—many of them realized after twenty years that the communist idea was not the best one, and they wanted to alter it. Not throw it out, but alter it. These guys were called "The men of '68." They also eventually suffered persecution, but it was nothing like what we had endured. Because, of course, we had wanted to defeat communism altogether, while these men simply wanted to alter it. They wanted to give communism or socialism what they called "a human face." We completely rejected this idea, and told them, "There isn't any socialism with a human face. There is only one democracy—and this is absolute."

After the upheavals of this time, the Prague Spring and its aftermath, another wave of repression followed, and, as before, I despaired of change. This was perhaps until 1986. I began then to notice interesting developments on the screen of world politics—I saw hitches in the system, hints that things were beginning to shift. And the changes that slowly appeared in the political arena could not be attributed to the work of dissidents, with their political leaflets and those kinds of things. Tyranny can never be changed by such things. Leaflets can never change tyranny. It has to be something stronger, something that compels change. In 1947 and 1948 certain diplomats and political people had laughed at me when I spoke about a Third World War. They said: "No, there won't be any Third War. They will come and put their proposals on the table, and then they will go." But I didn't believe them.

Then, in 1985 and 1986, I began to believe that democracy was possible after all. Democracy was undoubtedly advancing, and in 1988 when I saw the exodus of East Germans—well, by then it was all quite obvious, was it not? And there was no doubt whatsoever about what was going to happen after the first demonstration in Old Town Square in Prague on the 10th of December 1987—Human Rights Day. There were definite changes in the air, and each time we organized a demonstration there were more and more people on the square. Communism seemed to be crumbling, and though the authorities reacted in the only way they knew, we didn't care at all how much they beat us, especially on the 21st of August—Jan Palach day. And on the 28th of October Wenceslaw Square was full, full of people—a crowd of about 100,000. And you know what? The dissidents were upset, yes, upset—because they wanted to know who had organized the crowd! They asked, "Who wants to rob us of our leading role as dissidents?"

Democracy Today?

All those years ago, we joined the resistance because we wanted people to elect proper representatives who would improve the lives of the people, who would serve the people. When we spoke about politics in prison, people used to say, "We are fighting for democracy and Masaryk and a Republic." And I would say, "No, you are wrong. If we ever get out of prison, at least for two years we will need to be authoritarian, even dictatorial, and clean the Communists out of public life. Only then can we pass the power on to the people, and say to them, 'Now you can elect the representatives you want.'" If we had done this, suspended democracy for a short period, things may have been different today.

Yes, certainly, today we can travel, we can speak out, we can publish what we like. We have almost absolute freedom. But what is the value of this? For, you see, I believe that real democracy should be something more: it should embrace principles. I don't believe that people who are in politics here today have any political principles. They just want to hold on to their positions for the sake of money. If I had the power, I would send most of them to work with a pick and shovel because they are not suitable for anything else!

My idea of democracy is closely connected with the Christian idea of the progress of the world. At the end of the Bible, there is a clear description of how the world will end. And now, really, the general trend is one of deterioration—everything is getting worse and worse. When I was a little boy, when a couple got divorced, they were socially ostracized. Nobody would invite them anywhere. Today this is no longer so—we see decadence all around us. Look at homosexuality. People of the same sex being wed and adopting children. Well, that is awful, awful!

And apart from moral decay there is pollution—look at our world. Who will stop factories from pouring poison into our rivers and seas? No government will do this. The world, as I said, is reaching its end, as predicted in the Bible. But what has this to do with democracy? Well, the world is deteriorating not only morally and ecologically, but also politically. Politicians are concerned only with money and power, and not with improving social conditions.

As for me, I have given everything up. I am not interested in politics any more, though I still hate the communists. I am sorry, I hate them still. I know this is not very Christian, but I hate them. I despise them and I don't like them. Especially now when I see that nobody is going to stop the communists. At international meetings, Russia is again behaving in the way Brezhnev did all those years ago. The West is dealing with very dangerous people. Nothing has really changed much—the same kinds of people are still in power.

I am old now. I don't know how long I'll still be here, or what will happen after I pass away. Indeed, I no longer care. But it is far from over, for me. I have recently—now, now in my old age—been haunted by dreams that they are after me—either that they are after me, or that they have arrested me, and that I have a court hearing. I remember waking up one night some weeks ago, with images of myself sitting in a chair with my hands tied behind my back. And they were beating me. And, do you know, when I woke up I actually felt pain where they had beaten me. Ah! I still feel the pain.

8

Lola Škodová: The Idealist

The End of a Dream

I don't like to think back on these things, they happened a long time ago—and look at what my life is, today. I am old, and what has been gained? It was all very different in 1939, when I had hopes and dreams—even as the clouds were gathering in Europe, and the German army had already crossed the borders of my country. My aim then was to study medicine, but I had my first setback when I was a nineteen-year-old girl.

Hitler's occupying army closed our universities on November 17, 1939. I had to return from Prague to East Bohemia and start studying something else instead. This was to be the pattern of my life, being at the mercy of forces stronger than I was, having to do what I was told, with no regard to my own needs. You could say that my life was stolen from me—and it all began then, though I had no idea, at the time, of what I was up against.

I attended evening school and learnt typewriting and Czech shorthand. After about a year, I applied for a position, which I got. I was asked to learn German shorthand because my immediate boss was half-German—his father was Czech. He spoke perfect German, so it was better for him to dictate letters in German than to have them translated. I started to learn German shorthand, and it all worked out very well for both of us. Then, after the War ended, I became secretary to the managing director, who moved to Prague, and took me with him. So, in 1946 I came back to Prague again; my financial position was good, and I was happy.

I joined the Social Democratic Party in 1947, though you could say I did not have much political awareness then. I wasn't an activist. At school, of course, we had been educated against communism. And Tomáš Masaryk, our first president, whom we all respected very much, was also against it. So was his son, Jan. He knew a lot about communism—he knew what it was like in Russia.

My family were ordinary people. My father was a chief of police, and my mother was not employed. Instead, she worked with young children, teaching them physical exercises according to the beliefs of the Sokol Movement which was founded in 1862 by Czech patriots to promote good health; you know—

Lola Škodová as a young woman

the Roman idea of *Mens sana in corpore sano*. There has always been a movement to promote Czech consciousness—just as there was when we were under
Austrian rule. But after the coup d'état in this country in 1948, the Sokol
Movement was abolished. The Czechs have so often been under the rule of
someone else—this seems to be our fate, if you look at our history.

The Nightmare Begins

Though our lives were slowly beginning to return to normal after liberation
in 1945, there was a growing uneasiness about the activities of the Communists
and the influence of the Soviet Union. I remember once, in May 1945, when a
Russian woman in uniform visited the firm I worked at. She was carrying two
revolvers. She barged into the office and wanted to know all about the director,
what his name was, etc. He had to go with her, and was placed under arrest for
two weeks. Just before this happened, there had been complaints about the
merging of business enterprises which had been decided by the Germans during their occupation. Our director had been involved in one such merger, and
when he returned, people were distressed at what had happened.

We were very aware of the presence of the Russians, and of our country now
being part of a larger territory—a Russian territory. We felt very deeply that the
Russians were nothing at all like the Americans, who had liberated the western
part of our country. So, our fear began to grow, as we saw the Communists come
into power and gradually penetrate all corners of society and of the workplace.

I have never been an activist, neither at that time nor today. But my resistance against the communists was triggered by the events of 1948, and all that
followed. The Communists had won the election, and after this they tried to
seize all the best positions, all the best jobs—and they set out to influence our
people to join them and agree to all their plans. To make things worse, our
leaders were weak, and the general mood among the people I lived with, among
my friends, was one of embarrassment. President Beneš seemed to accept what

he saw as the destiny of the government. He had accepted the resignation of a number of ministers—so allowing the Communists to take over everything. And, of course, we were disturbed at the circumstances of the death of Jan Masaryk. Everyone felt these events as a defeat—and they were right to feel this.

How was it possible for us to protest against the coup d'état when the head of state, the President, did nothing? What could we do? And when we did try to protest later on, it was, I now realize, in vain. Looking back, I don't think that the resistance started immediately after the *coup d'état*. But it is possible that the idea may have struck people by then—for there was a general feeling of shame and anger at what was happening around us.

The streets were full of workers with rifles, guns at the ready—poised to step in if the *coup d'état* was not successful. It was very depressing. Extremely disturbing. So, people probably said to themselves, "We must do something against this because it looks as if we might be under pressure for decades." But at first no one did anything. Even though we were very, very distressed, very unhappy. We hoped that the West would step in and help us in some way—but I am sorry to say, they never helped us at all.

But there was growing resistance. People were doing all kinds of things. I got to hear about one such act in jail: a group of medical students had planned to blow up the offices of the secretary of the Communist Party Committee. Of course, though, someone must have told the Communists of the plan, because they found the wires that had been laid—and the student responsible was himself blown up. They had attached the explosives to his belly. I heard about this later from a fellow prisoner who was a nurse in the hospital. She said that the student had been very badly injured. He was desperate and asked her for a razor so that he could put an end to his horrible suffering. Because she could see that he had been fatally injured, she gave him a razor—and he killed himself. For this, she got five years. She sat in jail a full five years for what she had done. There were many people like her who landed up in jail—hundreds and hundreds of them, whose various acts of resistance made no difference to the way things were. People saw this, and were frightened into a state of passivity: they stopped doing anything.

I had in fact heard about the events around the 1948 coup while in bed—I was recovering from a knee operation. I could not walk, and people from the firm I worked at came to visit me, and they told me all about what was happening when I asked them for news. And so I heard about the banning of the Social Democratic Party. I heard about the Communists coming in, and Comrade Meier either greeting them, or asking them to leave—I don't know what exactly it was—but in any event, he was standing on the steps of a building, and they knocked him down. He fell down the steps, and his face was covered with blood. I heard all this from my friends—colleagues I worked with. People in general were angry at what had happened. And there seemed, at the time, to be a feeling, a sense, that nothing could be changed.

Surveillance

All this began to affect me, though—what could we do to stop it, I thought. And so, I became involved in a secret group. My main task was to type whatever was needed by the group. It mainly concerned information about the location of transformers in various industrial plants—information that could have been regarded as sensitive. Many of us disagreed with the activities of the Communists. We tried to do something to inform the West, because we still believed that they would help us. But in the end, of course, they didn't, and we were imprisoned.

I was aware that what I was doing was dangerous, that if the documents got into the wrong hands I might be in trouble. The work I was doing was forbidden—I knew this. But, like anyone else, I believed that I would not be found out. At the same time, though, I would worry, "Do they know anything? If I'm found out and punished will they give me longer than two years?" I consoled myself, thinking, "I'll be able to endure two years. I can go through with it." This was how I felt, and, well, this was my work.

Strangely, though, I was not afraid. I think that anyone who does the kind of thing I was doing always believes that nothing will happen to them. So, I wasn't afraid. Although, when I heard that some unknown person—a person who was head of activities against communism in Central Europe—when I heard that he was informing on our activities, then I began to feel afraid. I was afraid to think that this person—a provocateur—knew about our activities. And when, later, the head of our movement was imprisoned—then I was really afraid.

Of course, there were spies everywhere. Even so, I trusted my colleagues. They were not informants. But once, I remember, someone came to the house of the family where the documents were. He was a very suspect character—I didn't know him, and I didn't believe what he said. Soon after this visit, the head of our group went into hiding one night, and he was arrested the next day. I think it was the work of this person, that is my opinion. They had already imprisoned him and he must have talked about me and others. And so they must have known everything. They certainly knew that I was working against them.

But even though I was afraid, I could do nothing to save myself—it was impossible to leave the country. We were under surveillance—their eyes followed us all the time, wherever we went, whatever we did. They knew all about us, in any case, so it was impossible to think of fleeing. We simply had to wait to see what would happen.

I was afraid, even though my work was not that important. I was not involved in drawing up programmes or plans for the group. All I did was type whatever they wanted, that was all. I never took part in secret meetings—in fact I don't think they held any. And if they did, I never heard about them. I did not get involved in mass action of any sort. But still, they found me, and that was the end of my life as I knew it then.

Pankrác Prison

The authorities visited my landlord. They asked about me. You see, there were many people who were willing to be informers. They were all around us, in every house, and my landlord was one of the *Decitave*—or "one in ten" people who helped the secret police. Do you know, that even after my release he continued to give them information about me—the very same person! Anyway, the police had found out about me, and I was arrested.

Prior to my trial I was not harassed and no one tried to persuade me to change my mind about my political activities. The only thing they did was ask me to tell the truth: if I was willing to work against Communism, if I was involved in activities against them—but, in fact, they already knew everything, because some of our group had already been arrested and imprisoned the previous year. Also, they knew that everyone in the business I worked for was against them— this was, in any case, a well-known fact.

After my arrest, I spent four months in detention in Pankrác Prison. But this was nothing in comparison with the plight of married women who were detained for two years—and then exonerated from all blame at the trial. They would then go home—innocent women whose children had been without a mother for two years, all for nothing.

I never received written notice about my sentence, so I never knew what section of the law it was that they used against me. I think, though, that it might have been the Act for the Protection of the Public—law number 231 which was reintroduced after the 1968 Russian invasion. In any case, though, this law was originally drawn up for other offences—for armed rebellions and such like— not for the kind of subversive activity I was involved in. They misused this law.

Before the trial, we were allowed no contact at all with our families. We were not even allowed letters. And I want to emphasize that my mother had no idea at all why I did not return from my holiday in the mountains where I had gone skiing in March 1951. Until one day some people from the State Security arrived at her door and said that I was dead. That I had had a ski accident. They said this—and then they started to search our flat. They went into everything, my mother said, all our personal things, my wardrobe, even the library.

At first she was shocked at the news they had given of me, but when she saw how determined they were in their search to find incriminating evidence against me, she thought they might be lying, and that I had fled the country instead. This kind of thing often happened at the time. It was, in fact, only a month later that she received information that I was in jail. But my mother never blamed me for what I had done, for how it affected her life. When I came back home after more than six years, she never once blamed me. Not one word of blame.

All the while, I was experiencing a life that would have appalled my mother. Her only child, I was living in a cell that was cold all the time—even in the summer. We were not given enough to eat, and we were treated like dogs: our bowls were put on the floor in the corridor outside the cell. They tried to humiliate us, forcing us to take our food from the floor—but this had the opposite effect, and it simply made us defiant . We were given a jug of water which was removed from the cell at 6 PM—and if we got thirsty after this, no one cared. There were no taps, no bathroom facilities. If we needed water, we had to take it from the WC, I am sorry to say—though this was not for drinking, of course. I slept on a mattress laid on the floor. Next to an open WC. We had to lie with our faces towards the door so that the warders could see who we were. If they could not, they barged into the cell and woke us.

After interrogating us almost all night—until about 4 AM when we got back to our cells—we had to get up again at 6 o'clock. It was impossible to sleep during the day. And the following night, you would be interrogated again. After a few nights of this, you didn't mind lying quietly in your cell with your head near the WC. I remember one night, a woman was put into our cell who was not allowed to sit or to lie down. She had to stand all the time. She couldn't walk around because the cell was too small—the two mattresses took up all the space, so she had to stand all night. And she must have been instructed not to talk to us. She looked horrible, terrible. She was completely exhausted—I remember thinking that this could not have been the first night that she had been treated in this way.

During this time, until the day before my trial, I was put into solitary confinement for six weeks. You see, while walking to the courtroom one day, I noticed a girl from our group in the window of the hospital. I knew that she was very ill, that she had a tumour, and I wanted to comfort her—tell her that everything would be all right. And so I shouted to her, not very loudly, I said, "Don't be so sad—we'll soon be going home!" That was all. Later on, after the trial, I heard that a warder in the hospital room had noticed that I was wearing a ski outfit, and they then searched the cells, going from one cell to the next, checking to see who was wearing a ski-outfit. Because I had no idea why they were asking, I thought nothing of it, and said, "It was me," and then they called me out and told me that I would be punished for plotting a *coup d'état* against them!

I was given half rations—for breakfast, a small piece of bread; one unpeeled potato boiled in a very strange sauce for lunch; and dinner was cold—a small piece of *blatinger*. The black coffee we had was not coffee at all. We were terribly hungry. On Saturdays and Sundays we got our breakfast and dinner together. On the first Saturday of my stay I was so hungry that I ate everything in the morning—there was nothing left for dinner, which was bad. But I worked out a way of coping with the hunger. I could hear the jail clock strike every hour, and when it did, I took a tiny morsel so that my stomach would have at least something in it for most of the day. And it worked—it lessened the hunger pangs.

But there was another punishment that they gave me. Every second day my bed, mattress and blanket had to be taken out into the corridor, and I had to lie on the floor without any bedding at all. All this would have been worse if the so-called black holes—the cells used for solitary confinement—had not been full. I would then have been in complete darkness day and night.

Other prisoners suffered worse things, though. People who worked in the resistance with the church were particularly badly treated—like the young lady who had had contact with a priest from Moravia. I heard about her being called out by the authorities in winter. She was put in a basement where she had to stand for hours without clothes—naked. She had no shoes and had to stand on cement. Every now and then they released steam into the cell, and she thought that she would asphyxiate. It was so hot, and there was no air to breathe. And then it would get cold again—and this went on for a fortnight. She was menstruating, and she did not have tampons. She could not wash herself. She would hear voices behind the door, "Is she dead yet?," and the reply, "No, not yet." She never recovered from this ordeal. She was eventually released after six years, but about two months before she got married she had to have all her female organs removed. They were rotten. She would never be able to have children.

After months, my trial eventually came up. It was the June 22, 1951. On the day, I had nothing in my stomach, even though I was supposed to be given full rations after my solitary confinement. I did not receive written notice of the criminal charges against me, but I knew what they had against me—you see, they had previously stated my "crimes." In the first place, I was accused of typing a message that was to be smuggled abroad. Secondly, this was espionage—this typing of information. And finally, I had given a secret message: I had told the person who was to carry the message abroad that the leader of our group was no longer at home—he was staying somewhere else that night—and he should meet the group leader at a certain time.

The trial lasted almost the whole day. I think it started at 9 o'clock and we only left the court at 5 o'clock in the afternoon. During the two-hour lunch break, we did not receive any food. The courtroom was very far from our cells. We had to go through a basement, and along long corridors, and the warder could not be bothered taking us back to the cells to eat. So they just left us there without food, and we spent the whole day without a break.

I could not afford to pay for my defence, and I refused the services of an attorney. But I was told I had to have one—an ex officio attorney at no charge. He came to the trial but did not say one single word. He must have been instructed to remain silent. I did not say much in my defence because I knew that I had acted against them and that they knew everything. So how could I defend myself—particularly since I was in such a bad state because of the punishment I had suffered in solitary confinement. So, I simply did not defend myself. Also, we had been harassed for weeks, interrogated without being given anything to eat. I was questioned for days and nights without anything in my stomach.

I felt no guilt—in the moral sense—though I was aware that I had acted against them and that they would definitely not forgive me. Otherwise I did not feel ashamed about what I had done because I knew that this communist idea was bad. It was wrong, and it should be defeated. I knew that I would have to take responsibility—our plans had not worked out and information was leaked.

But I could not believe it when I was given my sentence. Twelve years—how could this be justified? Of course, I expected to be punished—but twelve years! I was stunned—this seemed so unjust and exaggerated when one looked at my three little deeds. I had expected two years—that was all I expected. The verdict said: twelve years imprisonment, confiscation of the whole property, forfeiture of civil rights and a fine of 10,000 crowns, though the fine was later withdrawn. I did not know what to think or feel. And I could do nothing, say nothing, to change things—to bring back the life I had now lost. Obviously, my emotions during the trial were in a turbulent state, I was deeply afraid and upset.

All justice had ended years before this, in 1948. After that nothing was fair. Everything was done for the Communist Party and none of these trials were fair. In some trials people were told to memorize answers. We weren't seen as important enough, but after 1951, some important trials were staged, with pre-prepared questions and answers.

As far as I know, nothing was published in the papers about our trial. I asked about this when I returned home, and all I heard was that some newspapers in Italy had published something. That was all. At that time, our newspapers were in fact going with the tide. They were against anyone who was against the Communists—they were all, in fact, pro-Communist. This was well known to everybody. No journalist would have been brave enough to write against Communism—and even if he had, the articles would not have been published. During the time of our trial we were, of course, not allowed to read newspapers—in fact, I did not read newspapers for the whole six years I was in jail.

We received no support before, during, or after our trial—it was such a bad time that people were afraid. They were afraid of everything. There was not a single family that did not have someone in jail. So, people did not demonstrate. They were afraid to talk, let alone do anything in support of people standing trial. It was impossible. It was such a bad time. Things were never worse than in the 1950s.

After waiting in Pankrác for some days, we were transported to the District Prison at Charles Square, which was for people who had not been sentenced by state tribunals. Together with eight other women, I was put into a very small cell. Two women had to share one mattress, on the floor. Here, for some days, we waited to be transported to Kladno, a town in central Bohemia, thirty kilometres west of Prague.

Kladno Prison

My two-year stay at Kladno began without fuss. We were put into wooden barracks which had originally been built for miners—they looked like Nazi concentration camps. The admission procedure was brief, and we were given

Kladno Prison in Kladno

what we needed: some blankets, better shoes than those that had been issued to us at Charles Square, some bowls—that was all. I stayed here for two years.

Kladno was not a political prison. There were other convicts as well: prostitutes, thieves, murderers. Only about one third of us—140 women—were political prisoners. We had no idea of who was who, so it was difficult to form friendships. For the first time, we had to be careful about who we spoke with in prison. We were, as a result, cordial towards other inmates—though we did maintain a reserve.

I found the prostitutes very nice and kind from the beginning. They were very frank towards us, and always ready to do something for us—to give us advice, or to help with something. The other prisoners weren't quite as open-minded. I remember when, at the court of appeal, I met someone who said to me, "Where are you going?" I answered, "To Prague." And she—she was a prostitute—said, "Have you got cigarettes for the girls there?" and I explained that I did not, since I was not permitted to open an account after only two months. She then said, "Well, I'll give you some; give the cigarettes to the girls in prison." She brought me twenty cigarettes, which she asked me to give to whoever I liked as a gift from her. She was very open-minded, very frank, and I really can't say a word against her.

Life in Kladno was very tedious. The inmates were ordinary women, and life was generally quite peaceful among the prisoners. There were no gangs, and I never came across anyone with high political status. Twelve women lived in a small cell. The barracks were full of bugs—it was horrible. There were holes in the wood and nothing could be done about the bugs—they couldn't gas them. The bugs had lived there forever, and ever, and ever. I could not bear it. When I woke up at night I tried to move my bed into the middle of the cell to escape from the bugs, and all the others woke up and were angry with me for waking them. So, this was very, very unpleasant—it was horrible.

After several months of doing nothing at all, and being given insufficient food and poor accommodation, we found it very difficult when we had to start work in the steel mills. My job was to cut 13 cm-long points on the ends of iron rods. These rods were both round and hexagonal in shape. They were very heavy, they were 4 m to 5 m long and 5.5 mm thick.

After the crane laid large piles of rods on the work desk, I had to roll out the round rods and pull out the hexagonal ones, which were very difficult to work with because they were always twisted after being burnt in the furnaces. The rod had to be dragged to the machine for about two metres and fastened there before being cut. The electric cutting machine did not work and I had to drive the machine with my own hands. Then the rods had to be dragged back to the desk and thrown down a big chute. We had to use all our strength because the rods were so heavy.

After this, I had to pull very large, very heavy chains from a heap for the crane to take away. Dragging these was very strenuous—it was in fact work that should have been done by the crane. But waiting for the crane would have cost me many minutes, and we had a quota, and if this was not met, we would be denied visits and letters—so we had to try to work as quickly as we could.

The environment we worked in was extremely uncomfortable. Behind my back there were four very large taps with boiling sulphuric acid which was used to treat the rods. The steam irritated our eyes and noses. It escaped through openings in the roof, and in winter it was extremely cold near the openings. The furnaces were turned off at the end of the year—at a time when we needed heat—and they were turned on in summer, and I worked in a part of the factory right next to red-hot metal. I was wet with sweat.

There were many injuries in the steel mill. Mostly, fingers were torn away. Every sixth day we were given a pair of linen gloves—though these only lasted for three days before they were in tatters. Threads hung from them and these could easily be caught by a rotating rod, which would catch not only the glove but also a finger—and sometimes, even, the whole hand, breaking bones and tearing sinews. Accidents happened when the rod-fastening came loose. This only happened to me twice in the two years I worked there, and both times I was lucky to be quick enough to take my hand out of the glove. This must have happened during day shift, because we were very tired at night, and I would never then have been so quick. During night shift we lost concentration. We would just find ourselves dropping off to sleep for short periods at any opportunity. I worked mechanically in a standing position, and when I closed my eyes—usually after two in the morning—I fell asleep, even if it was for two seconds at a time.

The reason we couldn't stay awake during night shifts was because of the conditions in the camp. Our sleeping conditions were dreadful. The cells were occupied by women who worked all three shifts. Those returning from work disturbed those who were supposed to be sleeping, and those on night shift had the worst time of all. They worked from 10 PM to 6 AM. These women then returned to the cells at 7 AM and ate a breakfast of black coffee that was not coffee at all, and a piece of bread. After this, they had to wash themselves. But there was no hot water in the camp—it had to be prepared by those who were on shift in the cells. It was warmed on the stove, and there was noise and movement all around.

The women returning from night shift had to go to bed at 8 AM and try to sleep while the camp was in full swing. Loudspeakers blared all day, telling people to report to the kitchen to peel potatoes, or to load coal, and sometimes people from Prague would tell us to come to the hall to see a film—always the same two films: "The proletarian" and "A man with a gun." And the gong would announce mealtimes—so there was not much quiet time for sleeping.

At other times, inspectors arrived from Prague to check if our underwear was folded correctly in our wardrobes, or if our beds were made properly, or if our straw mattresses were stuffed tightly enough, or if we had forbidden items with us such as pencils, etc. After these inspections the cells looked like the aftermath of an earthquake. The poor nightshifts! No wonder that most injuries in the factory happened at night.

Only one bucket of coal was allotted per day for each cell—even though Kladno was a coal-producing area. And only a third of this could be used to warm water after the shift. We could never heat the stove just to keep ourselves warm. No wood was given to us at all. We had to steal it from the factory, where wood was layered between the stored rods. We would hide single pieces of wood under our coats, next to our backs, and carry them back to camp. Sometimes—this didn't happen very often at all in summer—the guards at the factory exit took the wood from us.

The situation was far worse in winter, though, when there was no coal at all in the camp, and the warders checked us before we entered the camp and took all the wood and used it for themselves. The task of getting wood was given to the woman who was charged with duties for the week. She also had to wash the cell floor as well as the floor of the corridor and the WC. She had to do all the jobs that needed to be done, until the next week when someone else took over.

Since we were in a coal-producing area, one of our jobs was to unload coal and coke from wagons—two women per wagon for eight hours at a time. These were not ordinary working conditions, and we were not paid for the work we did. We were brigades and worked for nothing. We did this work once a month, on the only free day of the week. We had no day of rest. We worked from Saturday to Sunday, at temperatures of minus 15 degrees in winter. It was bad—really bad. Sometimes it was so cold that we could not even eat a piece of bread while we rested, because the bread would have frozen.

The clothing they gave us was completely inadequate. Our skirts and trousers were made of white linen—this was so that we could easily be seen if we tried to escape. The linen did not keep us warm in winter, and all we had was a jacket and trousers or a skirt made of a thick, coarse material that scratched our skins. We had to wear this skirt when we went to and from work, but we were not allowed to wear it while we worked. The material was so thick that it would have taken a week to dry—but, even though it was a very thick material, it did not keep us warm. Also, as you can imagine, our white linen clothing was filthy after six working days—and after working in the coal brigade it was so black that it looked as if it had been pulled through a chimney. We looked like ghosts, and none of us could even think of sleeping when we got back to the barracks—we had to go straight to the washroom.

We washed our clothes on washboards—all our bed linen, our clothing, etc. Everything had to be boiled because even the bed linen got dirty from our bodies – you see, not even bathing could remove all the coal dust from our skin and clothes. And the facilities were completely inadequate. For 130 of us, only three cauldrons were put at our disposal. We had to stand in queues, and after we had finished washing, we had to let the stuff dry and then iron it. If we were on night shift, we didn't sleep at all.

My mother visited me for about thirty minutes once every two months—as far as I can remember, this is what was permitted. During visits we sat opposite each other with other prisoners at a ping-pong table. A warder was posted for every so many prisoners, along one side. Visitors were not allowed to give us anything at all. We were not allowed parcels from our families. If one applied, it was possible to request a parcel containing soap or toiletries, but I never did this because I didn't want to take money from my mother. That I would never do!

I worried about my mother—I thought about her almost every evening after the lights were switched off, when all talking stopped, and we were left with our own thoughts, alone. Though I never feared that I might die in prison, I was terribly afraid that mother might die. That she might not live to see my return.

But I remained reasonably healthy. Since many doctors had been arrested and imprisoned, we had at least some medical care in Kladno. One doctor who was part of our group—though I had not met her before—did what she could for us, even though she had little at her disposal, and no medicines. The elderly and infirm did not work in the steel mills, or load ore or the old iron deposits left by the Germans, and the medical care these women got was usually adequate. When there were serious injuries, these were taken to Pankrác Hospital in Prague, or when iron particles got into our eyes, which happened frequently, we had to go to the town of Kladno where local doctors removed them.

The only other contact we had with outside people was through our work. Every machine had its civilian worker. Mine was a barber who had been trained to be a knife sharpener—but his knives were no good for cutting. He was not good at sharpening knives because he was only used to sharpening his razor. He wasn't only no good at work—he was very bad at communicating, too. He never had any news. He did not read newspapers. He did not listen to the radio—he simply didn't want to get into trouble.

There was so little opportunity to know what was going on outside. We were kept ignorant, and all we got was propaganda. The warders from Prague who showed us the films always wanted to discuss them with us—but we weren't interested. Once, one of them called a girl and asked her to comment on them, but she refused. She was, by the way, a religious teacher, with the name Mary Heaven (Maruška Nebeská), and she said she wouldn't say anything. The warder asked her why she would not speak, and she simply said, "Speech is silver, but silence is golden." All of us burst out laughing, and that was the end of the discussion.

There was no recreation at Kladno. But though we had no sports facilities, there was, at least, a library—quite a large library that we made good use of. We liked reading, and so we read quite a lot. I remember reading the works of Gogol, the Russian writer, as well as short stories by the twentieth-century poet, Vrchlický, and the beautiful poems of the German, Heine—we read Eisner's Czech translation of these: they were very, very good. This is all I remember—though I did in fact read a lot in prison.

They would not allow us to study at all—but we got round this problem quite easily. There were two girls who spoke French: one, a Slovak girl, had worked in the Czech embassy in France, and the other had studied French in Prague. It was therefore possible to speak and to learn French by talking to them—but no books in French or any other language were available to us. I remember, though, a book—*History of Art* by Professor Matějíček—that was sent to a friend of mine by her mother, whose request that her daughter be allowed to have it for six months was granted. The authorities didn't confiscate it, and so, I had it for about three months, and I used it to make carvings—I made a lion, and a hand, for example.

We were disciplined by being threatened with having our letters and visits taken away. We hated the idea of this—and also of losing the few privileges we had: being allowed to buy cigarettes, biscuits, toilet paper, tampons and tooth-paste. We were only allowed to spend forty crowns, no more—this was the sum allowed before the Money Reform Act in 1953. The amount would be less than this now.

There was no physical violence against us and we were not psychologically abused. Though it never happened to me at Kladno, some prisoners were put into solitary confinement—even for minor offences—for up to a week or so. But this wasn't so bad—it wasn't a tragedy to be in solitary for a week. It was nothing, really. There were no atrocities in Kladno, though I did hear of horrible atrocities in other places, atrocities which, for example, caused Ms. Pistová to commit suicide.

The warders at Kladno in 1948 and 1949 were different—sometimes very different—to those who came after them in later years. We called them *Bachaři*—a slang term for warder. They were people with heart. One of them once offered to take a prisoner's ring and earrings to her parents, and he wanted nothing for this service. The worst they did was shout at us.

The characters of the warders were rather low—though there were, of course, some exceptions. The camp commander in Kladno, called Jakeš, announced to us one day that his co-worker, Bančinec, and the convict, Hinda Bendová, who had been sentenced by a district court and not the state tribunal, were taking money for their own pockets. They did this by diverting money from our accounts to theirs—a total amount of 60,000 crowns. Both were subsequently transported to another prison, but the money was never returned to us. On three occasions I got permission to send my mother 300 crowns, but she never got the money. In my own case, an amount of 900 crowns disappeared—and this was only what I knew about. Imagine how much money had in fact been taken from prisoners in this way.

My fellow prisoners were, for the most part, good people, although there were also a few who had agreed to work for state security. Some of these were spies. Their method was to spend time in the cells of new prisoners, and to gradually gain the prisoners' trust—and then to betray them by disclosing any information that they thought might benefit the state. These spies would come and go, moving from one prison to the next—all in the hope of being released and going home earlier. But I don't know of a single prisoner who succeeded in getting her reward. Apart from these spies who moved around, there were also women who agreed to inform on their fellow prisoners.

Pardubice Prison

For some reason they decided to move some of us to Pardubice Prison in East Bohemia, a large prison with 800 women inmates. It was surrounded by towers, with armed guards. There were two buildings, each three storeys high—these were the old houses of correction—with a big garden and separate kitchen facilities. We lived in large communal cells that accommodated twenty-six of us. There was also a separate building for fifty men who were responsible for maintenance. The prison was originally built for murderers and women convicted by state tribunals. But in the year before my release, all kinds of convicts were being imprisoned there.

Our accommodation and conditions were much better than at Kladno. There were many work opportunities such as machine sewing, technical and mechanical services for Tesla Pardubice, a local factory, as well as vegetable gardening and bead stringing. The twenty of us who had come from Kladno were told to do sewing. This was the only group that worked in shifts: day, night, day, night. Here there were only two shifts, but this was worse because for half the year we lived in darkness. On the other hand, the work was not as hard as what we had previously been doing.

We earned money from the work we did—as we had in Kladno. But because our first job at Pardubice was making handkerchiefs for prisoners, we earned nothing, though after this we earned about six crowns a month. Later, I used to make eighty pairs of handkerchiefs in eight hours. They subtracted from our

Pardubice Prison in Pardubice

earnings what we owed for our food, and out of what remained we paid for necessities like toilet paper (one crown, thirty), tampons (two crowns), toothpaste (one crown, sixty), and a very poor quality—the worst—toilet soap (one crown). Altogether this came to five crowns, ninety. Since I only got six crowns from my first month's earnings, I did not have enough for a stamp for a letter to my mother—I had to borrow this.

But the next month was better, and the eight crowns I earned covered my expenses, including stamps. One year we sewed aprons for the prisons factory in Polaban, and because we were skilled, we earned fifty crowns a month. Out of this we could buy luxuries like a piece of butter, two little packets of soup, four eggs, and something else besides. At such times, life in prison was quite good—yes, it was very pleasant for us. But this was only the case after we had spent some time at Pardubice.

On the whole, the food was better than at Kladno, but there was never enough of it. We had coffee that was not coffee and a piece of bread for breakfast. Lunch and dinner were mostly potatoes with a teaspoon of horsemeat cubes and oil. It was hard to eat, to swallow this food, but we had to eat it because we had to work. We had to live. Generally, we got pasta or potatoes with sauerkraut, lentils or groats or some sort of gravy, but never with meat. When we did get meat—which was rarely, usually on a Sunday for lunch—it was a very small sausage, which we would usually share, and keep the other half for the next day. The only time we had a piece of meat was at Christmas time and at Easter. And once a week we got a small bit of raw egg. We never ate this at the time, but left it for our Sunday celebration, when we would beat it in with a piece of sugar to make a kind of dessert.

Unlike Kladno, where all we could buy was cigarettes and hard biscuits—we called them dog biscuits—at Pardubice we could buy cigarettes, biscuits and also half a litre of milk a week, so it was much better. The problem was that we only had one aluminium pot, which was used for food—for soup and pota-toes—so we couldn't use it to store the milk, which we had to drink at once. It was really a pity that we couldn't save the milk for later, for a time when we could enjoy it more.

The clothing we were given was the same as what we previously had. At first, we had a sweater or some warm underwear, but after two years we were forbid-den to wear this. We had the same rights regarding visits than at Kladno—one every two months, which lasted only thirty minutes. A warder was posted next to each convict during the visits, while both the convict and the visitor were forced to stand, with a net between them. We were not allowed to be given anything, or to be sent anything, or to be given any news of what was happen-ing outside.

But we worked out a way—a sort of code—to find out information from visitors. We were desperate for news, and whenever anyone came back from a visit, the first question we asked was, "When are we going home?" And when the person said, for example, "They said that they planned to decorate the flat in spring," we would read into this that we would be going home sometime before spring. So, it was something—but it was also nothing, of course. We relied on messages like this because we had no other way of communicating or finding information.

We were only allowed visits and letters from our families, though the letters were censored, and if they said something that the warder disliked, they were stopped altogether. Once my mother asked in a letter, "How are you?" and I said, "I am well, thank you, and how are you?" and she replied, "Oh, it is not good." And the warder got suspicious and asked for an explanation. All my letters had sections crossed out by the censors. Once, my mother wrote some-thing that they had crossed out, which I later read in the sewing room, the only place where a bulb was available. I held the letter against the light, where I read the words: "Everything comes to an end. Only God is timeless. All good people will be saved"—a Czech proverb which provides encouragement in difficult times.

But, while emotionally I often felt bad, physically I was in fair health. The medical attention we got was better than what we had previously had. The young doctor and the two nurses who treated us were, of course, all prisoners. They were given a good supply of medicines, and they were very kind to us, and so we were generally satisfied with our treatment.

Our relations with other prisoners were very cordial, but we never got to know the elite of the prison. University professors, and various kinds of doctors were separated from the others. There were twenty-three of them, and we called their cell "The Castle." The cell next to it—nicknamed "The Vatican"—was occupied by twenty-four convent abbesses and sisters. These people had their own special times for meals, walks and showers so that there would be no contact between us and them. This was a real pity, as these women could have educated us—but of course the influence they might have had on us was thought to be too dangerous! I never saw any of them.

The warders at Pardubice did not really abuse us. They had no reason, in any case, to be cruel towards us when we were working since they needed us to earn money for the prison. Some of them were quite decent—I remember, once, a particular warder even apologized for something he had done to a prisoner. I would say that the warders at Pardubice were on a higher level than those at Kladno. I remember the chief commander—we called him Sultan. He thought we gave him this nickname because the prison was like a harem of women—but no, this was not our reason. Sultan was the name of a dog in a novel by Bo•ena Nemcová, and we named him after the dog because it barked loudly all the time. You see, he was rather like the proverbial dog—the one who barks but doesn't bite.

Only one woman warder was notorious. We called her Elsa Koch—after an evil German concentration camp warder, a fictional character in a book, I think. Our Elsa was about twenty. One of the convicts had met her in a correctional institution in Kostomlaty, a place of safety where girls sentenced for prostitution were sent. Elsa was malicious and loved ordering us around, particularly to cut our hair. But when, eventually, we went on a hunger strike in protest, she was removed the next day—because everyone knew how vicious she was. They punished us by sending home our civilian clothing, mostly sweaters, and so we had nothing warm to wear in winter. Yes, they knew how to make us suffer: our cells and workplaces were not heated, and in the sewing workshop there was no glass in the windows.

Of course, there were other punishments as well—this would not have been a prison otherwise. But there was never anything very serious. I remember, once, when two young girls wanted to cook cabbage in a far corner of the cell. It was a large head of cabbage, so they brought in two large stones, to put the pot on. They made a fire with dead wood they had gathered from trees that hung over the prison wall—but almost immediately a warder came and stopped them. One of the girls—or possibly both, I can't remember—her name was Jitka, was put in solitary confinement for a week. All because she was cooking cabbage.

But there was one very effective form of psychological assault on us—it was calculated to emotionally isolate us from each other, to stop us from forming bonds with individuals. Every three months we had to move from one building to the other, and back again, and so on. This made it impossible for friends to live together for any length of time. Only one woman out of the twenty-six in each cell was allowed to remain in the same cell every time we were moved. And though we tried to work out what the pattern was behind their selection of this person, we never found out what it was—that is, if any plan did in fact ever exist. We wondered whether the length of a prisoner's sentence might be a reason for their choice, but it never became clear to us. What they did distressed us—it profoundly disturbed us.

This plan to discourage friendships affected me badly when we went on a brigade. This was unpaid work, and we would often be called out to work in the fields in winter, when it was very cold and the sugar beet had frozen in the ground. Our job was to kick the sugar beet out of the frozen ground with our shoes, and then cut it up. Though it was terrible work, and we were frozen, we all volunteered when they asked, "Who would like to go on a brigade?" We looked forward to getting out of the prison, where we could not see those horrible towers with the guns. It was a change, and very refreshing to get out into the fields.

Sometimes, when they saw how we suffered from the cold, the villagers we worked for gave us straw to put under our feet—though many did not care. We never spoke to the villagers—we had no contact with them, and it was only us and the warders in the fields. The work was hard, and we got so tired. We were exhausted by the time the bus had taken us the fifty kilometres from Lanškroun back to Pardubice. Often, we would then be told that we had to move to the other building where we had no bed, no straw mattress, nothing—we didn't have any of our things. And then, after moving our things, at four o' clock the next day we had to get up again for another day's work. It was terrible.

While we worked in these awful conditions, we of course formed groups of friends, people we talked to about how we felt, and who understood, and so lightened the burden—this is what friendship is, not so? But they would soon tear us from each other, and the only possible reason they had for doing this was malice. They always said, "It is forbidden to take anything with you apart from your personal belongings." And so we could not even take the comforts of friendship with us.

As a result of all this, no one cared very much—we could not afford to—about anyone else. If you were strong, and you could walk, you simply took everything you could with you when you moved to the other building. If you had a well-stuffed straw mattress, you didn't want to be deprived of it. Even beds—we took beds with us, and those that creaked the least were highly prized because these would be least likely to disturb our sleep when the person sharing the bed with you moved in the bed. You see, most of the beds creaked so badly that even the slightest movement would wake us up. These double beds couldn't be carried down the stairs by one person, so we dragged them down in pairs. You can imagine the sight of women carrying beds up the stairs and dragging them down—all at the same time. The noise was terrible, and the whole building seemed to tremble in the chaos as the beds were dragged from one building to the next, across a courtyard we called Wenceslaw Square.

The warders had no feeling for us—no sympathy at all. I remember an incident on Wenceslaw Square, when they were directing the movements of prisoners and their belongings. An official asked them how things were going, and a warder said, "Everything's going well." Just then, another warder arrived on the scene and said, "The ceiling on the first floor of the building has cracked along its entire length. The fire hydrant—the big, heavy marble one in the wash-room—has fallen from the first floor to the ground floor. The prisoners are okay, but it's left a huge hole in the floor." Other warders then arrived, and when they told them what had happened, the whole lot of them laughed—they found the whole thing a big joke. And all the while we stood in the square like pathetic fools, with our pathetic belongings, and our "home" a wreck.

Both floors had to be vacated, and for about six months we lived in a very large room that had previously been used to store textiles. We had no ward-robes. We had put everything under our beds. There was dust everywhere, and we were not given anything with which we could clean our rooms. We put our biscuits on top of a heater which never got hot. And we were so tired that when I saw a mouse gnawing at my biscuits I did not bother to chase it away. I just left it. I didn't care. We were like sardines in a tin: one on top of the other. The building we were in was derelict—it was not fit for humans to live in. It leaned over to one side, and they tried to prop it up with planks. But it was as bad as the leaning tower of Pisa, and so they had to bring whole pine trees in as extra reinforcement.

The warders harassed us in various ways—but there was never any sexual harassment in Pardubice. There were too many of us—800 women—not to be aware of it. And, where there were twenty-six women to a cell, it would have been impossible for women to form secret liaisons with warders. I never heard of a single case of this kind of thing happening there. In the smaller units, though, like at Obovice, where there were only nine people to a cell, we did hear of women who had contact with male warders. Some women traded sexual favors for privileges, to improve their conditions, to get passes. I remember a story about a girl from the state prison—a simple girl, she was not an intellectual—who fell pregnant and had to send her child away to be cared for by her mother.

I will never forget how depressing it was in Pardubice—especially after the first three years. Every year, the burden of it all got heavier and heavier. You saw four years go by, and then the fifth, the sixth, the seventh—and you thought, will it go on like this until the twelfth year comes? Such were my thoughts, especially at night, when we were left with our own thoughts after the lights were switched off. I lay awake, with the darkness above me and all around me, wondering, "What is it like for those with much longer sentences than mine?" But then the morning would come, and I would feel more cheerful.

The routine, the boredom, were unbearable. There was no sport, and no possibility of studying. We were not considered to be political prisoners, and so our status was the same as that of the other convicts. We had no privileges, no sports, no study, we were given no pencils, no newspapers, nothing to occupy the mind. Once, when they found notes I had made on Babylonia, they took them away and threatened me with the "hole"—a damp basement cell where I would be on half rations for at least a fortnight. Before my time, before the elite were separated from the rest of the prisoners, a Professor Růžena Vacková gave lectures on art. Of course, this was unofficial, and the lectures were not open, but limited to a small number of people who were interested. It was because of these lectures that the elite were eventually separated.

We felt very isolated, very deprived—we were experiencing prison life in all its boring drabness. We had no contact with the outside world. Nothing. Nothing could be said to us, and nothing could be sent to us. There was no contact with civilian workers. And, of course, there was no contact with the men who were imprisoned at Pardubice. We weren't allowed to talk to them at all—we lived in a separate part of the prison and knew nothing at all about their lives.

But there were also pleasant times. Once, we were invited to form a group for knitting, sewing and cooking, as well as for reading and artistic creation. The person who started this circle was Ola Keyes, a good artist. Her English surname originated with her husband's Scottish forefathers who had come to Moravia 300 years before, and stayed for good. I was very interested when she told us that the commander had asked her to make a puppet theatre for the local kindergarten and to enlist our help in making the puppets. It wasn't an easy job, but after many grey hairs we began to enjoy it.

The prison was our studio, and Ola asked us to make colorful characters, for example, a middle-aged queen, or a young girl, or a little boy, or a very old king. This wasn't easy—but we found it all very interesting. We had to make papier-mâché heads, which were light enough to be manipulated by the puppeteer, and we then cut, sewed and painted the material. We fitted these to wooden bodies with moveable legs and arms which had been made by the men, and the people made the clothes and shoes. Once the puppets had been made, Ola painted them. This work was really important to us, because it was the only time that we could forget that we were in prison—we were enjoying work that allowed us to be creative and transported us to worlds outside the walls with their gun towers.

While doing this work, we needed to discuss things, and we would move from one house to the other. We also met and talked when we were standing in queues for breakfast, for lunch, or for dinner. This usually took an hour or so, because it took a long time for 800 women to fetch their food. We also went from one house to the other for meals, even though this was not officially allowed, and we would talk about our puppet-making while we were eating.

When I think back on it, life at Pardubice was slightly better than at Kladno. In the first place, the work was better suited to us as women than the hard physical labor in the Kladno steel mills. And secondly, we didn't have to do our own washing—everything was washed for us. All we had to wash were handkerchiefs and small items. And, best of all, there was no danger of physical injuries. So, for me, it was better—I think that if I had stayed at Kladno for the whole six years I would have been in very poor health.

And while we were caught in the routine of life inside the prison walls, outside, the state was ensuring that we would remain ensnared long after our release. There was, for instance, the whole issue of prisoner's debt. In 1952 the state tribunal passed a verdict that state convicts would be obliged to pay for their trial defence. In my case it was 1,632 crowns—as I was later to learn when they informed me in Pardubice by letter. I had to agree to pay this by signing the letter. But, in the meantime, the prison accounting office would pay it on my account. For I was not in a position to arrange for payment personally. I was not able to draw money. I could not go to the post office to send it.

The Rehabilitation Act stated that the money for our defence would be returned to us when it was proved that it had been paid. Later, when I asked an official at the Ministry of Justice about this, I was told that a receipt was required as proof. I did not have this receipt in my possession, and I had to approach the Ministry of Justice with a letter the chief commander had given to me before my release.

But there were obstructions. When I went to claim the receipt from the Ministry of Justice, an official said that he had gone through all the papers in question and could find no receipt. He saw my disappointment, but just glared at me and said in a harsh voice, "The state is not a milk cow that pays for something for which there is no official proof." The court insisted that the receipt be shown. I then went to the chief of rehabilitation and, in my presence, she spent two hours going through the personal documents of seven people who had been at my trial, and eventually found the receipt for 1,100 crowns that was paid to cover the expenses of the defence at the main trial.

I did eventually get the money, though. And two months later an experienced jurist went to the Ministry again on my behalf and succeeded in finding the second receipt for the defence in the court of appeal. So it was obvious that no one from the Ministry of Justice had looked for the receipts at the time of my rehabilitation. It was easier for them to say that nothing had been paid, that no receipts existed, and that the state is "not a milk cow."

After my release I was forbidden to have contact with the family of fellow prisoners. I was forced to promise this—but this didn't stop me from visiting this mother and that mother, though I always asked them not to mention my visits in their letters to their daughters. They promised, but Mrs. Ječmenová wrote to her daughter, and I had problems as a result. She had promised, and yet she still wrote, "Mrs. Lola from East Bohemia was here and we talked a lot about you. She sent you her regards." And then, of course, the Censor wrote to this aunt, "Mrs. Lola is in fact Miss Škodová."

Release

I returned to what you call normal life, but really, for me things did not return to normal. My political involvement continued to affect my life very badly—in all ways. It affected my relationship with my friends, although—because I was not married—its negative effects were limited, you could say. My career prospects were dim; I could not study medicine because I had been imprisoned.

I went to a good friend to ask her if she knew of any job opportunities—it was very difficult finding anything. She said, "Well, tomorrow morning I'll be meeting my former boss, and I'll ask him. He might know of something or someone who can help you find a job." But when I arrived for an appointment the next afternoon, she said, "Can you imagine! I told him that you were back home again—and he cancelled our meeting. It looks like he's afraid to help you at all."

I was a pariah. I remember, another time, seeing someone I knew in the street. When he saw me, he quickly looked away and crossed over to the other side. I felt really bad about this, very embarrassed and angry. People were afraid to meet me, to talk to me—they were afraid of what people would say about them if they did. I gave up asking friends to help me find a job. You see, it was far too dangerous for them to talk to me at all, let alone to get me a position in their own workplace. It was in fact unthinkable. I soon realized how stupid it was for me to expect my friends to help me in this way.

Times had changed—and everyone was aware of the numbers of people that had been jailed. So people did everything they could to avoid suspicion. They simply avoided talking—not only with me, but with anyone who had been in prison. It goes without saying that they did not visit me in my flat. The only visitors I had were ex-prisoners, girls who had been with me at Pardubice. I could hardly complain about the way people behaved—I knew how afraid they were. And fear, we all know, is a very strong emotion.

I continued looking for a job, and went from firm to firm, but no one wanted to employ me. Eventually, though, I got a job for a month—no one else wanted it, you see. I had to type at night, and only got home at 4 am—it took me an hour to walk from Prague to my home. Then I washed myself and slept for an hour, and then had to get up again to go to the office. The material I was typing concerned a certain Act, and the number of political prisoners who had been imprisoned—it had to do with the Prague Spring of 1968.

All the while, the state tried to control all aspects of peoples' lives. And when I was released, they did not leave me alone. Once a year, sometimes twice a year, the state police would interview a particular person in the apartment block I lived in to ask about my behaviour and activities. And they would certainly have done the same thing in my place of employment. They wanted to know from informers who we communicated with, what we did in our leisure time, whether—and what—we were studying, and if we had any contact with prisoners.

With all this happening, I decided I should go abroad—even though I had got a better job typing invoices. Another problem was that I could not study in the evenings as I wanted to because as soon as they heard my name, my case for admission to a course was weakened. So, I was surprised when I applied to go to England that they said without any fuss, "Yes, you may go." Of course, I immediately applied for a passport, and I was given extended leave from my job.

I spent a year in England working as an *au pair*. Time passed quickly, and the sixties soon arrived. From 1962 things changed for me. I remember hearing a radio programme in about 1966 where a group of actors described the sixties as a period of evolution that offered better conditions for them. They could perform things that were previously forbidden. But for ordinary workers like me, and for ordinary factory workers, things had not really changed very much.

Why didn't I go into exile while I had the chance in England? Well, I did in fact want to leave, and I succeeded in bringing my mother over there. I also invited two of my friends, one from Brno and one from Prague, and they brought some of our things over to help us start a new life in England. And some of my other friends came over from Canada to see what they could do for us. With their help, I found a job in Canada—one of my friends was to be pensioned off, and I was to take her position.

My mother and I underwent medical examinations, and we were declared eligible to apply for emigration to Canada. But, as the time drew nearer, my mother became more and more unhappy. She cried all the time and wanted to go home. I could understand how she was feeling, since she couldn't speak a word of English. Also, she was seventy-seven years old, and at this age such colossal changes must have been very hard to deal with. So, I gave up my applications, and told her that we would be going home. I stayed in England for a further four or five months, until the end of 1968, and then I returned to Czechoslovakia.

In December 1968 when I returned from England, the Russian soldiers had been occupying our country for some months. The Prague Spring had come and gone. There was an air of oppressive suspicion throughout the country. The situation back home seemed to be worse than it was before. It was a time of political trials and tests, and all workers were forced to undergo political examinations—it was a really terrible ordeal.

Everyone from the firm I worked for had to undergo some form of questioning. We were all asked what we thought, what our opinions were, what we had done in 1948, what we thought about the arrival of the Russian soldiers, about Dubček—about everything. For those of us who weren't communists, this was a very difficult time.

Aftermath

I have no physical scars to show for my imprisonment, though I certainly still have emotional scars. Even now, several times a year, I dream of being imprisoned again, and, what is more, that my mother is with me—or, in another dream, she is alone in prison, without me. I wake up, terrified that my mother won't survive it all. These nightmares are horrible—and they still come, forty years later.

But other things I have forgotten. I find it hard to remember my prison number today. We had to introduce ourselves by our numbers—we were forbidden to say our names, it was just like the concentration camps in the Nazi era. They used numbers to address us, even though they had our names. I hated having to mark my underwear with a number: mine had four numerals, and

Lola Škodová in 2000

an extra four numerals—it was two centimetres long. It made us angry to have to do this—it was hard work. And then they would, for whatever reason, give us new numbers, and we would have to undo what we had done, and embroider it all again. There were many things that made me feel bad in prison—this was just one of them. They tried to take away our identity, but they never succeeded with me. I never felt that I was just a number. I always felt like a human being—and I still do.

Was it worth it all? No—on the contrary. My actions affected my mother very badly in her old age. She lost the flat that had been given to me in exchange for hers when I moved to Prague on January 31, 1951. Six weeks after this, on March 16, I was arrested, and the flat was confiscated because she had the same name as me: Škodová. She was moved to the worst category of flat—a one-room flat, sixteen square metres in size. The furniture that had previously fitted into a two-room flat had to be piled as high as the ceiling, into one small room. No, my mother deserved more respect from me. She should have grown old in far better conditions than those she died in at the age of eighty—and now that I am the same age, I can appreciate how much she must have suffered. I will never forgive myself for what I did to my mother.

And, of course, I have lost everything I had. No, I would never do it all again. Never, ever. Never, ever. Today, some Bolshevik lives in my flat, and I am forced to live in terrible conditions—in the same flat they moved my mother to. Though another room was added about ten years after my release, this is still the worst category of flat: it is without water, a bathroom, WC, gas, or a garage. It is on the third floor of a building that has no lift, and, just as my mother did, I have to carry coal up ninety steps. They say it would be cruel to claim my flat from the Bolshevik who now occupies it, but look at my life—is this not cruel? No, I would think about things more carefully today—and I know that I would never do the same thing again.

While we were in prison we were convinced that everything we had done was worth it, especially for the West. But, when, after years of imprisonment, we returned home, and especially after the Velvet Revolution in 1989—when we found out that nothing had been done to the authorities, or to the people in state security—we began to reconsider the value of our activities. These people were still the only people who had enough money to buy extra things. Their lives are still much better than ours. Nothing has happened to them.

Certainly, things are better, but we cannot talk of a victory—indeed, it is better not to even mention the word. We have still not been properly compensated. And nothing has been done to punish our oppressors. They have got away with everything—with the torture they inflicted. How can we forget what they did to farmers and priests in detention? Why have they not been punished for the atrocities? For stomping on prisoners' bellies to kill them before they came to trial? And what about the state security members who shot at escaping prisoners and brought the injured back to prison where they eliminated them?

Why is it that they have not been put on trial and witnesses called? Instead, they have been allowed to profit from their evil deeds. Some Bolsheviks went into business, and have fled the country with millions. Many others still occupy influential positions. And today, none of my fellow prisoners is part of the elite. Do you know, not one is included in the current group of leaders.

Let me say it again. After 1989—the Velvet Revolution—the circumstances of my life remained the same, and I experienced no substantial change. Of course, some things were better—I had lived to see the end of that regime. And as an ex-political prisoner I was given some compensation, though we were not happy with the proposal that this amount be paid over a period of ten years, because every year its value dropped. But, after the founding of the Confederation of Political Prisoners, we succeeded in getting the period decreased to five years. So, on November 1 this year, I will receive the last of my money. The total compensation was 190,000 crowns, though the Confederation succeeded in gaining for us free bus tickets—not only for local buses, but also for long distance travel. At my age, travel is difficult, but it is, I suppose, something at least—just last week, in fact, I travelled to Brno to see my friend, and it cost me nothing.

Today I am no longer interested in any form of resistance at all. And certainly, any claim as to the value of our resistance and imprisonment should not be exaggerated. But please—do not think that I have changed my mind or altered my political views. No, I have not—not at all. Prison did nothing to change my beliefs. I still believe that communism, like fascism, is a threat to mankind. And as far as political imprisonment goes, I don't think there is any room in contemporary politics for it. I still see my old prison friends at meetings of the Confederation. We meet once a month or so, though I only go every second or third month, which is enough for me. It is enough. You could say that I have in fact had more than enough of it all. And now, I am tired.

9

Jiří Stránský: The Rebel

Three Generations of Political Prisoners

I belong to a family with a long political background—for three generations my family has fought for democracy. You could say, in fact, that the history of three generations was written by acts of resistance and repression. Oppressive forces—whether Nazi or Communist—have blighted not only the life of my country, but also individual lives in my family: those of my grandfather, my father, my brother—and, of course, my own life as well.

I am the last in a long line of political prisoners—going back to my grandfather, who was prime minister in the time of the First Republic. He was a farmer, and was a leader of the Agrarian Republican Party, which was a party of farmers, but also of middle class townsfolk. It was the strongest party in Czechoslovakia at that time, and other parties—not only the Communist Party but the People's Party, the Christian Democrats, and the Social Democrats as well—regarded the Agrarian Party as the enemy.

My grandfather played an important formative role in my life. I had a very strong feeling for him—you see, I had always loved him very much. There was a close bond between us, and he chose me out of all the grandsons to take over the farming—though, of course, this was never to happen, as history took its bloody course and shaped my life so differently. My grandfather was very ill after returning from prison in 1946, and died in 1947 at the age of seventy-seven. As a boy, I had spent much time with him, and absorbed much of his wisdom, though I did not realize this at the time.

And then my father was thrown into a labor camp by the Communists—just as the Nazis had done to my grandfather when I was a child, at Auschwitz. Though I was only seventeen at the time of the 1948 putsch, I think I understood what was going on, mainly because of my family's political involvement. I had very strong feelings about it all, and I felt I had a role to play. I even joined in the university student demonstrations. I remember marching through the streets of Prague, trying to reach President Beneš, to persuade him that our fate was in his hands, that there was still time to rescue the situation, to save democracy. Because, you see, we all knew what real democracy was—we had had twenty years experience of it in the years of the First Republic.

Jiří Stránský in 1996

We also knew, of course, what totalitarianism was—we had lived through the War years and the Nazi occupation, the so-called Protectorat Böhmen und Mähren. I was fourteen when the War ended—I used to read all about it in the newspapers, because, you see, I read everything I could lay my hands on. But I had also seen things at first hand; I had witnessed the aftermath of the War. Because my father worked with the Czech National Council, as a sort of inspector for the Sudetenland region, I saw what happened with the crazy expulsion of the Germans. Though I was not actually part of any of this, I thought deeply about what was going on, because I didn't like what I saw. After all, we Czechs were supposed to be better than the Germans, and here we were, treating the Germans in the same cruel way as they had treated us. I was ashamed, and these things haunted me afterwards.

This was an important formative period, a very negative one. But there were many other positive things besides. I have already mentioned my grandfather, and there was also his circle of friends—who included Masaryk and many others. Also, because my father was a lawyer, he was in regular contact with Masaryk's American friend, Marcia Davenport, and I was fortunate to be around such people, to hear their conversation, to absorb their ideas.

A further major influence was my early contact with the outside world. The year after the War ended, I went to school in Switzerland. And in 1948 I got a scholarship to the United States because I spoke good English—though I had already travelled to Paris the year before to attend the World Boy Scout Jamboree in Paris, where I worked with the Americans, translating from French into English for them. And—let me add—I was also a member of the national ski racing team. But they cancelled the scholarship because of my family background.

My grandfather had predicted the 1948 putsch, so when it came it was no surprise. My family knew that the coalition would not succeed in managing the state and the society. My father even thought about emigrating—but we didn't because he was involved in politics and he wanted to stay in his own country. We knew from the beginning of the putsch that there was no way we could hope to try to bring about a new revolution against the regime or to try to change things by means of demonstrations. You see, first of all, the Ministry of the Interior and all its sections were in the hands of a Communist minister. And the army was under Communist control because General Svoboda, a Communist, was head of the army. He had fought in the Red Army, and he was fond of the Russians—obviously, he was afraid of any western democracy coming to our land. So, there was no way that we could hope to change things ourselves.

It was only those of us who were young, and who didn't know much, who had dreams about demonstrating and persuading Beneš to change what had happened. Little did we realize that this wasn't the eleventh hour—it was already five minutes past midnight. Our group didn't even manage to get close to Hradčany Castle—they stopped us at the Vltava River, and didn't let us cross the bridge. There were cordons of policemen, and when the students tried to get through, many were arrested. But I was lucky to get away, even though they beat me just as I managed to cross the bridge.

When I look back on it now, I have to admit that we never really believed we'd get through—we were young, you see, and part of our motive was the sheer fun of protesting, if you understand me. I remember another incident—we did such a strange thing. It was when the factories went on general strike on February 25. They stopped work at twelve o'clock, and the sirens gave the signal. At that very moment, we left school and began to clean the streets outside—just to show that we were working, you see. The punishment the school authorities gave me was pretty severe: two years later I was expelled, just before my graduation. This was the first time the Communists had interfered directly with me.

All this happened during what you might call the worst of times, the dark period two years after the putsch of 1948, when my brother and my father had already been thrown into prison. During the War we had lived in Prague, where my father was a lawyer, a solicitor. But because he was one of the leaders of the famous Czech Gymnastic Organization, Sokol, he was arrested soon after the Communist putsch of 1948. Altogether, they arrested 5,000 people associated with the organization—including ordinary members in the smallest villages.

Almost all these people died during their imprisonment. My father was released with the last sixty-five survivors, and as a boy of eleven or twelve, I would listen to their narratives, because they stuck together. Whenever they could, they would meet and talk about their ordeal. So, you could say that their experiences were absorbed into my blood.

Immediately after the war—it was a cruel time—the Communist Party accused my grandfather of collaboration with the Germans. You see, they wanted to get rid of him. Of course, none of what they said was true, he was absolutely innocent—and this became clear when they apologized for what they had done, when, after the trial, he was rehabilitated.

There were many military groups at the time. We knew that they were strong—but we also knew that we could do nothing to change this. We knew that they were very powerful—they had absolute power in their hands. This didn't stop us from expressing our opinions, though. And that was why we, as young people, accused our parents of being afraid, of being cowards. But now, after many, many years, I am able to understand these things much, much better, and from a different point of view.

But, at the time, even though I knew my father was on the list of "class enemies," even though he was soon arrested, I still thought that he had given up too easily, too quickly. Of course, we knew that they had no choice, that they had to give up—but still we thought that they should protest more, express their feelings, make it clear that things were happening against their will. We felt this—even though we knew that protest was futile.

I have since spoken about these things many times with people who have never gone through this kind of thing in their own countries, especially people from other continents, Americans, Australians, and so on. They just don't understand, because they think that a rebellion is something that involves people going out into the streets, not caring that they are unarmed, or that they are only armed with sticks or stones, you see. But we had already had experience with the Nazis, and we knew that a new totalitarian regime was on the way. And that there was no way of stopping it. All we students wanted to do at the time was show that we were against it.

It's true—but this is another matter—that there were, at the time, a lot of intellectuals that helped the Communists take power. And today, a lot of these same intellectuals try to explain their actions by saying that Czechoslovakia has always had a tradition of leftist intellectuals, and so on, and so on. I have nothing against this opinion. But in those three years of relative freedom we had—from 1945 to 1948—surely the intellectuals, especially the intellectuals, should have seen what was coming? They should already have seen this in 1946! Because by then the Communists in the Czech lands—though not in Slovakia—had already won the elections. All this means is that a lot of people—4 percent of the people—actually believed all the lies that were being forced into our ears and our minds. So, there is no excuse for them, you see.

But to return to my father's arrest and imprisonment: he was put into a labor camp, and from then on, my family was subjected to continual harassment by the Secret Police. I remember how they would knock at the door, and demand to see my mother. It was terrible for us—I had a younger brother, and I remember the expression on his face, his fear that mother would also be taken from us.

I was no more than a boy myself at the time, but to them this meant nothing. I remember three or four occasions when they even interrogated me. Of course, I was hardly a fit subject—but still, they persisted, asking me questions that I hardly understood, and when I answered I was aware that they were listening for some slip that I might make—anything that would give them a clue or tell them something they wanted to know about my father. I remember feeling afraid and confused, knowing that I might at any moment say something that would be very bad for my father. But the whole thing taught me a great deal about the mind and methods of our oppressors—it was an invaluable experience for the ordeal that I would soon personally face.

There were other experiences that robbed me of a carefree boyhood. I remember, for instance, the teachers at my school. They knew very well what my opinions were, and didn't try to persuade me otherwise. They never tried to argue against me. But they made life difficult for me at school. Many of them had joined the Communist Party, and they made the lives of boys like myself very hard—you could say that this was their method of persuasion. The pupils were in fact divided into two camps—those who were for the regime and those, like myself, who were against it. The communist supporters even had a slogan: "Anyone who isn't for us is against us." So, you see, for me it was all very clear, very easy. I was definitely not with them—so, I had to be against them. It was all very, very simple.

Our family were outcasts because of my grandfather's leadership of the Agrarian Party, which was banned. As a result, my family always kept aloof—our point of view was always a little different from those who were members of the three right-wing parties: the Social Democrats, the National Socialist Party and the Christian Democrats. But my family had a long view of politics—we had heard from Jan Masaryk about the rejection of the Marshall Plan, which was our last link, our last bond with the West. So we knew, we were already aware, and we thought a great deal about what was going on. We rejected the new regime, but still, you know, my father refused to leave the country.

Two years after my father was imprisoned, they arrested my brother as well—he was at the time a reporter for United Press, and the Communists accused him of being involved in an espionage group. They also accused Jiří Mucha (the novelist and son of the painter Alphonse Mucha) with him. I was seventeen, eighteen, nineteen years old at the time, and I remember the sense of deep fury I felt. And of course, before my brother was released and came home again, I was also arrested. My family had to go through the pain of yet another trial. The infuriating thing this time was that all the evidence was fabricated, but none of us could do anything about it all, and so I was sentenced to eight years in prison.

1953: Arrest

They came for me on January 16, 1953. I had done nothing to justify my arrest. Nothing. It would have been utterly senseless to get involved in anything political with my father and brother already in prison. My only "crime" was that I happened at the time to be working in an office where a couple of my colleagues were setting up an illegal group. When they tried to recruit me, I refused—you see, I wasn't a member of any political group. Opposition party members had by this time either fled the country, or were in prison. I had nothing in common with them—they were just people who worked in the same office. In any case, I walked a lone path because I knew that—given my family background—connecting up with anybody else would put that person in danger.

What happened to secure my arrest was that one of the guys who worked with me in this office had been arrested. He was eventually sentenced to death, and he told them what they wanted to hear. I don't know if I remember it any more—the circumstances were unbelievable, one could say. I was arrested not because I had done something, but to save a life. You see, this colleague had been involved in an illegal plan to get a whole trainload of people over the border to the West. And they did it—but I had refused to join them because both my father and my brother were already in prison at the time. Things were dangerous, and I had already had my own experiences. Nevertheless, they caught them, the whole group, and because my colleague was the organizer of the group, they sentenced him to death. He asked for mercy, and they promised him that they wouldn't hang him if he gave them more information. And he fabricated thirteen stories about thirteen co-workers, and the story he made up about me was the worst. They had been out to get me in any case, though, and when he made up the stories and I happened to be the subject of one of them, my fate was sealed. As you can imagine, they weren't at all interested in hearing my own story. They had succeeded in their goal of getting another member of the Stránský family, and they gladly went ahead with their accusations and sentenced me to eight years.

When they arrested me I was with the army—I was a non-combatant, in the PTP, and we worked in mines and buildings, amongst others with pilots from the Air Force who had served in Great Britain. Well, it was just after Christmas and New Year, so I have to say I was a little drunk after a celebration we had all had, and so, when they came for me, I didn't mind very much at all. But in a very short while they started to beat me, and I soon realized the mess I was in. I had no idea at all why they had arrested me. And they wanted me to sign a confession, admitting to what I had done, but I had no idea what they were talking about, and so I didn't. But because I did not tell them what they wanted to hear, this cost me a lot of beating—I was beaten a lot, I was beaten terribly. The first two months were terrible. It was so bad. I lost nine teeth, and often had to be carried into my cell. They were pleased with themselves at reducing me to this state, because I had been in perfect shape physically, what with being in the national ski team, and playing basketball, and doing gymnastics.

I remember a wise old man who was put into a cell with me. He told me: "You must admit whatever they say. You must sign whatever they give you, because if you don't , they will kill you. They don't care at all. To save your life, admit to whatever they want." So I did.

You get used to doing these things. It's very strange, you get used to hunger, you get used to everything after a while.

The friends I had before my arrest all thought the same as I did, we had the same opinions—and because I was educated, my opinion was absolutely clear. My family had always known what the communists were about, what they wanted, and what their real intentions were. After the Nazis were defeated we knew that we had to struggle to put things right in the country, but we weren't so desperate as to blindly believe the promises of the communists. To me, it was perfectly clear what they were doing. I don't for a moment believe those leftist intellectuals who today deny knowing what the communists were up to. Please! I was only seventeen years old at the time, and I saw what was going on. So, why didn't the intellectuals—people who were ten, fifteen years older than I was at the time. No, it's all nonsense, rubbish.

I was imprisoned for seven months before my trial, at Bartolomějská Street Prison, which had been a monastery. I was also taken to Pankrác, of course. The first time I had any contact with my family was at my trial eights months later. Our accommodation was dreadful—we didn't even have a bed to sleep on, just a straw mat, nothing else. And the food was terrible—just black coffee with a piece of bread in the morning. And lunch—well for lunch we had something that was barely recognisable—you had no idea what food you were eating. It was the same for so-called dinner.

The only time we were allowed to take a shower was when they decided we could. The first month I didn't shower at all. The first time I showered it was terribly uncomfortable. You see, I was covered in a layer of blood and sweat. I was filthy. If we wanted to shower, we had to get their permission first, and they would press a button and we would have just a few short seconds to wash.

For one severe episode of physical torture I later needed medical attention. It was when they punished me for being too stubborn, for refusing to tell them what they wanted to know. That was in the very beginning. They sent me to a place—I think it was Litoměřice, but I'm not sure—it was a prison that had "water cells." I was thrown into a cell without windows, whose floor was covered with 10 or 15 cm of water. I couldn't lie down at all, and was forced to walk in water for five or six days. This experience absolutely destroyed all my urinary functions and severely damaged my kidneys. I suffered afterwards—and I have been suffering for the past thirty years, even after they operated on me years after my release.

The physical torture they inflicted on us was carefully designed—they were too clever to lay themselves open to charges, and so we were never given electric shocks, or suffocated or beaten with sticks. But they did hit us with their fists, and they kicked us as well. As I have said, though, the pain became bearable as soon as I decided that I would not allow them to get any joy at all from my suffering, or from my situation. I would never allow them the pleasure of breaking me. This helped a lot. And the moment you reach this decision, you no longer care.

I very soon learned that it was nonsense to let them continue to beat you. You see, I was lucky to have the experiences of my family to draw on—for my family had, as I have said, always lived under someone's boot. So, to save my life, I pretended to faint. Even at moments like this, it was possible to help yourself. These people were filled with class hatred. They were bureaucrats who had been given power, and they didn't have the brains to see through the tricks we used. What they did, was to pour water on you. That's all they knew. And even when they let me out of my cell to do sit-ups, I would pretend to faint after five or six. I didn't care if they poured water over me, even though it was cold. The cold water washed you a little—and this was welcome, since they wouldn't allow us to wash at all at times like that.

As I said, I was detained before my trial at Bartolomějská Street Prison where I was interrogated. I was one of the lucky ones, though, because my detention wasn't very long. Some people were detained for two, three, even five years before being tried. I was put in solitary for the first six weeks, and then they put me in with another man who was also a political prisoner. I devised various ways of coping. So I talked French to myself, or English. And, because I was a writer—I had already written my first big novel at the age of seventeen—I created alternative realities in my head, I imagined things. It was a way of creative thinking, of looking at things in a "what if" way. What would happen if this or that was the case? This also helped me, it helped me very, very much. Many times, at moments when you are covered in blood, your are beaten, and so on, it helped a lot. Because the moment you make your brain work, it is good. There's an old proverb: "When the soul works, the body no longer cares."

When my trial eventually came up, I was charged with high treason and espionage. You see, they had a story from my colleague who didn't want to be hanged. He told them that I had left the country and spent six weeks in a training camp for spies in West Germany, and so on, and so on. Yes, all this—and then I was said to have come back, with espionage equipment. But there was no way they could prove this—never. Because they knew very well that during the period I was supposed to have been out of the country, I was in fact in Prague. It was all ridiculous, of course. There I stood, before I had even turned twenty-one, not yet an adult, accused of high treason. And because they couldn't sentence me to death for the things they accused me of, they only gave me eight years. Later, in the concentration camp, where many prisoners had twenty-five years, or even life sentences, everyone told me how lenient this sentence was—although, to a twenty-one-year old, it seemed excessive and cruel.

At the time, my father had just been released from prison, and was working in a forest—this was the only kind of work ex-political prisoners were permitted to do. He arranged for someone he had worked with before in the solicitor's office, a reliable man, to be my lawyer. But it was all for nothing. They wouldn't let him speak. He wasn't able to say one word during the trial. Our trial wasn't in the news at all—we weren't important enough. No one knew—or cared—whether it was fair or not—and of course, it certainly wasn't.

I stayed in Pankrác for about six weeks after the trial. A friend of mine, Boža Modrý, who was a famous member of the national hockey team, was in prison with me, and he arranged for me to do some decent work. But it wasn't long before they discovered what I was in for, and soon afterwards they sent me to Leopoldov.

From Leopoldov to Ilava

I spent about two weeks at Leopoldov, where I was a working prisoner. I belonged to a maintenance group doing building repairs. After work, we were put in separate cells, and my only contact with the other long-term inmates was when we did exercise and for meals. We weren't regarded as political prisoners—we were put with thieves, murderers and people like that. They actually saw us as worse than murderers—they said that we had the blood of their mothers and I don't know what else, on our hands. So, you see, we were seen as class enemies, murderers. From Leopoldov I was taken to Ilava in Slovakia. But we first went to Ilava by bus for twelve hours, with only one stop, and we were accompanied by armed guards—you see, Eduard Goldstücker and a lot of other important prisoners were with us.

The prisons were full of the best brains in the country, the best intellectuals. I was very fortunate to meet very clever people who told me: "Forget your hatred. Forget your lust for revenge, because if you don't forget it, you will be its first victim—you yourself." And they were right, I soon realized—revenge is a devastating emotion, it's not a good feeling to have.

But these feelings of revenge and hatred were, in a strange way, a gift. They got me through the cruellest moments of interrogation. Because, you know, the moment you become resigned to your hopelessness, and accept that you will never leave prison—in these moments of resignation you lose your life. And you don't only lose your life—you lose your brains, you go mad. So, always—as I later wrote in my short stories—I was convinced that even when you are down and your nose is rubbed in shit, you must know, be aware, that there is a tiny piece of blue sky which you must try to reach.

Yes, and the moment you gave up, you were lost. It was not a matter of telling them what they wanted or not, it was a matter of keeping sane. I would do all kinds of things to exercise my brain—I would try to think in French or in English. I tried to memorize things. And writing my novels and poems also helped a lot—even though most of it was garbage, rubbish. I was lucky to meet real, excellent writers in prison after my interrogation phase—they were like a breath of fresh air. They gave me a great deal to think about, and in this way helped me. What also helped were my recollections of the stories I had heard as a boy from my father's generation at Auschwitz: they stopped me from sinking into a state of self-pity.

I remember a professor who told me, during my interrogation, "Try not to wait for anything"—because if you did, you would go crazy, you would lose something of your life. This was a very bad period in our lives, but we just had to get through it—without waiting or thinking of what they might do to us in the future. Because the moment you did that, you were lost. Of course, we did think of the future, but we always stood with both feet on the ground—even though this was just the floor of a cell. No matter. You just had to accept this as part of your life, and, strangely, in this way you grew as a human being.

I shall never forget Jiří Krupička, who gave me a survival strategy. He told me that there were four ways of getting through prison: first, you could decide it is a dream, and that you would awake from it. Second, you could decide that the prison experience is merely provisional—that it is not the real part of your life. Or, you could decide that prison is a kind of waiting room for your civilian life. But the fourth way was the only way that would get you through it all: you had to adopt prison as a normal part of your life, and do everything you could to make the best of it.

All those clever people told me: "Everything you do is a matter of your own choice. This is not something the communists are able to teach you. Wherever you are—whether in a cell or in a concentration camp—you have your own free will. You can decide on the course of your life." And do you know, even now, when my children or friends have problems, I always say, "It's simply a matter of deciding, of choosing. You must decide what the first, second or tenth thing is that you are going to do in a bad situation. There is no such thing as 'it can't be done.'" You see, I believe that, whatever our circumstances, we are, finally, in charge of our lives. I learned a great deal about life and survival in prison. And so, when, after my imprisonment, people asked, "What was it like in prison?" I could always say, "For me it was a good experience. It was the only university the Communists allowed me."

They soon decided at Ilava that I was too young, too healthy and too strong just to be in prison, so they sent me to a uranium concentration camp. The camp looked exactly like a German concentration camp, with fences and barracks and everything. These camps were built to house workers for digging uranium at the West Frontier of Czechoslovakia at that time. There were about twenty concentration camps. But I was lucky to arrive at a time when the political prisoners were really the leading intellectuals in the country—I was with writers, priests, and philosophers, extraordinary people. Among the people I met was one of my best friends—the head of the biggest monastery, the Premonstratsky Monastery at Teplá. There was also Jan Zahradníček, one of the best Czech poets, and, of course, many politicians whose names I don't recollect because I didn't care very much at the time.

We had wonderful discussions, and we learned a lot from each other. The discussions were organized as they were, let's say, in Auschwitz: the moment you got there you managed your time so as to make the most of the people you were with. You might know, for instance, that there was a professor of philosophy, and you tried to arrange a lecture with him. And not only that, you went to work with him—you descended into the mine and you worked side by side with him. All the time, you would be talking about things—all kinds of things. I was very interested. And when I became the President of the Czech PEN Club in 1992 many started calling me Doctor because they assumed that, just because I was a political prisoner, I must be some big shot, a graduate. I always say that I am not that sort of a doctor—that, if I am a doctor of anything at all, I'm a doctor of prison science.

The people I met—people with wide experience and powerful intellects—influenced me in many ways. Remember, I was at the time a stubborn twenty-one-year-old who refused to listen because, you know, young people don't like to listen to older people. But still, something told me to listen to these people in prison with me, and I am grateful I did. I was in fact unbelievably lucky to meet the right people—and very soon, too. It was not long after I was jailed that I met Jan Zahradníček, a famous poet, who had been sentenced to twenty-five years. It was he who first said to me, "My son, cast off your hatred, throw away your lust for revenge. If you don't, it will eat you up."

What they were talking about were tangible realities. I was surrounded by, immersed in, feelings of hatred and revenge—these were the realities of my life in prison. But when I crossed to the other side of the river—my personal Rubicon—and stood on the other bank, I felt such relief, real relief. I was lucky that my stubbornness had not prevented me from listening to these people. You see, they were right. And from that moment I gave the same advice to other prisoners—something I have continued to do to the present moment. It was this principle that enabled me to keep going, it was a kind of optimism—a path that I had in fact been educated to follow as a boy.

I call it a prevailing optimism of the soul—something that I had learnt from my grandfather, who was not only a politician and a prime minister, but also a farmer, and therefore a realistic man. It was also very important for me that my grandmother was also a farmer's daughter, a real lady who was not only a farmer's wife, but also a farmer who took charge of farming when my grandfather was doing political work. She was a very clever woman, who shared his realism, his optimism of the soul. I remember, once, when I was a boy of six or seven years old, when she listened to arguments between Jan Masaryk and Karel Čapek.

They were discussing complex philosophical issues like optimism and pessimism, and she then said, "Well, I am listening to you gentlemen. I'm an ordinary woman, so I don't understand everything you are saying. But I think the argument is much simpler than you think. My opinion is that an optimist likes more things than he detests, and a pessimist detests more things than he likes!"

They had to feed us properly because we worked so hard in the mines, digging uranium. So, to say that we starved wouldn't be true. They didn't let us starve—though of course the quality of the food was terrible. You just ate because you had to eat—the food had no taste, and there was no pleasure in eating. If we didn't fulfil our quotas we got less food. You see, they divided us into three groups, and the lowest group got the worst food. So, you made sure that you fulfilled your quota so that you wouldn't be put into the lowest group.

I noticed a strange thing when I first arrived: the prisoners drank gallons and gallons of tea—which I thought at the time would kill them, that their stomachs, their kidneys, wouldn't be able to stand it. But, interestingly, we later learned—secretly, of course—about the findings of a World Congress of Radiologists that the best way to resist radioactivity is to drink tea. So, you see, our bodies even knew intuitively what was good for them in prison.

There were lots of things that helped us get through our ordeal. Music was regarded as illegal, but this did not stop us from listening to good music. Some prisoners were musicians, and they had concerts—illegal concerts—at night when we returned from the afternoon shifts. We would go to a jazz session or something of that sort. This all helped a lot. And things improved even more for me when I began to write my own poetry—in my mind, of course, since you would be sent to solitaries immediately if they found a piece of paper on you.

We all avoided the solitaries. You would be put into a tiny cupboard of a cell, without any heating. You got food only every third day—the punishment was really hard. But you had to keep your feelings to yourself. From time to time, though, you would find a bold civilian who was able or willing to smuggle something to your family with a letter.

We were always really anxious to read something, anything. There were many writers—some as young as me, and some older, and we would talk about literature, and about the history of literature. Do you know, the regime never allowed me to study. Even when I was released, they wouldn't let me study. So, I educated myself by using the education of those who were in prison with me, university professors, and so on, those who had had the privilege of studying. So it is really a fact that prison was my university, where I attended seminars on ethics, aesthetics, history of art, whatever, for seven years. Few students have the privilege of attending seminars such as the ones I attended—and that for seven years!

Every camp had its own hospital, where we were given medical attention. The doctor was also a prisoner, and he really cared about us. But his head was an officer of the screwers, as we called him—and these didn't care at all. You just couldn't get good medicine—it was very, very rare to get some. I also suffered through a dysentery epidemic which they somehow managed to deal with.

Among the prisoners there were many priests and religious people from various churches. They had their own circle of believers who not only supported them, but also met for secret church services, masses and so on. I was pushed into a rather queer dilemma, because, you see, my grandfather had been a leader of a party of ordinary, rather dull farmers, many of whom were devout. And two of my aunts—my father's sisters—were nuns, heads of the Anglican virgins, a strong women's order. So, the various churches jumped at me.

I tried not to join any camp, whether it was religious or political—though I did find out how helpful a really strong faith could be. Religion always helped. Especially very ordinary people—it helped a lot just to believe, to have faith. That was very important. But there were, of course, people who just waited, and had trouble getting themselves out of this frame of mind, of just waiting—and it destroyed many of them. Some of them became suicidal.

One shouldn't forget the terrible pressure that was put on prisoners' families. It went on all the time. They tried to persuade the wives of prisoners to get divorced. Even children, they put pressure on children, claiming that the wife was not able to take care of the family—and they would put the children into an orphanage or something like that. They even did this to us—they put pressure on my family too, and it was horrible. You see, the family was for many prisoners the only link with the world outside the prison walls, and the moment the family went to pieces, they went to pieces.

During our first years in prison, the warders tried to set the various groups of prisoners against each other—and, in the beginning, they succeeded. At the concentration camp, they formed murderers into groups which called themselves "The Black Commandos." At night they attacked our barracks, the political prisoners. They would do this to punish us.

They tried to blackmail us by promising that we would be given an early release if we did what they wanted. I had a terrible quarrel with my father about this, when he tried to persuade me to take their offer, and when he came to see me in prison, I asked him, "Do you want to be humiliated, do you really want to be offended?" I was relieved that my family listened to me, because a lot of people were completely broken down afterwards. They weren't able to help their family members in prison at all. You see, you couldn't just live, wondering every day, "What if they let me go?" and so on, fantasizing about what might happen if you signed your willingness to co-operate with the state. Sure, sure, you will go home, they would say—but of course they also needed us in the camps as slave labor. Often we would see fellow prisoners succumbing to the pressure, and suddenly changing—and we would pounce on them, and demand of them, "Tell us what you said to them. We don't blame you. You were under pressure—but please, just tell us what you told them!"

The warders were very, very simple people, many of them from Slovakia, who usually just obeyed orders. Many were youngsters who were recruited from prisons for juveniles, and educated as warders. Others came from the civil service or from lower ranks of the army. They were uneducated, and without mercy. In prison, they found that they were suddenly somebody, and they insisted that we address them as "Mr Chief" or "Mr Headmaster." In some concentration camps they tortured prisoners. One of my friends, Karel Pecka, a writer, told me about a murderous warder in the concentration camp he was in—this warder was so mad that he would even shoot people. I was one of the lucky ones, though, because I never encountered such a crazy warder.

Obviously, our experiences were not pleasant, but we scarcely thought about them—in fact, it would have been a luxury to dwell on them. The whole experience has hardened me, you could say, and I have little patience with people in civilian life who complain about emotional problems. You see, even now, when my daughter told me the other day that she felt depressed, I said, "For heaven's sake, what is it? What is wrong with you?" I never had time to feel depressed, you see. You had no time for such indulgences in prison, no time at all. And when you did have time, it was dangerous for you to give in to feelings like this.

It was far better to work, to keep your mind busy. There were many suicides, and things like that. Because the moment you decided to wait for things to improve, it was already a death sentence for you. You had to accept prison life as part of normal life. Of course, you knew that certain situations were completely abnormal, but you just had to accept it all as normal. You had to. It was all part of your life, whether it was normal or not—it was all just part of your life. And you had to accept that it was your duty to live, to get through it all somehow.

For me, it wasn't too bad, because I was always an optimist. So I always believed that I would get through it all, somehow. I never, ever believed that I wouldn't get through it all alive—but, you see, I was young, of course. Though I must say, this optimism remained with me, because when I was imprisoned again some years later, I felt the same optimism that I had felt before.

We were allowed visits from our family, but not very often. In the first year I met my family for the first time during the trial. Then, when I left for prison after six weeks, I met my mother again—but this happened purely by coincidence, because I had met a good officer who arranged a meeting with my mother and my younger brother. I saw them again after three months. The next year I saw them only twice—and this was for twenty minutes, at the most.

I suppose you could say that we were lucky to have some sporting facilities—we were allowed to play basketball. We formed teams, and used the area between the barracks as our field. We had to make this field ourselves—the authorities didn't help us to maintain it at all, so we did this ourselves. They allowed us to buy a ball with the money that we earned—though we never saw any of this money ourselves.

We were also allowed to read books, but only the books that they selected for us. As you can imagine, these were mainly books by officially approved Russian and Soviet authors, and Czech communist writers. There was nothing else, although from time to time other books appeared—books that slipped through because of the ignorance of the authorities. And so we were able to read writers from the United States whom they thought were communists—Howard Fast, Dreiser, people like that.

But they never allowed us to study at all, though this didn't stop me from deciding that I would try to learn all I could about philosophy, about sociology, about the history of art, about ethics or about the history of literature. And about languages, of course. I already knew three languages when I went to prison. As the son of a political prisoner who had been at Auschwitz, I was lucky to be offered a scholarship at a Swiss school, where I learned English, French, and Italian. And I had grown up with German, which was, you might say, my second language. So, while I learned many things in prison, I also taught languages. You see, this was the only way I could give something back to my teachers—and many of them were eager to learn languages. There were professors who spoke perfect German, but who wanted to know English or French.

From time to time they came—the people from the State Police or the Secret Police—they came to the camp to interrogate us. They chose a few prisoners they found interesting to them, and because I was such a rebel, I was usually one of them. I was always in trouble. Once I was even involved in a prison rebellion, a mutiny. We rebelled because they decided to make us stand in queues after our shifts, and when they gave us terrible, bad food after one shift, we simply refused to eat it. They saw this as a revolt, and they were stupid enough to try to force us to eat the pasta, but we wouldn't eat for three days.

They interrogated and beat us, and this became known as "the pasta affair." They even put up posters in the shop windows of Příbram, with pictures of weapons, to persuade people that we had caused a revolt. It was all ridiculous. Afterwards, we were given a collective punishment, though some of the longer serving prisoners' sentences were extended by another ten, twelve, or twenty years. I was already a marked man because I was always rebelling against something or other. But because I was such a good worker, a good miner, and because I was

Prisoners leaving the "correction cell" (reconstructed for the film "Boomerang" — directed by Hynek Bočan).

The barracks (reconstructed for the film "Boomerang"—directed by Hynek Bočan).

young and strong, they couldn't just mistreat me. They needed me, you see.

But of course this doesn't mean that they didn't punish me—I was punished many times, put into so-called "correction," a cell where they locked you up for ten days, and sometimes even up to a fortnight. I only got food once every three days, with only one blanket, with no heating. That was really hard, very hard. It meant that I came back weighing five kilos less.

Theoretically, we had the right to complain to the prison authorities, but it was dangerous to do this because there was always the chance that we would be the victims of revenge. This happened to me indirectly when, on one occasion, my father, who was a solicitor, made a claim—and they punished me! They took revenge on him by victimizing me!

But, as I have said, I was a rebel, and so they often punished me. I would spend periods of up to ten days or a fortnight—and once I even spent twenty days—in solitary confinement. Altogether, during the eight years I was in jail the first time, I spent over a year in solitary confinement.

Our cells were crowded, with sixteen beds to a cell. Most of us were political prisoners, and the rest were in for economic crimes—including the gypsies who were thieves, of course. From time to time, there were also sexual offenders. At least twice a year, we had to change barracks—they would simply call us out, and put us in line, and we had to leave the place for a new cell where we were put with strangers.

Our daily routine centred round work. We worked on shifts: morning shifts, afternoon shifts and night shifts. For the morning shift they woke us between 3:30 and 4 AM. Breakfast was black coffee and bread, and if you were lucky you got enough bread to take a piece with you down the mine. We had to be ready

Uranium concentration camp (reconstructed for the film "Boomerang"—directed by Hynek Bočan).

to go down the mine at 6 AM. We came up at 3 PM again for lunch. If you were on the afternoon shift you had lunch at 11.30 AM and then went down the mine again. The night shift started at 10 PM.

When we got back from the morning shift we had to make sure that we weren't seen by the warders if we wanted to have some free time. You see, they could catch you at any time and put you to work on brigades, where we would do things like peel potatoes, or move huge heaps of coal to the furnaces for the central heating. This work would take hours and hours—so we were very careful not to be seen by the warders.

The civilian miners we worked with were afraid of having contact with us, because they could be caught at any time and charged and sentenced. But nevertheless, from time to time you got a brave one who arranged for illegal contact with your family. In this way, we were able to send material to our families that we hoped might once be published. If you were lucky enough to work with a civilian who was prepared to risk bringing you a book to read, or a newspaper, you could count yourself lucky.

They allowed us news from outside from time to time. We were allowed to listen to the radio, but usually only in the evening. And there was nothing else apart from this. On Sundays, after about two o'clock in the afternoon, we were allowed to listen to concerts on the radio. We could also ask for newspapers, but because the only available newspaper was the Communist newspaper, nobody bought it. So, I suppose you could say that we did not have access to newspapers at all, really.

Prisoners were always making escape plans. All the time, there was someone or other trying to escape. But it was all in vain: a lot of people were shot and killed,

Uranium mine near Příbram

in fact most of the escapees ended up dead. A very small percentage succeeded in getting away. I never tried to escape because I saw how risky it was. I thought it was ridiculous, it was stupid to try to escape with the odds stacked against you. It cost many people their lives, you see, and I didn't want to die this way.

There were always secret organizations in the prison. Those of us who were young used to make fun of these organizations, and we would say that in each concentration camp there was a President of the Slovak state, and a Government of the Czechoslovakian Republic. You see, there were so many former politicians among the prisoners. At first, they believed that they would be freed by the Americans, but this hope slowly died. There were also very strong political parties in the camp, and I thought it amusing that, because of my name, Stránský nearly all of them wanted to recruit me. There was also a very strong Catholic movement in the camp, and they often had midnight masses in the barracks—even in the mineshafts.

Release

I was released four months early because of a Presidential amnesty. We were all released, nearly all political prisoners—apart from those whose offences involved weapons. These prisoners were charged with terrorism. When I arrived home, I felt very emotional, as you can imagine. But reality soon hit me, as I realized I only had three employment possibilities. The regime would only allow us to work in the building industry, in mines or in agriculture. Nothing else was permitted. At first, I lived with my parents who at that time had a very small flat. So I found a building firm that was not too far away, and I worked there for nearly three years.

But because I had problems with my health, I did not work for the first four or five weeks. You see, I had low blood pressure, and my blood count was very low. I had good doctors, and so I think I was lucky at the time because many of my co-prisoners had real psychological problems and found it difficult to adapt to civilian life.

Even though I was free, the police still harassed me. They would often call me in and warn me that it would be very bad for me if I did anything against the regime, and so on and so on. I had a very strong mind, though—this was my advantage—and I didn't let things trouble me or get me down. So I adapted very quickly to civilian life—just as I had adapted to prison, and to the uranium mines.

What built me up was my family background. Also, I was a sportsman. And I was young. You see, there were people who were older and had more troubles, or had kids, small kids. Of course, the second time I was in prison, I understood these things much, much better, because I also had kids then. But the first time, I felt joy that I was able to return. I felt a sense of primary joy and a lust for life, and that was all I had, and nothing they did bothered me or could take that feeling away from me while I was free.

My girlfriend and I had gone through troubles before my imprisonment. Our problems started when we were both involved in ski-racing. We hardly saw each other, and she soon felt that I wasn't the right man for her—she was, in fact, much younger than I was. She told me that I wasn't reliable, even though I was nearly five years older than her. But, you know, the moment they put me into prison, she wrote to me and said that she would stick by my side. I never forgot her, and she waited for me, even though she was a university student. Her mother was afraid all the time that the moment the news spread that she was visiting her boyfriend in prison, and that her boyfriend was a political prisoner, and so on, that it would harm her terribly. She had trouble throughout the years before our marriage with her family. It was not easy—for them, for her, or for me.

So that was why we married very soon after my arrival. And then the kids came, and so on. But I was really working hard because I was just an ordinary worker. It was not easy to earn a living, because I had nothing. They had taken everything, you see. Not only my stuff, but also my family's belongings. I had no shoes, no socks, nothing. I'm not telling this so that I can claim against the state. I just took it as it was.

My wife was working. She is an architect, and though she stopped studying for a while, she continued when we got married. So it was not easy. I worked twelve hours a day—just trying to earn more money. And that cost me even more problems—with my health, my stomach. It soon happened that I had to go to hospital, where I stayed for two months. I also had terrible trouble with my kidneys. This was because of being forced all those years before to walk in water—I had to do this for six whole days and nights in the water cell. In winter. The whole experience was a disaster for my kidneys and urinary system, which continually gave me trouble.

But, in a funny way, this experience of illness helped me, because I started to write again. I had a lot of things ready for publication when I was released. But nobody was interested. After three years, though, a story of mine was published in a magazine. Fortunately, one of our best Czech film directors read it and wanted to meet me so that I could be his scriptwriter. And so, towards the end of 1963, I worked for the film industry, first as an assistant director, and then as a scriptwriter.

Very soon, though, they found out that I was a former political prisoner. And so, because culture was under the Communists' supervision, I was expelled from the film industry. I had no option but to work at a petrol station. What happened then was that a former director of the film industry who liked me very much helped me to write a film script about the petrol station. In this way I succeeded in writing a film that eventually won a prize at the International Television Festival at Montreux in Switzerland. I soon developed a name as a scriptwriter, and from time to time I wrote something. I earned my living in this way, but it was mostly with stuff that wasn't very important.

I was, shall we say, "free," for only thirteen years, until 1970—for a period of nearly seven years. This was the time that the New Wave film began, with world famous directors like Miloš Forman, Jiří Menzel, and so on. I mention this because this was a time of, how shall I put it—smoothing things out. The pressure of the regime was not so strong, especially in culture. There were many writers, names like Škvorecký and Hrabal, and so on. They were able to publish texts that were against the regime, that told the truth. It was the same with film. Although, as far as I was concerned, as a former political prisoner, I was not able to publish. I did succeed, however, in writing eight film scripts, but only one of these was shot. I had contacts, but that was all. They wouldn't allow me to publish.

Things went better for me, though, with TV. I wrote scripts which were screened, scripts that went all over the world. Eventually, I had quite a good name in TV, better than in anything else, and TV was, in a way, a strong medium.

And then 1968 came: the occupation, and so on. And to tell the truth (it is very important to tell it), I did not believe too strongly in the so-called Spring of 1968. I was absolutely certain it would all fall to pieces. You see, I had already had my experience with this totalitarian regime, and I could not believe that the Soviets—the Russians—who had so deliberately tried to get rid of us, would simply give us democracy as a gift. A lot of my friends were very angry with me because they were filled with euphoria and plans for the future, and all I said was, "Steady, steady, steady, you'll soon see what will happen." They were surprised at my attitude—I who had always been such an optimist in the bad times. For here I was, telling them things that seemed pessimistic—but were not in fact so. You see, I was merely being a realist.

Even though there were, you could say, two sorts of communists, this in no way meant that we would be able to jump out of the communist system or jump out of the communist bloc. So that was why I didn't let the "socialists with a human face" use me. You see, I was a person with public appeal. I had not been contaminated by the Communists in the previous regime. I was clean, *carte blanche*, and so the people from radio and TV wanted me for the news, to use me for commentary, for publicity, and so on. But I didn't give in to their flattering offers—because I knew what was coming. It wasn't that I was afraid—no, it was just that I didn't believe any of what they said.

I had in fact joined K231—the political prisoners' club—but I was more or less made a member, even though I had told my fellow ex-political prisoners that it would end in disaster. It wasn't a question of emotion, you see—it was a question of thinking rationally. I didn't join in any activities of the club, because this would mean communicating with the Communists, which I refused to do.

K231 applied for rehabilitation, just as I had done, though unsuccessfully— but that is another story. As I later discovered, it made the regime, especially the State Police, furious that I was warning people against having any dealings whatever with the regime. But let me make it clear: I was no dissident—I didn't even publish in Samizdat.

Second Arrest

I infuriated them because I refused to have anything at all to do with them, and so they took the first chance they had to catch me, and that was that. They took their chance when they uncovered a scam at the petrol stations. Some of the workers were part of an elaborate secret scheme to exchange petrol for foreign currency with foreign drivers, and so on. And even though I had left the petrol station nine months before, and was in fact working as a dramaturge at a small theatre at the time, they came and arrested me! And to this day, I don't know on what grounds they arrested me.

They accused me of organizing the foreign currency groups that were stealing, and so on. They said that I was the only person who could have organized things with the foreign drivers because I spoke four languages, and the ordinary workers didn't know any other languages. Though I had heard rumours of their plans to arrest me, I hadn't believed any of it because I was no longer working at the petrol station, you see. It all seemed far too preposterous.

At the time of my arrest, I was working with a very famous film director, I was at home, writing a script for his film. And it was there that they came to arrest me. I soon realized what their real reason was. You see, I wasn't arrested by the Criminal Police, but, once again, by the State Police. Their first words to me were, "You see, we finally got you at home anyway!" They then gave me over to the Criminal Police, who accused me. In their eyes I was guilty by association, just because I had worked at the petrol station—even though they couldn't prove that I had stolen a penny. I infuriated them, and they didn't care about procedures—they just thought that I was guilty, and then tried to get information out of me.

Interrogation at Ruzyně

They took me—once again—to the interrogation prison at Ruzyně, which was one of the worst prisons. I was there for nearly fifteen months, but they didn't get anything out of me. In all, I spent fifteen of the twenty-four months that I eventually ended up serving, in that horrible interrogation prison. So, now you can appreciate that something was drastically wrong. I knew nothing, and could tell them nothing.

The interrogation technique they used was more sophisticated than the first time. They didn't torture you; they didn't beat you. They could no longer just behave as they had done before, you see. They had to try to prove to the world that they were behaving legally, and so on. Also, they knew that I was a relatively well-known person, with my family background. So, they didn't torture me. In fact, they did nothing—they even let me write in prison.

Though I had no direct contact with my family, I could write letters to them. I also had a really good connection with my lawyer, through whom—I couldn't believe this!—I could smuggle all my writing. You see, I had already been interrogated by the Criminal Police, so this was not their problem. They didn't care. Nobody had the imagination to suspect that I was smuggling my writing—over 1,000 pages of it! They just thought I was giving my lawyer papers relating to my trial. So I was able to send all my writings home—and this was the one thing at Ruzyně that made it much, much better. The second thing that made things better was the fact that, because I was a former political prisoner from the fifties, they didn't try to bribe or threaten me.

An important factor in my experience was that I now had a family, unlike the time before. Suddenly I was a prisoner who had his own family, small kids—I think my daughter was eight years old and my son was twelve—and I knew it was very, very dangerous to be in this situation. Because of my former imprisonment, my family was very tightly knit, very close. And the kids were terribly upset. That is why I wrote a series of short stories, fairy-tales, for my daughter, to help smooth her sorrow. It was not easy to go through all this.

They tried to accuse me of being an ordinary criminal because the State Police were not able to prove any political charges. So they tried to heap shame on me by saying that I had ended up as a common criminal. They did the same thing with another of my friends, Jiří Lederer, who was accused as a criminal, and not as a political prisoner. It was their way of humiliating us, you see. That was perhaps why I was at Ruzyně for such a long time—because the thieves, the people who had really stolen the currency, had all the information. After fifteen months at Ruzyně and after hundreds of hours of interrogation, all they got from me was three or four pages, because I had nothing to say. If you really hadn't committed an offence, what could you possibly have to say? My answer was always, "Why are you asking me these things, when you know that I have already spent eight years in prison? You know what

I think about all of this. You know that, before even stepping into your office, I know all your tricks." This infuriated them, because, you understand, they knew I was not a fool—I was an experienced prisoner, I was hard.

Second Trial

My second trial? Well, that was pure theatre, once again—especially because of who I was. They tried to degrade me: "Look at him! A former political prisoner! And look at how he has ended up—a common criminal!" They even tried—unsuccessfully, of course—to make me out to be the head of the criminal syndicate—the brains behind the group.

Nevertheless, I was convicted as a criminal on a charge of trying to destroy the national economy, and sentenced to three and a half years. I was sent to Bory, where I spent the rest of my sentence among common criminals. As in prisons all over the world, the regimen was strict, the warders were cruel, and the prisoners had their hierarchy—even helping the warders to run the prison.

But I had a big advantage—I was respected. Even the hardened prisoners and the warders respected me. They knew that I had spent eight years in prison in the fifties. I survived this so-called stone prison for hard cases and even harder warders by just biding my time, not asking for anything, not showing what I felt.

I worked in the metal industry, and did an eight-hour shift every day. There was a factory inside the prison that belonged to Škoda, so we had no contact at all with people outside, only with prisoners. As long as we filled our daily quota, the authorities were satisfied. They didn't care about anything else, so, in a way, it was easier than it had been in the fifties. In comparison, Bory seemed to be a sanatorium, with family visits allowed every second month, and permission to write letters every week, and to receive mail at any time—and I could even receive a big parcel every month. You couldn't compare Bory in the seventies with my experience in the fifties. We had baths every week or so, and had to be clean shaven all the time—everything had to be very clean. But in the fifties they didn't care about such things at all.

The warders saw themselves as just doing a job. You weren't really a human being to them. You were just something that they had to take care of and make sure didn't escape. They just carried out orders. It wasn't like it was in the past, where you would occasionally meet someone who was human, who was normal, who even tried to help you, and risked arrest. The older warders had been replaced with new workers. The regime detested any sign of independent thinking or intelligence in warders, and so they recruited workers from factories. They also came from militias, you see, people who were not only blindly obedient, but also cruel—inevitably so, because the system itself was inherently cruel.

But many of the older warders were opportunists, and saw that they could build careers as officers, and also benefit financially by working in the system.

For instance, they would steal food from prisoners—they gave us less than was allocated, and kept the rest for themselves.

Most of the new wardens were Party members—they infiltrated the prisons, just as they had everywhere else, the ministries and offices and the army. But the warders—even when they became members of the Party—they were not the so-called fist of the working class. These people—the warders in the concentration camps—were former workers from factories, so there was no need for them to have special training. They hated us—they hated all the political prisoners because we were educated.

The only person I had any kind of relationship with was the prison psychologist. I told the authorities, "If there is anyone I am going to talk to at all, it is the psychologist." You see, he was an intelligent man, and saw immediately that I would not speak to him about my case. He was up-to-date in his methods, in any case, so I didn't pretend too much. I think that he felt flattered, pleased that there was at least someone who wanted to talk to him, and that he could talk to. We spoke about many things, even about socialism. He had nothing to do with politics—he was just a doctor, you see. Then one day he got a message from a psychologist friend of mine, who told him that I was his friend. And after this he would phone my wife every three to four months to say that I was okay, and so on.

It was a very bad time for my wife, who had the responsibility of our two children. Nobody cared for her or helped her—and some people even put obstacles in her way. I was plagued with thoughts of my family. Even though I knew they were not suffering materially, I knew that they suffered mentally—because, of course, they knew that I was in prison for nothing, for absolutely no reason. And, what is more, I was living among criminals—real criminals. But somehow, we got through it all.

Second Release

I was released after two years, towards the end of 1975. And after that, with the help of my friends, I was hidden as a stage worker in the state dance and folklore ensemble, where I stayed until 1989. I was forbidden to publish anything during this time, though, and even the collection of short stories from prison that I had published in 1968 was banned. I was banned—absolutely banned—everywhere, and still they tried to get me.

As a writer, I was always a potential danger to them. Even the mention of my name on TV was dangerous. Though I had continued to write while in prison, and all my colleagues knew that I was writing, and tried to get me to publish in Samizdat, I did not, I could not, you see, because I respected the wishes of my wife. She begged me not to as it was very dangerous and I could be thrown into prison yet again. So I refused to publish in Samizdat. I even refused to be a member of any dissident group.

Nevertheless, the situation of the 1970s repeated itself. They knew very well I was not a member of any dissident group. And yet, when I happened to speak with Václav Havel, for instance—you see, we were friends and neighbors, and we would often meet while walking our dogs—or with Mr. Smrkovský who was also a neighbor, they immediately suspected me of acting against the regime. They knew I was not active, but still they regarded me as a potential threat, a potential danger to the regime.

So, I refused to publish anything—because of my wife, my family, you see. I did not even sign Charter 77. In fact, Václav Havel advised me not to sign at the time. But not even this helped me. At least once a month they came to visit me, to see what I was doing, and to interrogate me. And always they asked the same questions: "How are you? What are you doing? What is new? Can you tell us anything new?" Always, always, the questions, the harassment, never leaving me to live a normal life.

How has prison altered me? It has irrevocably changed my life. But I am fortunate. I have my family, and my wife continues to be a great support to me. I write a great deal, and I am president of PEN Club. I have always been involved in film, and I have written many scripts. And here, my prison experiences of living in a world of my own creation—of imagining "what if?"—have helped a lot. After all these years my relationship to property has radically changed. When, for ten years, a toothbrush is the only thing you own, how can you have a really heartfelt relationship with property? I therefore look at material things with a sense of irony. You see, I don't care much about any of it.

Postscript

Each of the stories we have read forms part of the larger narrative of humanity, and each voice has surely found an echo in our own individual experience—however slight—of deprivation and defiance, bitterness and triumph. We have listened to humble tales of suffering and loss, as each narrator has struggles with memories of human rights abuse that, in the words of Nelson Mandela, should never, never and never again be repeated. We have also glimpsed something of the private truth that compelled each to confront the public lie.

We have seen how people of different cultures, imprisoned under two very different, yet similar systems learned to cope with the brutality that has been identified as the essence of evil. The note of victory in the voices of the South Africans is unmistakable, while the grim stoicism of the Czechoslovakians lingers darkly. A legacy of oppression is sharply etched as the tales of two disparate countries, each today as emergent democracy, gradually unfold. And each narrative comes to exercise a cautionary function as old rivalries re-emerge on the world stage: socialism vs. capitalism, internationalism vs. ethnicity, the local as opposed to the global.

Two of the six narrators never lived to see their stories in print – though Joseph Faniso Mati and Johnson Malcomess Mgabela were firmly convinced that their stories would one day be heard. For truth will out, as it inevitably must, as the dark side of history comes to light, foiling the attempts of those who hope to perpetuate the lie. It is up to the individual to keep truth alive, in the way this has been done from time immemorial, by going out and telling the stories that need to be told, and in this way to struggle against that silence that is nothing less than a form of consent to the forces of evil. This is the only way that we can ensure that the horrors of the past are never resurrected.

"After Auschwitz, it is no longer possible to write poetry." There have been many holocausts since Theodore Adorno made this claim, and modern-day tyrants continue to appear before the international court of justice. This does not mean, however, that human creativity dies in the massacres, and is buried in the mass-graves that litter our world. There will always be romantic poems, as long as men and women love, and nature reveals her wonders. Adorno's words suggest, instead, that poetry of more innocent times has given way to different forms that better reflect the horrors of our times. In an era that teeters so precariously between hope and despair, poetic insight emerges today in a variety of forms, and may be found in prose recollections such as those contained in this book, in the stark images, the confessional tones, and the rhythms of regret and rebellion. There is, indeed, both truth and profundity in the simple tales of these six ordinary yet truly exceptional people, each of whom reminds us not only of who we are, but also of what we may become.

Glossary

[A = Afrikaans; X = Xhosa; Cz = Czech]

Abakhwetha. [X] Young men undergoing circumcision.

Baas, 'seblief Baas, kan ek 'seblief in die kombuis werk, Baas?
[A] Master, please Master, may I work in the kitchen, Master?

Baaskap. [A] Control that stems from white supremacist attitudes.

Bandiet. [A] Prisoner.

Binne-in julle koppe? [A] Inside your heads?

Bouspan. [A] Building team.

Broederbond. [A] Secret organization for the advancement of Afrikaner men.

Die troos van die boere—soet koffie. [A] Sweet coffee—the comfort of the
Afrikaner.

Dompas. [A] "Stupid" pass book.

Ek het nog nie 'n hou ingekry nie. Ek wil ook slaan! [A] I haven't had a go. I also
want to hit!

God, die kaffers is dom. [A] God, the kaffirs are stupid.

Haai! As daardie kruiwa nie loop nie, gaan ek julle moer! [A] Hey!
If that wheelbarrow doesn't move, I will hit you!

Here! [A] Lord!

Hulle ken nie skoene nie. Kyk hoe loop hulle; kyk hoe dra hulle hulle skoene!
[A] They don't know about shoes. Look at the way they walk; see how they
wear their shoes!

Iimpimpi. [X] Informers.

Ingcibi. [X] The person who performs circumcision.

Julle is bandiete, en bandiete is niks anders as goed nie! [A] You are prisoners,
and prisoners are nothing but things!

Jy is 'n bandiet hier. Moenie maak asof jy die baas is nie. [A] You are a prisoner
here. Don't act as if you are the master.

Jy vloek my! [A] You're swearing at me!

Kom aan, man, jy gaan te laat wees! Waar is jou stok? [A] Come one, man, you
will be too late! Where is your stick?

Kom eet! [A] Come and eat!

Kom jong! Kom jong! [A] Come on! Come on!

Kruiwa. [A] Wheelbarrow.

Kyk hierso, dis Robben Eiland hierdie! [A] Listen here, this is Robben Island.

Kyk hoe loop hulle! [A] See how they walk.

Los dit! Los die bandiete! [A] Let go! Leave the prisoners alone!

Man, dis somer! Hoe kan jy 'n trui dra in die somer? [A] Man, it's summer! How can you wear a jersey in summer?

Mukl. [Cz] Man destined for liquidation/death.

Nee, kak, man! [A] Oh no, what shit!

Oom. [A] Uncle.

Pap. [A] Porridge.

Poqo [X] We go it alone. (Military wing of PAC).

Pusa amasi. [X] Sour milk.

Pusa mandla. [X] Soup.

Semels. [A] Bran.

*Sinktronk/*zinc *tronk.* [A] Corrugated iron prison.

Sit! Sit! Sit! Eet gou, jong! Ons wil toesluit! [A] Sit! Sit! Sit! Finish eating! We want to lock up!

Span. [A] Work team.

Tshayile. [X] Stop working.

Tronk. [A] Prison.

Ukuthawusa. [X] Naked search.

Umkonto weSizwe. [X] The Spear of the Nation (Military wing of ANC).

Val in! [A] Start working!

Vat jou goed en weg hierso! [A] Take your things and be off!

Verkramp. [A] Conservative.

Verlig. [A] Progressive.

For Product Safety Concerns and Information please contact our EU
representative GPSR@taylorandfrancis.com Taylor & Francis Verlag GmbH,
Kaufingerstraße 24, 80331 München, Germany

Batch number: 08158516

Printed by Printforce, the Netherlands